THE LATTER DAYS

THE LATTER DAYS

A Memoir

JUDITH FREEMAN

PANTHEON BOOKS, NEW YORK

All photographs in this book are from author's personal collection.

Library of Congress Cataloging-in-Publication Data
Name: Freeman, Judith, [date] author.
Title: The latter days : a memoir / Judith Freeman.
Description: New York : Pantheon, 2016.
Identifiers: LCCN 2015042317. ISBN 9780307908612 (hardback).
ISBN 9780307908629 (ebook)
Subjects: LCSH: Freeman, Judith, [date]. Women authors, American—20th century—
Biography. Ex-church members—Mormon Church—Biography. BISAC: BIOGRAPHY &
AUTOBIOGRAPHY / Women. RELIGION / Christianity / Church of Jesus Christ of
Latter-day Saints (Mormon).
Classification: LCC PS3556.R3915 Z46 2016. DDC 818 / .5403—dc23.
LC record available at lccn.loc.gov / 2015042317.

Jacket photograph courtesy of the author
Jacket design by Oliver Munday

Printed in the United States of America
First Edition

2 4 6 8 9 7 5 3 1

For Todd, with love,
and
in memory of Roger Blakely

She had attempted to be someone she didn't really understand. A powerful but fragile female character. If she knew that to be forceful was not the same as being powerful and to be gentle was not the same as being fragile, she did not know how to use this knowledge in her own life.

—DEBORAH SOLOMON, *Swimming Home*

We live in a world ruled by fictions of every kind . . . We live inside an enormous novel . . . The fiction is already there. The writer's task is to invent reality.

—J. G. BALLARD

THE LATTER DAYS

PROLOGUE

I have an image of myself at twenty-two: I have recently decided I am going to be a writer, but instead of writing I am working in the cookware department of the church-owned department store in the town in Utah where I grew up. My mother works in the same store, in gift wrapping. It's just before Christmas and both our jobs are temporary, meant to last only through the holidays. I have a son, now four years old, who has endured two heart surgeries, one when he was three weeks old, another when he was two and a half. According to the heart surgeon who performed the second operation, my son should not be alive, so serious are his problems, but he is alive, thanks in large part to the superior skills of the heart surgeon.

The heart surgeon, who is already a rising star in his field—the field of pediatric thoracic surgery—has become my lover, though he is married with three children of his own. He is a number of years older and lives in Minnesota, which is where my son had his surgery, but he is planning on coming to Utah very soon to visit me. I have recently left Minnesota myself, where I lived for the last few years, and I am in the process of divorcing the man I married five years earlier, when I was seventeen. I have returned to Utah with my son to live with my parents. I came back because I didn't know where else to go, because I have no money and no education and no way of knowing what sort of work I can do, and because my parents agreed to let us live with them until, as they put it, I can get back on my feet.

❖   ❖   ❖

I am on my feet all day long in the cookware section of the church-owned department store, which is called ZCMI—Zion Cooperative Mercantile Institution. It's the biggest department store in town, located on the main street, and everyone shops here. The year is 1969. Things are happening in the world. But I'm not really thinking of them. I am thinking about my son and his slow, steady improvement following his heart surgery, and I am thinking about the heart surgeon, whom I love very much, and I am thinking about a cooking pot I really want that sits on the shelves at the front of the display in the cookware department which I know I cannot afford but which I have not yet given up on owning. The pot is heavy cast iron, with red enamel on the outside and a lid to match. It's a Graham Kerr pot. Graham Kerr is an English chef who has a cooking show on TV called *The Galloping Gourmet* that I watch sometimes. He's not only an exciting chef but he's also a very funny one, always cracking jokes on his show, and then there's his accent—the way he talks with that English accent—which makes him seem even funnier than he really is. I don't know why I want this pot so much, but I do.

Sometimes I think of my son as the blue-lipped boy—the beautiful blue-lipped boy—although since his open-heart surgery his lips are no longer as blue as they once were. He was born blue, his color caused by a lack of oxygen due to a malformation of his heart. He has a congenital defect, what's called a transposition of the great arteries, meaning his aorta and pulmonary arteries are switched, causing the oxygen-deprived blood coming back from the body to be sent out again without going to the lungs to be replenished, while the blood returning from the lungs full of oxygen is simply sent back to the lungs. Were it not for a small hole between the ventricular chambers in his heart, which allowed for some of the oxygenated blood to mix and go out to his body, he would not have survived. An attempt by nature, perhaps, to offset one abnormality with another.

His heart, due to the surgical reconfiguring, now pumps back-

ward, reversing the normal flow of blood. And still it works, this
fragile heart, stitched together from inside and pumping backward
day and night, keeping my son alive.

He has blond hair and pale skin and little bulbous fingers also tinged
blue and he is a small boy because the lack of oxygen has made it difficult for him to gain weight. His teeth are dark as well because they
too have been deprived of oxygen. Oxygen is what he doesn't get
enough of and what is causing all his problems. He is among the first
children with a transposition to survive after undergoing a recently
invented surgery to reconfigure the inside of his heart since the arteries themselves cannot be switched. Still, there's no guarantee he can
have any sort of active life, with his damaged little heart. He will be
a pioneer, the heart surgeon says: if he survives he will be a model
for what is possible. Since I come from a long line of pioneers, this
somehow seems appropriate.

He has already confounded expectations: before his first surgery,
at three weeks, his father and I were taken aside by the surgeon, a man
with very large hands—hands with thick, blunt fingers and black hair
growing on the backs, not at all the hands of a surgeon who would
be operating on a heart the size of a walnut—and told that should he
survive, our son would most likely be mentally retarded, due to the
lack of oxygen to his brain. But he is not mentally retarded. At four
he is a very bright little boy. Very, very bright.

Sometimes my mother takes a break from gift wrapping and comes
down to see me in the cookware department, which is on the first
floor, between luggage and cosmetics. We haven't always gotten along
but we're getting along okay now, even though she isn't happy about
what's happening in my life, meaning the divorce, just as she didn't
approve of me getting married in the first place, at seventeen. I married my older sister's former boyfriend, who was twenty-three, six
years older than me. I don't know why you'd want to take hand-me-

downs, she said to me when I told her he had proposed to me while
we were out horseback riding on a winter day. My father only looked
at me and said, I don't think you've got both oars in the water, doll,
if you think this one is going to work out.

Occasionally my mother and I take our lunch breaks together and
go to the restaurant on the second floor of the department store and
share a sandwich, and sometimes her friend Ada comes with us. Ada
works in gift wrapping too and is more or less my mother's age—
late fifties or maybe even sixty. Ada isn't really that smart, not like
my mother, who has to do all the addition for Ada when it comes
to figuring out what to charge a customer for the special gift wrapping. My mother has only a high school education but you'd never
know it. She's sharp: growing up, whenever I've wanted to know
something—how to spell a word, for instance, or the capital of a
foreign country—all I had to do was ask my mother. She has given
birth to eight children and she's never worked outside the home
before, or at least not since she was married. But now all of her children are grown and gone except for her youngest son, Gregg, born
when she was in her forties. My father has recently begun having
health problems: he had a grand mal seizure that almost killed him
and had to retire from his job working in civilian personnel for the
Air Force. Now I am back in Utah living with them and my younger
brother Gregg. My father said my son and I could return but I had to
pay a hundred dollars a month rent, which is why I have the job in
the cookware department. He said it wasn't about the money, which
they don't really need; nor is it about space—the house I have moved
back into has six bedrooms and only my little brother is left at home.
It's about teaching me a lesson, my father said, that I won't get something for nothing.

I'm not very good at selling cookware or kitchen appliances, or
the fancy sets of dishes and silverware that people like to register
for as wedding presents. I hardly know how to cook, am not really

interested in it, which is why it seems odd, even to me, that I want this Graham Kerr pot as much as I do. Maybe it represents a future I think I'll have one day, with a well-equipped kitchen, and a nice house to go with it. Maybe I just like the color, the beautiful orange-red of the enamel, the heft and weight of the thing. Or maybe I just like it because it's *a Graham Kerr pot,* a signature item with his name embossed on the metal bottom, a special thing tinged with the good times its celebrity namesake seems to be having on TV in his kitchen. It seems like I could have my own good time in a kitchen if I had this sort of pot. If I had a kitchen of my own again.

Even though my parents, who are both good Mormons, don't really approve of my current lifestyle (the divorce, the affair with the heart surgeon, my estrangement from the church), they've been very kind in allowing me to move back home for a while. I think it's because they know how hard the last few years have been on me. How when my son was born I came home from the hospital without him because he was so blue and frail and sick and because the exact nature of his congenital problem had not yet been diagnosed.

They know how the blue-lipped boy spent most of his first six months in an incubator in a hospital in Salt Lake City with his father and me visiting him every day, sitting beside the glass box, watching over him, sometimes opening the plastic portals and putting our hands through so we could stroke his hair, touch his tiny hands. They know how hard it was to help him survive until he could weigh enough to be put on a bypass machine for the second operation since he could not have the experimental open-heart surgery until he weighed thirty pounds, and he was sick so much of the time he simply couldn't gain weight, so that for a very long time we were trapped in a catch-22: must gain weight to have the surgery, can't gain weight until he has the surgery. They also know how two days after he was operated on he developed a terrible complication, requiring that his chest be reopened and left open so that the wound could heal from the inside out; how precarious everything was for many months.

They know all this, but what they don't know is exactly how it was that the heart surgeon and I became lovers in the first place, in the months following the surgery, though they know about our affair, because the heart surgeon sends me letters and sometimes calls me in the evening. They never ask me any questions, but I can tell how they feel about my affair: on the one hand it's shameful; on the other they think it's extraordinary that such a sophisticated, wealthy, respected doctor has fallen in love with their daughter.

The heart surgeon was born in Europe. His grandfather was an ambassador from a Central American country famous for its corruption and violence. He grew up in Italy, France, Germany, as a boy attended fashion shows in Paris with his elegant, wealthy grandmother. A friend of his mother's seduced him when he was fifteen, introducing him to sex, and this is not hard to believe because he is still an exceptionally handsome and sensuous man at the age of thirty-eight. He speaks Spanish, German, French, Italian, and English. He wears shirts with his initials monogrammed in script on the pocket. He is worldly and funny and charming, and he is as foolishly in love with me as I am with him. I have left my husband. Can he— should he—leave his wife? What about his three children, the youngest of whom is only five? Almost the same age as my son.

This is a lot of what I think about during the day, as I stand amidst the pots and pans in the cookware department of the church-owned department store, trying to answer questions about items I know almost nothing about. I think about the affair. The heart surgeon. My future.

I think about this, and I think about my son and whether he's really going to be okay now, and I think about how I'm going to become a writer, though I really have no idea how I'm going to do this. I just know it's what I'm going to be. Over the past couple of years living in Minnesota, I have become a reader—a real reader—for the first time in my life. I have discovered Willa Cather and Virginia Woolf, Thomas Hardy and D. H. Lawrence, and many other writers as well, and reading these writers' books I feel I have discovered what I want to do. And the heart surgeon, during the many evenings we have spent together in rented rooms, in motels with names like the Paul Bunyan Inn, has encouraged me. He says I must try to do this. He says he believes I can.

After Christmas, my mother is no longer needed in gift wrapping because gift wrapping shuts down. And I, too, am told my job is ending. We knew our jobs were only temporary so this doesn't come as a big surprise. Still, we both feel a little bad that it's over. Me because I need the paycheck I've been getting in order to pay my father the hundred dollars a month rent so I'll learn the lesson that I won't get something for nothing. My mother because I think she enjoys the camaraderie of Ada and the other women in gift wrapping, the way they can sit and gossip and tell jokes while they work and take breaks together, the way it gets all of them out of the house and gives them a weekly paycheck, what my mother calls *a little mad money*. The way they get to go out and eat in the café and let someone else wait on them for a change.

On the last day in the cookware department, I decide to steal the Graham Kerr pot, because I cannot afford to buy it. I tell myself I've been paid such a ridiculously low wage by the church-owned department store that somehow I deserve this pot as a kind of bonus for standing on my feet all day, flogging blenders and silverware and waffle irons, punching in and out on the time clock for even a short break, and getting docked if I'm five minutes late. I tell myself the church is very rich: every day it rakes in millions in tithing alone, 10 percent of everything its members make, and it doesn't even have to pay tax like I do. The church owns insurance companies and huge tracts of land, department stores and commercial buildings, even cattle ranches. The church is a rich corporation with stock holdings in C&H Sugar and Pepsi-Cola and lots of other companies while I don't own anything, certainly not any stocks. I tell myself no one will miss the pot, it was overpriced anyway, a luxury item, too expensive for people to buy, and it will probably go unsold for many more months. People here mostly don't even know who Graham Kerr is. I tell myself all these things and yet I know what I'm about to do is wrong but somehow I don't care. It's wrong in the wrong way. Or right in the wrong way. Still, I'm nervous. What if I'm caught? How embarrassing would that be? How humiliating? To be caught stealing in the department store where my mother works. A department store owned by the *church*. But I'm reckless now, feeling careless. Things have been messed up for so long. It's been so *hard*. Marriage isn't at all what I thought it would be. I thought my sister's ex-boyfriend and I would join the Peace Corps after we got married and go overseas and have adventures and help poor struggling people. But instead I got pregnant a few months after the wedding, then had a baby who was so sick, and we became the poor struggling people. And who knows what will happen in the future? With my son? With the heart surgeon? Or with my plan to become a writer? I *want* the pot. And I'm going to have it.

When it comes time for my lunch break on the last day, I simply put the pot in a shopping bag and walk out to the parking lot with it. My heart is beating fast, but nobody stops me, nobody even notices me, as usual: Same as before, no apparent reason, I think. This is a line of dialogue I recently heard on TV, on the *Lone Ranger* episode my son was watching. Same as before, no apparent reason, the Lone Ranger says to Tonto as they sit on their horses and scope out a lonely homestead. I put the bag with the pot on the floor near the backseat in my mother's Buick, and then I close the door and walk back inside and go to the restaurant, where I've agreed to meet my mother for our last lunch together in the department store. The restaurant is crowded with employees and shoppers and the loud voices overwhelm me, make me feel even more edgy. I have this feeling someone is going to come up behind me and tap me on the shoulder and lead me away. But no one comes: there's just this cold feeling at my back, a fearful presence quivering there. When we're finally seated we share a sandwich and each have a cup of soup, which is what we usually do, and I begin to relax.

I feel excited now. I feel guilty. I feel ashamed. And I feel high, flush with the newness, the immediacy and boldness of my crime. Because in spite of what my father has told me, the thing he is trying to teach me, I realize it is possible to get something for nothing. I have just done so.

Later that night, when everyone is asleep, I get out of bed and go out to the driveway in the dark and get the bag with the pot out of the car and take it back inside, to the room in the basement where I am sleeping. I put the pot on a high shelf in the closet where I know it won't be discovered, and then I shut the door and climb back into bed. All the excitement of the theft has now passed, burned off as the day and night wear on, and all that's left is the little residual feeling of shame, that I have stolen a thing I can't even use. A thing that will, as it turns out, sit on the shelf for a very long time, in the darkness of a long-forgotten closet.

PART ONE

◈

The Story

ONE

When I was little, one of my older brothers used to listen to radio broadcasts of car races from the Bonneville Salt Flats, lying in bed in the dark in the room next to the one I shared with my sister in the basement of the house where I lived until I was nine. The broadcasts often featured a man named Ab Jenkins, a Mormon born in Utah in 1883 who was the first man to begin using the Salt Flats as an automobile racecourse. I had never seen the Salt Flats in person but I wished I could. From listening to the broadcasts I knew they were white and made of salt, and they were perfectly flat and went on for miles and miles, more miles than you could walk in one day, or two, or even three. I imagined if you walked out on those Salt Flats you could kneel down and put your tongue on the salt. You could lick the earth and your tongue wouldn't even get dirty.

Ab Jenkins was the holder of more unlimited world records than anyone else in the history of sports, the only man in his lifetime who ever drove an automobile continuously without relief for twenty-four hours. He once raced an excursion train across the Salt Flats, from Salt Lake City to Wendover, Nevada, and won. His car was called the *Mormon Meteor*. In 1950, at the age of sixty-seven, he made his fastest lap ever—thirteen miles at 199.19 mph. He attributed his accomplishments and stamina to the fact he never in his life tasted liquor or tobacco. An announcer named Hot Rod Hundley was the radio sportscaster. Ab Jenkins! he cried. He has just broken his own record in the *Mormon Meteor*! And at the age of sixty-seven!

Hot Rod Hundley asked, Tell us how you did it, Abe?

Clean living, Abe Jenkins said. I have never tasted liquor or tobacco in my life.

The *Mormon Meteor*. It sounded like the most fantastic car, like a special holy automobile rocketing across a universe of salt, with cosmic flames bursting from its tail. I had no idea what it really looked like, but the next day I decided to make my own *Mormon Meteor*. It was green and sleek and long, made out of an oversized cucumber I found in the garden. I gouged it out with a spoon to make a cockpit for a driver. I stuck two twigs through each end for axles and made wheels out of unripe gooseberries. When I had finished I set it down in the sandbox in the backyard, resting it on the pale sand which I pretended was really white salt, and then I drove my own *Mormon Meteor* in a large circle, guiding it with my hand so it went faster and faster, imagining that I, too, was capable of record-shattering speed, until the cucumber fell apart and the gooseberries were shredded.

This was when I was six. Even then I knew I wanted to go fast— very, very fast. I thought all I'd need is the right machine.

TWO

I was born into a large Mormon family that was already big when I arrived. I was the sixth child and the second girl: two more boys would be born after me, the last when my mother was forty-three, making the final count two girls, six boys.

I don't think my mother's last child was planned: she hadn't intended to get pregnant again in her forties. But then I don't think any of my mother's pregnancies were necessarily planned, though they occurred with a kind of clockwork regularity every two years or so. They simply happened, I think, because little was done to prevent them. My mother loved babies. She once confessed to me that during her childbearing years every time she'd see a newborn baby she'd think, Oh! I must have another, even though she might have an infant only nine months old at home. Such was her hunger for babies.

My father, on the other hand, once said to me he felt he never should have had eight children. I didn't have the temperament for such a large family, he said, then added somewhat ruefully, If I hadn't had eight kids I might have become a *real* musician. He told me this when I was old enough to appreciate such a comment, and also be stung by it. What child wants to think she kept a father from his dreams?

Sometimes when we were growing up he would tell people that he had six sons, and each of them had two sisters, which made it sound like he had dozens of kids, and I am sure it must have felt like that at times.

Many of our neighbors had even larger families. The Harlines had fourteen children, the Stringfellows ten. Children are like special gifts to Mormons, who believe not only in an afterlife but in a pre-existence as well, an ethereal realm where souls are lined up, as if in a crowded celestial anteroom, waiting for a chance to pass through the veil and come into this world. To create a baby is to open the heavenly portal and let a spirit pass through. Most Mormons I knew wanted large families, because every child was seen as a special heavenly blessing. Mormons are not prohibited from using birth control like Catholics are, but when I was growing up in the 1950s and '60s it seemed the only rhythm method used was the one dictated by God. In this picture only seven children are shown with my parents: my youngest brother, Gregg, hasn't yet been born. I am the smallest girl, the one with her hand covering her face.

I was raised in Ogden, Utah, a city in the northern part of the state, nestled between the Great Salt Lake and the massive snowcapped Wasatch Mountains. Water on one side, tall granite mountains on the other, and in between a tidy little Mormon metropolis.

The city was named after Peter Skene Ogden, a trapper for the Hudson's Bay Company who in the nineteenth century was successful in trapping out much of the beaver in the Intermountain West. Originally called Fort Buenaventura, Ogden was the first permanent settlement by people of European descent in the region now called Utah. Until then the Utes and the Paiutes and the Shoshones pretty much had the country to themselves. And then the Mormon elders came in 1847 and bought Fort Buenaventura, bringing their wives and their babies and their animals with them. They planted crops, began irrigating the land and laying claim to it, calling it their Zion, and their "Deseret," the name they gave their new kingdom, which means honeybee, and that's how they worked the land, like honey bees, making the desert bloom just as their prophet had predicted they would.

In time Ogden grew into the second-largest city in Utah, after Salt Lake City thirty miles to the south. Still, it was a relatively small place, almost completely populated by Mormons. That would later change when Ogden became one of the main railroad hubs in the West, a town known for the many Negro porters and railway workers who settled there.

The Negro porters were not Mormons. And they didn't care to become Mormons. Even if they did join the church they knew they'd always be treated differently, since black men were forbidden from holding the Mormon priesthood, a doctrine that did not change until the late 1970s when the gains of the national civil rights movement made the practice of denying blacks the priesthood stand out unpleasantly and the president of the church had a revelation in which God told him it was okay to finally let a black man hold the holy priesthood.

In Ogden, the black railroad workers and their families settled in an area near the Union Pacific depot at the western edge of town, near 25th Street, where the bus station was also located. This street had gained a bad reputation by the time I was growing up, lined as it was with bars and cheap Chinese restaurants and run-down hotels where red lights hung in windows. There were stores that specialized in tarot card readings and fortune-telling. One had a phrenology head in the window, a sculpted plastic model of a skull segmented into neatly numbered sections, from which your personality and fortune could be told. I used to look at this skull in the window and think, From the bumps on my head my future can be read.

There were many more black people living in Ogden than in most Western cities because of the railroad. The porters who came through could see it was a nice place to live. The air was fresh and clean, the mountains nearby—it wasn't crowded like cities in the South or the Northeast. They realized the Mormons didn't bother them: they left them alone to make their own community and by and large they were nice friendly people. And so the blacks ended up settling on the west side of town, below Washington Boulevard, while the whites lived on the east side, and rarely did the two ever meet, except when some liberal-minded person—a person like my own father, in other words—made an effort to bridge the divide.

My father used to take his car to an automotive shop owned by an affable black mechanic who had his own business on the west side of town—he enjoyed this man's company, the easy, jivey banter they had with each other—and once, when I was a teenager, he invited this man and his family to our house for Sunday dinner, which I remember as a rather strange and awkward affair. But I think that invitation affirmed some sense my father had of himself as a man of the people, a man without prejudice, someone who understood the working class, who also had the soul of an amateur musician and thus cultivated what passed for a bohemian sensibility within the confines of the careful sameness of the Mormon culture that surrounded us.

He was an interesting amalgam of sensibilities, an old-style Democrat, the kind who believed in labor unions and racial equality and assistance for the poor, and yet he was also a faithful member of the Mormon Church, into which he'd been born, as were his father, and his grandfather, and his great-grandfather before him. His ancestors had joined the church in the nineteenth century when the church's founder, Joseph Smith, was still alive: that's how deeply our family was rooted in Mormonism. His forebears had known the prophet Joseph and followed him from place to place: they had suffered the early persecutions with him and remained devout throughout the troubles. My father's ancestors had been Southerners, and also slaveholders: it was my great-great-grandfather James Madison Flake who lent his black servant Green Flake to Brigham Young in 1846 to accompany him on the first expedition into the West in search of the new Zion, and it was Green Flake who stood next to the prophet at the mouth of the canyon overlooking the valley of the Great Salt Lake as he uttered his now famous words *This is the place.*

The slave who bore my family's name was among the first to hear those words and realize the difficult exploratory journey was ending. He must have felt relieved. He had made it to the Promised Land, even if it didn't appear all that promising to him.

In the nineteenth century, Mormons were sometimes referred to by the press and the less-than-sympathetic Eastern establishment as "White Muslims," because they were thought to keep harems and, like Muslims, they had their own "Bible." The founding stories of both religions are oddly rather similar. Both Joseph Smith and Mohammed received a series of revelations from angels who appeared to them in wilderness settings—Mohammed in a cave, Joseph in a grove of trees. These revelations became the doctrinal foundations of new religions and resulted in holy books, the Koran and the Book of Mormon. Both Mohammed and Joseph Smith were polygamists and both became prophets. Both men and their followers were also persecuted and shunned for their beliefs and eventually forced into exile.

There weren't many Democrats like my father in that mostly Mormon town of Ogden, where Republicans tended to make up the vast majority and decide every election. But my father seemed to have no problem being a Mormon and a liberal. I believe he relished the feeling it gave him of being an outlier, just as his love of music instilled in him a winking little sense of being special and caused him to affect the nattiest clothes and hats. He never met a pair of plaid pants he didn't like.

Once, I remember, he bought up a whole display table of outrageously patterned and colored trousers that were on sale at one of the better men's stores in Ogden—pants that obviously hadn't sold for a good reason—and he kept these pants in the trunk of our car, itself a riot of color, a 1954 yellow and green Buick Special. When he met someone he liked, he'd say, Come around here to the back of my car for a minute and let me show you something. Then he'd open the trunk and get out some of the pants and drape them over the fender of the car and insist the person choose a pair as a gift. Often you could see how people really didn't want these boldly patterned pants, but they usually accepted them anyway, just to please my father. Once he talked himself out of a speeding ticket while we were driving across the Navajo reservation by doing the same thing. I remember how embarrassed I felt, looking out the back window of the car as we sat by the side of the road in the hot and barren landscape while my father laid out the pants on the rear fender for the Navajo policeman who had stopped us for speeding, all the while keeping up the patter of a born salesman, until the cop, grinning widely, having finally been won over, accepted a pair of red plaid pants and let us go without a fine.

Later, much later, when my father had retired and formed a little combo in which he played the drums, beating out snappy rhythms at lunchtime at a local senior center, wearing his hipster hats and grinning happily while the elderly couples propped each other up and circulated slowly on a dance floor, he said something to me I've never forgotten.

You know, he said, giving me that look he always gave me when he was about to say something important, evil came into the world with syncopation, because that's when people started moving their hips.

He made evil sound fun, like some game involving gyrating to the sound of drums. He made evil sound exuberant—abundant, bounteous, and overflowing, a zesty sort of possession—and maybe that's what it was to him, and why it was so dangerous. It could make you forget yourself in a frenzied fit. It was the realm where you lost control, not only of mind but of body, the place where you started wiggling your hips, and who knew what that could lead to?

THREE

I was the only one of my mother's eight children to be born in a Catholic hospital—to come into the world with the help of nuns.

Later my mother would say that perhaps this had something to do with the way I turned out, but of course this can't be true. She was just making a little joke. Still, if all her other children had been born in a Mormon hospital, why did she choose a Catholic hospital to give birth to me?

Because it was new, she told me when I once asked. It was brand-new, she said, and I wanted to try it out. Later she would say that the nursing sisters—the Catholic nuns—had been so nice to her. She had loved giving birth in St. Benedict's Hospital and remembered those nuns fondly for the rest of her life. Sister So-and-So, she would say, Sister Blah-Blah-Blah. Oh, they were so wonderful. They treated me so well. It had been the nicest experience of her childbearing life, she said, having me in that Catholic hospital. When I was born the nuns told her they had never seen a more beautiful baby.

Me.

The beautiful baby.

Born in a hospital run by the Church of the Devil—for this is the way the Mormons openly referred to the Catholic Church when I was growing up: it was *the Church of the Devil*.

Mormons don't baptize their children until they reach the age of eight, the age at which, they believe, children will be held accountable for their sins, having been given a free pass for all transgressions up until that point. But they do give babies a blessing at the age of one month and at that time they also give the child a name.

The baby is blessed in front of the whole congregation, on fast and testimony day, which takes place on the first Sunday of every month. The child is cradled by the father and surrounded by several other male relatives who all hold the priesthood (women, of course, can never participate in such blessings, because they cannot hold the priesthood with all its special powers). The men place their hands on the baby's head and offer up a blessing, with the father or grandfather usually saying the prayer, and the name is then bestowed with quiet solemnity.

Later I was told my father blessed me on the first Sunday in November 1946.

I give you the name of . . . Judith Ann Freeman, he said.

Judith, a Hebrew name from the Old Testament, one favored by Jews. Judith who seduced Holofernes, luring him to her tent only to cut off his head in order to save her people.

A Catholic hospital. A Jewish name. A wrathful sword-wielding woman.

How did they imagine I'd turn out?

We lived in a small white frame house on a street called Orchard Avenue in an older neighborhood in the northern part of the city.

All the houses were modest and set close together but they had deep backyards and the old trees that lined the street gave the neighborhood a shady and pleasant feel. The house had a basement where the children slept and where a coal-burning furnace was kept going day and night throughout the winter. Our house was set back from the street on nearly an acre of land with many fruit trees and a big garden and a chicken coop at the very back end of the property. The hens were bantam chickens and they laid tiny blue eggs. The big lawn became the perfect place for all the neighborhood children to gather

for games of Hide-and-Seek and Mother May I? and Red Rover that went on until well after dark on summer nights.

We played Mumblety-Peg with a pocketknife, flipping the open blade into the grass so it would stick in the turf. Where the blade stuck is where your opponent had to move his foot until his feet were splayed so far apart he could move no farther. Often we played on the grass with bare feet. Who would now let their children play such a game? At the edge of my childhood there always lurked a faint danger we openly courted and which our parents did little to dispel.

We were a tribe, on our own, left to ourselves much of the time, organizing our affiliations and activities according to rules that were always changing, rules inevitably established by the oldest members of the group, whom we looked up to and were obliged to obey.

For a while when I was very young we had a cow but the cow was kept in a shed on another lot nearby: I remember going with my father when he went to milk the cow and how he squirted the warm milk into my open mouth with the stray cats circling at my feet. We

kept rabbits, stacked up in a hutch near the sandbox where they mul-
tiplied unremittingly. I thought of these rabbits as pets but sometimes
they were slaughtered and turned up at the dinner table, where I
refused to eat them because I could still see their shapes—their lean
rabbity outlines, bunnies now lying skinned and naked in a puddle of
sauce.

We also had six geese—six horrible geese that I felt existed only
to torment me, chasing me as soon as I came out into the yard. They
came at me, these huge white birds almost my own size, honking
loudly with wings spread, running across the grass on their terrible
orange feet, ready to nip at my small fleshy legs.

My first memory is of the swan I threw a rock at as she floated with
her babies on the surface of a pond near the Old Mill and who came
at me with such fury, grabbing on to my thigh with her beak and pulling me into the water before my father rescued me. This happened
not long after I had learned to walk.

Birds: the angry swan; the swarming geese. They instilled in me
the earliest feelings of primal fear. These same birds I would later
come to love for their elegance and beauty.

An irrigation ditch ran in front of our house, full of fast-moving
water, with a little bridge for the driveway that had to be crossed
each time we came or went. Yellow forsythia bloomed in the spring
next to the house. In the winter heavy snow piled up on the fitzers
beneath the windows, and when a bird landed on a branch it sent
a shower of snow springing into the air. From inside the house, it
looked as if a small explosion had occurred, with glittering bits of
mica-like flakes glinting in the sun.

Another early memory, a more painful one.

I am very young, not yet five. My father owns a small store in a
little nearby town called Layton, one of the many smaller communities that ring the larger city of Ogden and border the muddy shores
of the Great Salt Lake. The store is on Main Street and is called Free-

man's Men and Boys Wear and it mainly carries three things—Levi's, cowboy boots, and Stetson hats.

The store has a pink neon sign with our name on it and is just down the way from the movie theater where I will see my first film, a scary monster movie that leaves me more excited than afraid.

Freeman's Men and Boys Wear is devoted to Western clothing because my father considers himself above all a Westerner. When he's not affecting his natty bohemian style, he wears bolo ties and a big turquoise ring and cowboy boots and a white Stetson and he likes to talk about his childhood in Arizona, driving teams of horses and hauling freight with his father and brothers between the towns of Snowflake, where he was born, and Holbrook, to the north. He grew up with lots of animals—goats and chickens and milk cows, herds of cattle and horses. His grandfather was a much-respected horse trader who rode until he was well into his nineties. My father has a way with horses and a love of them that I will inherit.

When I am still very small he gives me my first pair of cowboy boots. They are yellow and I love them with such an inordinate pas-

sion I refuse to take them off except when I have to, at night when I go to sleep, and if I could I would even wear them to bed. But something happens. I do something wrong. I no longer even remember what this thing is but I am told I must be punished for it. And the punishment? I cannot wear my yellow cowboy boots for one week. They might as well have said, We're going to chop off your feet for what you've done.

The anguish is terrible. I suffer in the extreme. This, I understand, is what it means to be very bad. You will be hurt not on the outside but on the in-. And the inside hurt is much worse than the outside kind because you can't do anything about it. It doesn't go away like a wasp sting does when you put mud on it. It doesn't grow a scab and stop hurting. It bubbles in your head continuously and you think everyone can see it, this pain, and you know this is the beginning of the thing you will later call shame.

Growing up, everyone I know is a Mormon. The first friends I make are all Mormon because I meet them all in church. Church is the center of our life. All my mother's and father's friends are Mormon, even the couples who sometimes come over in the evening and play cards with them and eat nuts and drink Pepsi-Cola (technically the Pepsi is forbidden, even though the church owns a lot of Pepsi stock—no caffeine is allowed by the church's Word of Wisdom—and card playing isn't exactly encouraged either, though everyone does it).

All my aunts and uncles and cousins—every one of my relatives— are Mormon. We are all Mormons, everyone in my family, everyone I know, everyone at school, all the politicians, and the schoolteachers, and the people who own the businesses where we shop, except for the Japanese farmers (known as the Japs to my parents) where we buy our produce in the summer but they are an entirely different people, the Japs, and we don't expect them to be Mormons, just like the black people on the other side of town aren't Mormon and we don't care about that either. But everybody else we know

or see or do business with is Mormon, devoutly Mormon, churchgoing Mormons who never miss a meeting. There is never a time when we think of ourselves as anything but Mormon, first and foremost.

But as I get older and start kindergarten I realize there are, in fact, a few people in the world who aren't Mormon: these people are called "gentiles" because they do not belong to our church. They are not just outsiders, as I slowly begin to understand, but in some sense they are *less* than us, some kind of heathens or lost souls because they do not have the advantage of belonging to The One True Church and they do not have a testimony of the Truthfulness of the Gospel.

The outside world, apparently, is full of heathens.

We don't worry, however, because we have our world to ourselves, and the heathens seem far, far away.

In time the heathens will begin to interest me. When I was still a teenager, my mother accused me of picking only rich kids for friends and also of choosing friends who weren't Mormon, and this was probably true. She said it meant I didn't think my own family was good enough for me, implying that I was growing into some sort of snob. But I didn't think this is what it meant at all. I thought it meant that I was, from a very young age, always looking for the *other*.

Around this time, when I first start school, I meet a girl my age called Brenda Butterfield. She is an only child and she moves with her parents into a house a block away from ours. I notice her the first day she comes to school: she is small and lively and has a brown ponytail and when she speaks her mouth twists to one side and she says funny things. I like her right away. When she invites me to come to her

house one day after school, I discover she is not a Mormon, and neither are her parents. In fact her parents smoke and drink and this is
dreadfully interesting to me because these things are *totally forbidden*
by the church and I have never been around anyone who drinks or
smokes. I'm fascinated by the way Brenda's parents light their cigarettes, sometimes holding the smoldering end of the one they've just
smoked to the tip of a fresh one while sucking on it with their cheeks
puffing vigorously in and out. There's such suspense to this: will they
get the new cigarette going off the old one or not?

I find the smell of cigarette smoke to be totally alluring.

As I spend more and more time at the Butterfields', I discover there
are in fact many things about Brenda Butterfield's household that
begin to interest me, including that she is an only child. I have no idea
what this would be like. Not only that, but her parents are younger
than mine and they're always goofing around with each other. Sometimes when Brenda's mother stands at the sink doing dishes her father
sneaks up behind her and puts his arms around her and begins kissing
her neck.

This is not something my parents ever do.

Another time I see Mr. Butterfield lift up Brenda's mother, holding
on to her buttocks while she wraps her arms around his neck, and he
swings her around and around until they both get dizzy and fall over
on the couch laughing.

My parents do not do this either.

The Butterfields make alcoholic drinks and keep liquor bottles and
funny-shaped glasses in a cupboard and sometimes they let Brenda
mix their drinks for them. Soon I get to help her with this task,
measuring out the strong-smelling liquids into a tiny silver cup and
dumping them into the glasses, then dropping in maraschino cherries
or olives or special little onions that come in a tiny jar.

This is called "cocktail hour" at the Butterfields' and we don't have
one of those either. Instead we have Family Home Evening, where we

gather in the living room and sing hymns and read special messages from the priesthood or the Relief Society, the church organization for women, about keeping your faith and your family strong, and then we have refreshments and eat the cake or pie or cookies my mother has made and have some Kool-Aid to wash it down.

I begin spending a lot of time with Brenda Butterfield, in part because she shares a love of the same things I do. She likes stupid jokes, especially knock-knock jokes, and we spend hours making these up. She loves to play outdoors, and she especially loves horses, and together we make stick horses, tying yellow yarn or black yarn to the special sticks we've chosen for our horses to make their manes, and then we make little reins out of pieces of rope and we ride up and down the sidewalk with the sticks thrumming between our legs, holding on to the reins, turning our horses and racing this way and that, running up and down the concrete with the sticks vibrating against the sidewalk. Such pleasure, to play this way with our horses, without ever imagining where a part of that pleasure is coming from.

My mother doesn't like it that I spend so much time at the Butterfields', though she has nothing against Brenda, thinks she's a nice little girl in fact. But she also thinks I ought to invite Brenda to come to church with me. Wouldn't that be a good idea? she says. To introduce her to the gospel? But Brenda doesn't want to be introduced to the gospel, and her parents aren't hot on the idea either. In fact her father laughs out loud when I mention it the next time I visit their house and suggest that Brenda might come to church with me next Sunday. He ruffles my hair and looks down at me and says, We're the wrong species, kid. I don't quite know what this means but I'm sure it's a no.

When Brenda and her parents invite me to take a trip with them to visit Brenda's grandfather in Jackson Hole, Wyoming, amazingly my parents agree. It's my first trip anywhere without my family and therefore it's immensely exciting, especially because it means I'll be with the Butterfields, as part of their family, for five whole days.

We set off in the car, with Brenda's parents chain-smoking in the front seat, and suddenly I don't find the smell of cigarette smoke so alluring anymore. In fact I feel quite sick but of course I can't ask them to stop smoking, though I do have to ask them to stop the car, but only once, and then I don't really throw up, I just stick my head out the open door and take deep breaths until I feel better.

It takes us the better part of one day to get to Jackson Hole, where Brenda's grandfather lives in an old log house not far from the center of town. He's called One-Eyed Jack because he only has one eye. The other is covered with a black eye patch. Every year he plays the part of the outlaw in the town's annual Fourth of July shoot-out on Main Street and he's become famous for this, a well-known figure in all the bars and restaurants, and I'm impressed when he takes Brenda and me around town because he seems very famous. We get to go into the Cowboy Bar with him and sit on the barstools that are made out of real saddles, even though technically kids aren't allowed in the bar, because everybody seems to make exceptions for One-Eyed Jack. He's got a craggy face and wears a black cowboy hat and he's old and wizened and all in all he looks quite sinister with the black eye patch, but he turns out to be a very nice man who, when he finds out how much Brenda and I love horses, takes us out to the big barn behind his house and rigs up a saddle with ropes attached to the front and back and tied to the high rafters and then he swings us from one end of the barn to the other while we take turns sitting astride the saddle and clinging to the horn. This is fun, rather dangerous fun, but not as much fun as if One-Eyed Jack had real horses in his barn, something I've been led to believe he does. The disappointment is rather bitter.

Still I have lots of fun in Jackson Hole with Brenda and her parents and her one-eyed grandfather, though when I get home my mother smells the smoke on my clothes and then holds them away from her and goes, Eeeew! Where have you been?

With the heathens, I want to say. Having fun.

FOUR

There wasn't much privacy in the house where I grew up. Eight children might not have really been that many children compared to some other Mormon families we knew but it felt like a lot to me.

It felt like a lot because of the impersonal lives we led, the way we were often shaped and molded as a group, getting bathed in twos and threes when we were small; eating meals with a dozen people at the table; riding in cars where we sat on other people's laps, or else nestled on the floor near the center hump, or sometimes fit ourselves onto the shelf near the back window. A leveling sense of sameness pervaded the house: when I was very young we each had the same kind of bedding, army-issue green wool blankets my dad bought at the surplus store in Plain City. What I remember is how they itched in the night when they touched your skin.

It also felt like a lot because of the bathroom we shared and how it seemed like you could never be in there for more than thirty seconds before somebody knocked on the door and said, I've got to get in there! Years later, when I discovered people actually ran baths I was amazed, because nobody ran a bath in our house. Nobody ever had the time or luxury of allowing the water to fall into the tub before they did. I remember sitting down on the cold porcelain of an empty tub on Sunday mornings, turning on the taps, and splashing the dribble of warm water that came out onto my shoulders and chest, shivering and waiting for enough water to accumulate in the bottom of the tub to take the chill away, only to have the hot water run out altogether long before that ever happened.

It felt like a lot because we were always getting hand-me-downs, clothes that had gone through someone else and still had their slight impression—a jacket that drooped in the front because someone else's fists had been shoved down into the pockets, a rump-sprung skirt, or a blouse with tiny sprigs of cotton bursting from the collar.

My parents were always dashing around in their garments, the holy underwear worn by all good Mormons, trying to make it from the bathroom to their bedroom across the hall without anyone noticing. There was little mystery about what the other sex looked like: we were always getting caught naked when we forgot to lock doors and people sitting quietly on the john had the door suddenly opened on them and could only yell, Hey, I'm in here! There were always, forever, these surprises, these interruptions and intrusions, these reminders of the inescapable crowdedness—the leveling influence of a lack of privacy. And then of course there was the religion, which strove to make us all the same in thought as well as deed.

There was, however, during those early years, a feeling of an idyllic and uncomplicated world, an egalitarian realm where everyone seemed more or less alike. No one was terribly different from us. There were no rich people and poorer people to compare ourselves to as there later would be when my family moved to a new subdivision in a different part of the city. There was no sense of the envy I would later feel in my father, the envy as well as the resentment of the rich, meaning anyone better off than we were. As it turned out, there were lots of these people in the world. In the brand-new subdivision there would be doctors and lawyers and college professors, dentists and successful businessmen. The people, in other words, who could make my father feel as if they thought they were better than him—or rather that he was not as good as they were.

My father was a scavenger by nature. He couldn't resist picking up items he saw lying on the sidewalk or alongside the road.

Sometimes he would come home with one boot—an old rubber galosh with metal buckles—or one glove he'd found lying around somewhere. This is a good boot, he'd say, if anyone can use it—or Here's a glove that might fit someone. As if we were a family of amputees.

But the truth is someone often could use these things. Just wear an extra sock, he'd say if the one boot didn't quite fit, and then he'd add, You can make a pair out of that other boot lying around. And it's true we were always losing one mitten or glove, so an extra often came in handy. I remember one winter going sledding with friends wearing old woolen socks for gloves because I hadn't taken enough care not to lose my good ones and was told they would not be replaced.

We were frugal in the extreme. No bit of food was ever wasted. Nothing was thrown out if it could be reused. Odd bits of lumber were scavenged from construction sites and recycled as firewood. There were riches in the world for gleaning if one knew where to look. And my father knew where to look. Later—much later—I would understand that the gleaning and scavenging and recycling were in his genes, the result of descending from Mormon pioneers, settlers to whom objects were precious if not priceless. These were people who set out to cross the plains in overloaded wagons, jettisoning goods as they went along in order to save their trail-weary animals. Who arrived in a new world, found nothing awaiting them, and thus were required to build a life from scratch. People who carved bowls and eating utensils out of wood, who might own one dress and often no shoes. A small industry grew up around the enterprising men who, once settled in the new Zion, began backtracking along the emigrant trails, picking up the stoves and pots and pans and chairs and bedding that had been left behind in order to resell these items in the new colonies: sometimes people must have bought back their own belongings.

That was the world my father had come from. A world of gleaners and survivors and recyclers. And that was the world he still lived in.

My father had grown up in the small Mormon settlement of Snowflake, Arizona, a town named after his grandfather William Jordan Flake and another early leader of the church, Erastus Snow.

Snowflake is located in the high, cold, windy country of northern Arizona, between the Navajo and Apache reservations and near the Painted Desert. The Little Colorado runs nearby and Silver Creek provides the irrigation water for the town. The landscape is dotted with cedar and piñon pines from which the natives traditionally gathered pine nuts. It's a harsh and unforgiving country, and it was settled by Mormon pioneers like my great-grandfather who was among the first whites to occupy the territory.

In 1872 William Jordan Flake was called by the prophet Brigham Young to settle in the Arizona Territory and because he did not question what the prophet asked of him—because he had not questioned the prophet when a few years earlier he had commanded him to take a second wife, as difficult as that had been, and because like all the elders of the church he had taken a vow of obedience—because it was important that the Kingdom of Deseret be expanded into the surrounding areas—because of all these things William Flake obeyed the prophet and left the log house he had recently built in Beaver, Utah, and the fields he had planted, and with a party of other Saints made the arduous journey south, crossing the Colorado River at Lee's Ferry, and traversing the Kaibab Plateau with his two wives and his children and in-laws and his large herds of cattle and horses, and founded a new town in a place where there had been none before.

Snowflake. The town that carries my great-grandfather's name. The name of the polygamist patriarch who created a community where eventually, years later, my father would be born.

❖ ❖ ❖

Just north of Snowflake another Mormon settlement was created, called St. Johns. Miles Park Romney, the great-grandfather of Mitt Romney, was one of the early settlers of St. Johns, as were the Udalls, families, as it would turn out, who would end up producing politicians. My great-grandfather Flake and Miles Romney knew each other well. Both were polygamists (Flake had two wives, Romney eventually had five). When polygamy was outlawed by the federal government in the early 1880s both men were arrested. Their bail was set at a thousand dollars each. Since Miles Romney did not have the money to make bail, my great-grandfather borrowed two thousand dollars so they both could go free while awaiting trial.

But Miles Romney never went to trial. With a group of other Saints from the area he fled to Mexico with his wives and children and established a Mormon settlement in the state of Chihuahua, called Colonia Juárez.

My great-grandfather did not flee to Mexico. He was tried in Prescott and found guilty and sent to the Yuma Territorial Prison for six months, after which time he came back to Snowflake and continued living with his two wives and his many children and resumed his position as a community leader, eventually becoming one of the first state legislators.

Miles Romney never did repay my great-grandfather the thousand dollars he'd loaned him to get out of jail. He stayed in Mexico and got rich.

FIVE

My father was raised in a family of twenty children. His father's first wife had died, leaving behind nine children. The neighbor girl who had helped care for his ailing wife, and also tended his children, became his second wife. When he married her, she was eighteen, and he was nineteen years older. This was my grandmother Emma, who bore her husband eleven more children, one of whom was my father.

His father, John A. Freeman, was a farmer and merchant. My father grew up working on his father's farms and in the small general store called Freeman Trading Company that was located next to the family's two-story brick house on the main street of Snowflake.

In high school, the love of music was instilled in my father by a teacher named Rufus Crandall. All my life I would hear about this music teacher and what a formidable influence he had been—the greatest influence, my father said, outside of his parents. Later he would say that when Rufus Crandall played the organ in church, improvising during the passing of the sacrament, my father would sit in a nearby pew openly weeping at the beauty of his playing.

Music became the love of his life, the thing that brought him happiness and made his life richer and which informed the private sense he had of himself as someone special—more special, really, than anyone could know, because he was a man with music in his soul. It was one of the burdens he had to bear in life that, in general, people just couldn't fully appreciate this: they could not understand what an artistic person he really was, that buried beneath the layers of demanding and often dull work, and the endless family routines, there existed a very unusual man, with special gifts that he very much wanted to have recognized.

It must have been Rufus Crandall who told my father that evil entered the world with syncopation because that's when people began moving their hips, an idea that took hold in him and which he would repeat to people throughout his life. He latched on to this idea so forcibly, I think, because it held some mysterious attraction for him, as if evil had its uses as well as its pleasures, and music in some highly exciting and slightly verboten way might hold the keys to both.

Actually, he *liked* verboten. He courted it in various small ways, from taking the occasional drink of alcohol to breaking traffic laws. Laws, for the most part, didn't apply to my father: they were made for people less special, less able to see the hidden liberating rules of life, the higher laws imposed by an underrecognized intelligence and questing spirit. This was the same spirit that would give him a passion for running wild Western rivers in little rubber rafts, defying rapid after rapid as he charted a course through the churning water.

He never went to college, nor did my mother: I'm sure this was never even a possibility, never a consideration. Like all his siblings my father was expected to go immediately to work when he graduated from high school, or serve a mission for the church. In 1930, at the age of nineteen, he accepted a call to serve a two-year mission for the church in eastern Kentucky, and it was here that he met my mother.

My mother, Alice, had grown up in the small mining town of Magna, located just west of Salt Lake City at the foot of the Oquirrh Mountains and near the southern end of the Great Salt Lake. She was also descended from early Mormon pioneers, Cornish people who had joined the church in England in the mid-1800s. Her father, Edmund Paul, had been a miner who worked in the Bingham Canyon

Mine: later he developed lung disease—he felt he had been "leaded" in the mines—and supported the family as a carpenter, though there never seems to have been enough money and his health was often poor. She came from a close-knit family, passed her youth as a high-spirited and fun-loving girl, dark-eyed and pretty, and worked as a salesclerk in a five-and-dime store in Salt Lake City before she decided to accept a mission call to eastern Kentucky.

It was not so common for girls to go on missions at that time. It was said that only old maids, women too unattractive or unlucky to get married, ended up going on missions for the church. But this was not the case with my mother. I think she *wanted* the world, was hungry for it. She was twenty-two, possessed an adventurous spirit as well as a devotion to her church that caused her to burn with the desire to spread its message.

This is where they met: Sister Alice Little Paul of Magna, Utah, and Elder LeRoy Collins Freeman of Snowflake, Arizona. They were forbidden, of course, like all the elders and lady missionaries, from dating or having any intimate contact while in the mission field, but later they would talk about the attraction they felt for each other from the beginning. The spunky Alice Paul, who had no difficulty standing on street corners in Lexington, reading from the Book of Mormon and giving impassioned speeches about the Truthfulness of the Gospel, and the handsome Elder LeRoy Freeman—said to be the most elegant missionary in the field—who used his musical skills to try and attract potential converts. Here they are shown with their fellow missionaries; my father is seated on the lower right while my mother stands at the left on the back row.

For over a year they worked in the mission field together, always keeping an appropriate distance, even during the one time when they broke the rules and took a streetcar with fellow missionaries over into West Virginia to a resort and went swimming and had spaghetti afterward, something for which they later received a reprimand from the mission president. They were supposed to be toiling in the fields

of the Lord, not swimming and eating spaghetti and having fun, and yet looking at the pictures of them in the mission field, it seems they are always having fun, no matter what they're doing: they are young and handsome and full of the fire of their preaching, surrounded by other young men and women who will become their friends for life.

The family of a missionary—not the church—is expected to pay most of the expenses for keeping a son or daughter in the mission field: that was the case when my parents were on their missions in the 1930s, though more recently, in 1990, the church revised its rules and a new program was introduced to help equalize the financial responsibility and ease the burden on missionaries from less affluent families. My mother's family could have used help: they had little money and found they could no longer afford to support my mother on her mission, and so she was called home early, after a year and a half. She returned to Utah in 1932.

My father completed his mission, which lasted two and a half years, then returned to Snowflake and got a job working at a gas station in a town thirty miles away. A year or so passed without much contact between Alice and Roy (as his friends and family called him) until one spring, having heard that my mother was about to get engaged, he made the trip from Snowflake to Utah, taking the train to Barstow and switching there for Salt Lake City, where he proposed to my mother the first night they saw each other again. They were married during the Depression, in September of 1933, and settled in Salt Lake City, where my father began looking for work, going from door to door, accepting anything he could find. He worked as a waiter, a shop clerk, and even a bartender though he himself didn't drink, and then he found a job working as a shoe salesman for Thom McAn, a job he would hold for some time, climbing his way up to manager, an experience that would give him a lifelong interest in people's feet and make him a self-appointed expert on proper-fitting shoes.

Later he would work a series of different jobs. The store he started in Layton, Freeman's Men and Boys Wear, wouldn't last that long: business wasn't really his forte. But he was never out of work. Like most Mormons, he was raised with an acute sense of industriousness (the *honeybee* thing, the State of Deseret) and he always managed to find a job to support his growing family. In the 1950s he worked a desk job in the purchasing department of Thiokol Chemical Corporation and later for Hercules Power, companies that built rockets and missile defense systems under federal contracts, and then he got a job with Kennecott Copper, the very same corporation that had operated the mine where my mother's father had acquired lung disease. But he became disillusioned and bitter working for these corporations. Kennecott, he said, was turning the world into a trash heap.

In my father's self-published memoir, *Reminiscences of LeRoy C. Freeman,* which he wrote as a series of essays in the later years of his life, he explained his feelings about his time at Kennecott and Thiokol and Hercules Power:

The more I learned about Kennecott Copper, and its philosophy toward employees—the ruthless manner in which they fouled the atmosphere and their abuse of government subsidies—the more I became diametrically opposed to this giant, seemingly merciless, virtual monopoly.

And so he quit Kennecott, only to go to work for another giant, seemingly merciless virtual monopoly—the U.S. Air Force, where he accepted a job in civilian personnel, traveling from Ogden each day to a nearby Air Force base. His office was in a metal Quonset hut.

Since we had only one car my mother would often drop him at work in the morning and pick him up at the end of the day, and sometimes I would go with her. We would stop at the little guard station at the entrance to the military base, each time required to give our names and state our business, and then were allowed to drive onto the base, with the big planes parked on runways and rows of ugly barracks and wooden buildings, and we'd pull up to the odd-shaped metal building, the humped and corrugated Quonset, which looked more like a warehouse than an office, and my father would be waiting for us outside, in his dark suit and his loud tie, looking tired after a long day of work.

He would come to despise what he always called the military-industrial complex as much as he despised what he saw in the ruthless mining corporations. I've always thought it ironic that my father, with his leftist liberal leanings, spent his life working for entities he came to hate, which represented the interests of the rich and powerful rather than the little man, while his true love, music, was left to find its own modest and stunted outlets in the hours left to him when he'd finished his paying job.

Perhaps this was part of what made him the moody man he was. He had a tendency to isolate himself when upset. He was a man capable of going silent for days—sometimes weeks—and never even revealing what it was that had upset him. This was hardest on my mother, but it also affected us children as the mood in the household grew dark with all the unspoken troubles. He shut everyone out for long stretches, and when this happened I could often hear my mother weeping alone behind the closed bedroom door as she tried to figure out what to do.

I later came to believe he'd endured a stark emotional desolation in his youth due to his own father's harshness and severity. My grandfather Freeman, whom I remember as a stern, humorless man, had been hard on his sons: if one of his boys failed to feed the work animals on time, the boy's dinner was withheld. He was demanding and sullen, and as he aged his face grew sadder and longer and ever more stern until it became a hard and frightening countenance. You can see his severity in every picture ever taken of him. My grandmother, on the other hand, was a sweet, gentle woman who kept a constant expression of bland benevolence on her face. She called her husband "Daddy." It would have been unthinkable for her to go against his wishes.

In his memoir, my father described his dad as *brutally frank, an honest, ingenious person who loved his daughters more than his sons, and who showed the most consideration for his animals.* It must not have been easy being the son of such a dour, demanding man, one who so clearly favored his daughters as well as his horses and cows.

When my father entered one of his dark moods, he had no way of expressing his troubled feelings except to fall silent until he had worked through these feelings or until they had somehow lifted. At one moment he could be funny and amusing, the next sharp and cutting. He had a nasty habit of lifting his children up by the hair at the back of their necks when he was angry over something they'd done, and he was angry often enough that this prospect became terrifying to me. He called this punishment "the turkey trot" because the child being lifted by the hair would begin scrambling on tiptoe in an attempt to keep her feet on the ground.

Still, he was in general a fairly genial man, but he seemed incapable of controlling his anger. He dominated everyone and every situation with the intensity of his bottled-up emotions. The boy who cried in church listening to his music teacher play the organ grew into a man who could no longer so easily show his feelings and as a result the emotional voids in our household grew deeper and his behavior couldn't be predicted. A child troubled by incontinence would be humiliated repeatedly and forced to sleep in the garage after being publicly shamed and berated for something he couldn't control. A razor belt would be brought out to deal with certain other infractions. His temper would flare and his hand would reach for the hair on the neck and a child would find herself lifted off the floor, just for a few seconds, suspended by the tender follicles that seemed to be slowly ripping away from her scalp.

And then there he would be, a short while later, smiling and suddenly fine again, maybe even a little more than fine due to the remorse or guilt he might feel, happily tending a bonfire in the backyard, a toothpick clenched between his teeth, asking you if you'd like him to sharpen a stick with his special pocketknife so you could toast a marshmallow over the open flame.

Throughout all this my mother was stoic. Stoic, and resourceful, and very loving with her children, as if to make up for her husband's moodiness, his bouts of anger, his long silences and physical abuse. For the most part she was a joyful person, at least when her children were young before certain events later in life brought her more sadness and even then she always had a ready smile, always wished above all to make other people feel good. She was also skilled in running a household on not much money, often cooking up big pots of pinto beans—what my father jokingly called "Arizona strawberries," harking back to when this dish had been a staple of his childhood—beans that came in fifty-pound sacks and which my mother had to pick through carefully in order to take out any bits of dirt or rock before cooking them. One evening a friend came to visit while my mother sat at the kitchen table, a mound of beans spread out before her, carefully picking through them, and my friend later asked me, Are you so poor that your mother has to count the beans before she cooks them?

She didn't, but she might have, so frugal was she in husbanding our resources.

Who can say what makes a marriage a good one or not? What do we see and what do we not see of our parents' lives? I think often of my mother crying behind that closed bedroom door, emerging red-eyed, attempting to affect a heroic cheerfulness for the sake of her children. I think of how my father often went to bed early on week-

nights, retiring to his room right after dinner while it was sometimes still light outside, how he would lie in bed on his back in the crepuscular light with his hands clasped behind his head and his eyes closed, listening to the music coming from the small portable radio sitting next to him on the bedside table. Sometimes my mother, when my own bedtime arrived, would urge me to go into his room and kiss him goodnight, something I never really wanted to do, for it felt like I had to enter a place of almost deathlike stillness where my father lay on a bier of his own making, not really moving at all, just listening to the music with his eyes closed. Those times when I did enter the room to kiss him, mumbling Goodnight, Dad, he'd offer me a cheek, cool and firm as marble, and without opening his eyes murmur his own muted Good evening.

SIX

Why did I get married at seventeen?

I've been asking myself this question lately. It seems to have been such a stupid thing to do and I was not a stupid girl. I have no one to blame but myself. And this knowledge has left me with a little niggling feeling of shame.

For a long time—for most of my life in fact—I never thought of myself as a teenage bride, let alone a teenage mother, as if those terms applied only to poor girls from disadvantaged backgrounds, girls who didn't have other choices. But that's what I was—a teenage bride, and a teenage mother, and it's as if one day, not so long ago, I woke up from some deep slumberous state of denial and finally recognized this obvious fact that had been there all along.

Lately another question arises: Why did I choose to marry my older sister's ex-boyfriend, the man she had rejected after promising to wait for him while he went off to the Naval Academy? What was I thinking, marrying someone so much older, let alone someone who had loved my sister before he loved me?

She was a beautiful child, my sister Marcia, petite, with big dark eyes and very delicate, pretty features. Four years older than me. The first girl born to my parents after the births of three boys. She was their darling, the girl they had longed for, the child who would always hold a special place in their affections.

It seems odd to me that I can't remember much about my relations with my sister when we were young. There is an ineluctable, somewhat blurry distance between us that prevents our relationship from coming into focus. She always seemed to belong to the older siblings—my brothers Bob and John and Ron—as if they had already laid claim to her in some way I never could. Lee was the child born two years after her, the one located between us in age, the brother who felt more like a friend to me when we were young. But Marcia? We seemed to have had no natural affinity, sisters only in name. Many of the things that interested me did not interest her. Perhaps the four years between us formed too large a gap to bridge, especially with so many other children in the family, and particularly since we often functioned as a group, bound up by a collective mentality rather than close sibling affinities—at least that was my experience. Or was it simply the case that Marcia and I were, from the very beginning, two very different personalities, with disparate interests and dispositions, not to mention inclinations?

I remember how Grandma Freeman came to visit us once in the late 1950s, making the two-day car trip from Snowflake with her oldest son, Leo, who was by then divorced and living at home with her again. Marcia was fifteen at the time; I had just turned eleven. In the daily diary she kept throughout her life my grandmother recorded details from that visit—how my mother bought five dozen eggs at a time, how there were fourteen people at the table for dinner, how we all gathered around the piano in the living room after the meal for a little group singing.

She also recorded her observations of my sister and me. In her diary entry she wrote, *Judy is a horse girl. She and another girl went for a ride. Judy has her pony.*

Of Marcia she noted something quite different: *I had a rare treat, heard Marcia give a very impressive family prayer, proving she was used to doing so. How happy it makes us to see Our Dear Ones thus trained.*

One a horse girl with her pony. The other a dear one well trained,

capable of offering up a family prayer that could leave such a deep impression.

A photograph from around this time shows us standing in front of our new house where the lawn hasn't even been planted yet, me with my eyes closed, looking boyish and tanned, and Marcia with her pale skin and red lipstick looking demure, gazing rather sweetly into the camera my father holds. We're dressed for church, wearing our Easter dresses, and beneath them the rigid petticoats our mother has starched into stiff bell-like shapes. In this photograph, the difference between us, in spite of our similar outfits, right down to our corsages and cummerbunds, is rather evident.

And yet, during my early years, as the only girls in a family of boys, Marcia and I shared not only a bedroom but a bed, snuggling close to each other at night. Our room was next to a larger room where our brothers slept in bunk beds. The room had knotty pine paneling and often I felt afraid at night when the light faded and the knots in the pine began to look like faces with dark eyes staring out at me. Then Marcia would comfort me and help dispel my fear.

The bedrooms in the basement were next to the furnace room, where a coal fire burned throughout the winter. A truck brought the coal. It came in large, heavy lumps. The truck backed into our driveway, lowered a chute to an open window in the basement, and the coal slid down the chute into a big bin. From this bin the coal was then shoveled into the furnace as needed. You could open the door to the furnace and see the bright hot red coals and flames of fire, a beautiful inferno that made you want to stare into it. When a mouse was caught in the traps kept in the laundry room, it was taken to the furnace and thrown into the blasting hot fire. Dead or alive, in it went, striking the coals with the tenderest of thuds as the children gathered round to watch it burn.

From the time I can remember my family kept a two-year supply of food in the basement. We had been instructed by the church presidency to do so, because we were Latter-day Saints, of the Church of Latter-day Saints, and we took that latter-day part seriously.

We believed the latter days were now, or could be now, or anytime, tomorrow or the next day, if not next year. The world was full of troubling signs. We were living in the last dispensation. All Mormon families had been instructed by the General Authorities to keep a two-year supply of food on hand because at any time bad things could happen. Very bad things, like nuclear war. To help everyone stock their shelves the church even started a bulk food distribution program as part of a highly organized welfare system involving the processing of food at special church-owned canneries. The Relief Society women helped can the food. The kids were used to help harvest crops on large church-owned farms. I remember as a teenager being taken to a church-owned farm near the mouth of Weber Canyon with a group of other kids and thinning beets, crawling down rows on hands and knees, all the while hating the hard work in the hot sun, but this was called "service" and it's what we had to do.

Growing up in the fifties we know bad things are going to happen, and if not today, then maybe tomorrow. And if not nuclear war, something else—famine or plague or lord knows what, so we'd better be prepared. And we do prepare, starting with our two-year supply of food.

We know that we will be the ones who can survive, with our shelves of canned goods, our cases of tuna fish and bins of onions and potatoes and dried beans. We are absolutely prepared for the worst because in some way the worst is what we're waiting for— what we're expecting. We're almost looking forward to it, because it could mean Christ will return any day. *And we will be ready*.

I remember saying to myself, I don't think it will be enough to have a two-year supply of food when the awful thing happens. What about gas masks? What about a bomb shelter? I know enough to know about nuclear war: you need more than food if you expect to survive the Big One. And that's what we're thinking about. How to survive. Because we're told we can. We all can, as Mormons, by helping each other, and by being prepared. Other people might not make it. But we will.

However, we don't have any gas masks or a bomb shelter. We just have lots of tuna fish and Campbell's soup, fifty pounds of pinto beans, a hundred pounds of potatoes and onions, and shelf after shelf of fruit my mother has canned, jars that sit in the dark in the cool walk-in room in the basement we call the "fruit room," the pears and apricots, the cherries and peaches, floating in their beautiful jewel-colored juices like precious orbs.

We are told that one day the Constitution of the United States will hang by a thread and it will be a Mormon, or a group of Mormons who have ascended to high positions in the government, who will save the Union.

This phrase, *the Constitution will hang by a thread,* and the idea of Mormons saving the nation, are repeated over and over again until they become embedded in our minds.

No one knows when this will happen, but we know it's the future because the General Authorities have told us so, and the prophet and his counselors and the Twelve Apostles have also predicted it. All the children and all the adults are made to understand this.

When the disaster doesn't come right away, we simply go ahead and eat the food from the fruit room and then replace it with newly canned bottles and jars of fruit and new cases of tuna fish, and this is the way it goes throughout my childhood—always recycling, eating the older food, laying in the new, always preparing for Armageddon, for the day when the Constitution will hang by a thread and Mormons will save the nation.

SEVEN

Growing up, all the kids were assigned chores around the house and sometimes we also had small paying jobs—delivering newspapers, picking fruit, selling donuts door-to-door, babysitting, yard work, whatever brought in spending money, and no matter how young we were or how much money we made we were taught to pay tithing to the church on whatever we earned.

All devout Mormons, even children, pay 10 percent of everything they make to the church, and we're talking about gross income, not net: God gets his money before Uncle Sam.

If I earned four dollars babysitting, I put aside forty cents for tithing.

If I made eight dollars cleaning Helen Plowgian's house on Saturday, I put away eighty cents for tithing.

The tithing was collected by young boys, thirteen- and fourteen-year-olds who had been inducted into the Aaronic priesthood and achieved the rank of teachers, who came around on the first Sunday of the month with flat brown envelopes and knocked on the front door and waited while my mother wrote out a check and gave it to them to put in the envelope, along with any money the kids owed. Sometimes we paid the ward clerk who sat at a little desk in the church foyer on fast and testimony day, like an old-fashioned scribe accepting people's tithing and in return giving them a receipt.

Even when I was young I wondered if this was right, people having to give the church so much money. Requiring that even children pay tithing. Was it right to make money off children? But right or wrong, it was a way of teaching kids from the get-go that they would forever be expected to give 10 percent of everything they ever earned to the church.

And what would they get back?

A feeling of righteousness.

The promise of blessings.

And a place at the table.

I began to question things, such as why I should have to pay tithing on my meager earnings to a church that already had so much money. I gained a reputation for being a rebellious little girl, tough-minded and capable of holding her own against the bigger kids in the neighborhood.

Jimmy K. was a bad boy who lived on our street. He said bad words and did bad things, like torturing cats. I thought it was because he was fat and awkward and had big fleshy ears for which he was constantly being teased and this had made him mean. He was especially cruel to stray animals. One day I caught him winding an elastic band tightly around a gray cat's neck and I hit him on the head with my lunch bucket. He looked surprised and fell over on the sidewalk, holding his big ears.

I was not afraid of boys who were twice my size, especially not Jimmy K. Even then I could not bear the idea of cruelty to animals and felt the need to defend them.

I didn't mind being called a tomboy or being thought of as tough. When I thought of my father he seemed tough and when I thought of my mother I knew she wasn't. I thought of her crying behind a closed door and I did not want to be that person, though I did not want to be my father either. But if I had to choose I felt I would rather be like him. I did not see that my mother's intelligence was that of a happy child and I might have been better off emulating her than a man with a cruel streak running beneath his amiable persona.

◈   ◈   ◈

I thought all children were raised by a father who lifted them off the floor by the hair at the nape of their necks when he got angry or if they did something he felt was wrong, that this was somehow normal behavior, the prerogative of men who set the tone in a household where everyone was expected to obey or be punished.

We were not a family who had time to read books, nor were we inclined to do so. We didn't have children's books, or books of fairy tales, and my parents didn't read novels or other kinds of adult books. The books we did have were mostly of a religious nature—the Book of Mormon and its two companion volumes, The Pearl of Great Price and the Doctrine and Covenants, as well as other books with titles like *A Marvelous Work and a Wonder* and *Answers to Gospel Questions.* These were books that did not appeal at all to a child.

There was one book on our shelves, however, that I do remember opening and looking through when I was young: it was called *Heart Throbs of the West: A Unique Volume Treating Definite Subjects of Western History,* published by the Daughters of Utah Pioneers. I liked these stories, which had titles like "Riders of the Pony Express," "First Shoes Made in Utah," and "An Indian War Soldier." These were adventure stories. Stories that had animals and descriptions of nature in them, and children who did daring things.

Later my mother subscribed to Reader's Digest Condensed Books and every month we'd get a new volume, containing the abridged versions of a couple of popular novels. The religious books and these condensed books were the only volumes I remember my family owning. They were kept on a small built-in bookshelf just inside the front door, beneath a planter where pink plastic geraniums had been arranged in a tray of tiny white rocks. I never saw anyone open one of these Condensed Books. They seemed to be there only for show, as if these abridged versions of popular novels were proof of a kind of lit-

erary taste, but they also attested to the fact that we were all too busy
with church activities to sit down and actually read a complete novel.

From the time we were very young all the kids were expected to
help out with household chores. One job I had was polishing our
houseplants with mayonnaise. Where my mother got this idea, and
how she could have thought it was a good one, I don't know. She
would give me a little cup of mayonnaise and a clean cotton ball and
I walked around the living room, dipping the cotton ball in the mayonnaise and rubbing all the leaves on every houseplant, one by one.
They were all slick-leaved plants and with a coating of mayonnaise
they shone pure and clean, as if they'd just been pulled out of water.

But the mayonnaise also made the dust stick to the leaves and this
meant they had to be polished more frequently. It seemed a fool's
errand and I was the fool, wandering the house with my little cup of
mayonnaise and cotton ball, making sticky leaves for dust to land on.

Ours was a very tidy household. My mother kept our house very
neat and clean, as most Mormon mothers do, and all of us worked
hard at our assigned chores. Clean clothes were sprinkled and then
frozen in big plastic bags in a huge chestlike freezer until your turn
at ironing came, and then the frozen bags were taken out and as the
clothes thawed out they were perfect for ironing. I remember standing at the ironing board for hours on hot summer days, pressing
thawing shirts and pants—the family wash—listening to pop tunes
on the radio.

My oldest brothers, Bob, John, and Ron, were all so much older
they almost seemed to belong to a different family. I don't remember
them paying much attention to us younger kids. It was Marcia who
seemed to hold some pivotal place in the family, connecting the older
boys to the younger kids. Growing up I felt closest to my brother
Lee, two years older than me, and Jerry, eighteen months younger.
Gregg, the last child, was eight years younger than me and not until

we were older did I feel a connection to him: he was simply the baby.
My mother spread her pregnancies over more than twenty years.
Twenty years of babies, of satisfying her hunger for them.

And yet my mother was not overly maternal. It was as if the religion and the family were equally demanding of her time. They were
inseparable, really, two sides of the same coin. She had no time to
nurture every one of her children individually, though she often did,
when she could and still devote herself to fixing meals, and keeping
house, and doing laundry for a large family, as well as attending to all
her church activities. More often than not we were trained to think
as a *group,* and we were nurtured as a group. If I had been a jealous
child I would have been jealous of the church, not my other siblings.

But I was not a particularly jealous child, at least not at that age. I
was happy to be left alone. And with so many children in the household, this wasn't hard to arrange. Especially for the sixth child, a
small girl buried so far back in the pack.

EIGHT

When did I first hear The Story? The Story that tells me who I am, where I came from, why we are here on earth as well as where we are going, and what we need to do to make sure we get there?

It's a very *big* story. And it's the first and only story I hear for a very long while because we don't have books of fairy tales or other children's stories in our house. We just have books that tell about The Big Story, the one I hear most often, and of course that makes it seem like the most important story anyone could tell, more important even than the other stories I'll later hear, the ones from the other black book called the Bible.

Fortunately it's a magical story, one that appeals to kids, with talking angels and buried treasure and special magic glasses and stones, and the way it's told in Sunday school and also in Primary, which is a special weekly meeting for kids after school, and the way it's told at Family Home Evening and dramatized with figures on a flannel board in Sunday school makes it seem like a very exciting story indeed, even for little kids.

Basically the story goes like this: A man was looking for the true religion, he was all confused—really he was just a boy, a teenage boy—and one day an angel comes to him and says, I will help you find the truth and lead you to a place where a box is buried, and inside that box are special golden tablets that tell the story of the true religion, but I can't take you there yet, you're too young, you have to wait a couple of years, but I'll come back again, and the angel does come back, just like he said he would, and he leads the young man to a place called Hill Cumorah, which is in upstate New York, and tells him where the box is buried, and the young man digs it up and finds some golden plates with funny writing on them which he can't understand, but there are special magical glasses in the box, and a breastplate with seer stones, and if he wears these glasses and uses these seer stones he can read the writing on the golden plates. The angel has told him he must not show these plates to anyone else, only he can see them, and he should write down what they say in English with the help of the magic tools, and then take them back and bury them again, and this is what he does and when he's finished he has the Book of Mormon, which is OUR book, our Special Book that no one else has, and if we read it and believe in it we'll go to heaven with our moms and dads and all the other good people we know and once we get there we'll have something called Eternal Life which means we won't ever die, not like our cats and dogs do, which we will never see again, because in this place called heaven we see only people, everybody we ever knew, if they were good, like we're supposed to be, they'll all be there, and it's because of this book, the Book of Mormon, that this can happen. We have the only true religion and it will be our job when we grow up to try and tell the rest of the world about this so that they too can be baptized and saved.

In Sunday school we're taught a little song called "I Want to Be a Missionary" and we sing it every week. When we sing it, we draw out the one most important word and say, I want to be a *MISH-ON-AIRY*. To me it sounds like a foreign word and something I'm not sure I want to be.

Mormons train for public speaking early, which is why young people often feel so at ease in the mission field, knocking on doors cold and trying to get people to listen to their message about the gospel. You have had *experience* in putting yourself forward that way. By the time you're five years old, you're prepped to stand in front of a congregation and give a brief speech, what's called a two-and-a-half-minute talk. Parents usually write these talks out for their children and go over them repeatedly, helping the child commit them to memory. The stories are from either the Book of Mormon or the Bible—Joseph Smith discovering the box of buried golden plates, or Jesus walking on the water, or magically multiplying the loaves and fishes, or raising the dead—stories that naturally appeal to a child's sense of the fantastic. The first time I was asked to give a two-and-a-half-minute talk my mother taught me the story of Jesus driving the money changers from the temple and night after night we rehearsed it until I could repeat her very short version of these events almost perfectly, word for word. But when I finally stood at the pulpit in front of the congregation, I remembered something else I'd been taught, and said, much to the amazement of the congregation:

> I'm a cute little girl
> With a cute little figure
> Stay away boys
> Till I get a little bigger.

But they did not stay away, not the boys, or the men for that matter. One male relative in particular, a large fat uncle, had a penchant for grabbing little girls. At extended family gatherings he would trap us in his meaty arms and hold us on his lap, pressing us tight against him, rubbing us back and forth. Snatch us as we ran by and prevent us from getting away. Always wanted to hug. Always surprising you, then not wanting to let you go. His largeness felt so intimidating to me: it seemed impossible to get away from such a big man.

I think my mother knew he might be a problem and she watched us closely when he was around. What I remember about this man is how repulsed I felt by his size, by the softness of his belly flesh, and the taut suspenders that held his pants up which in some way seemed obscene to me (what would happen if they snapped?), and the way he pretended to tease me when really I felt something sinister running beneath his jibes. Nothing happened, really. He never did anything to me, and yet there is still a feeling when I think of him of a terrible predatory presence, or perhaps not so terrible, just sad.

Later I would hear other stories about this uncle. About his visits to prostitutes, though where he found those in Utah I'm not quite sure, and the way he hung around the pool of the condominium complex where he and his wife ended up, flirting with the little girls playing in the water, a sad old fat man whose strong and sensible (and long-suffering) wife would pointedly rebuke him when his behavior finally became too obnoxious. From the time I was quite young I came to understand that a number of people around me led double lives, presenting themselves as good churchgoing Mormons while privately indulging what would be viewed as unacceptable behavior. That's eventually what I would come to do as well, as a means of surviving my teenage years, and in admitting this it becomes more difficult to judge my uncle.

The kitchen was the center of our lives. White shoe polish was kept in the cupboard above the oven, with the Wheaties and Cheerios, the salad oil and potato chips and the small bottle of olive oil that was never used for cooking because it had been consecrated for anointing and healing the sick during the ritual of the laying on of hands.

I polished my own shoes on Sunday mornings, which were always rushed and chaotic. First the men got up and used the bathroom, dressed, and left for priesthood meeting at eight o'clock. With the men gone, my mother started washing the younger kids and helped them get dressed in their Sunday clothes. The older ones she told what to do, and tried to get them to do it faster. Two of us often took a bath at once. After our hair was washed, she poured a rinse made of vinegar and warm water over our heads to condition our hair and make it shine. It gave us the faint smell of pickles.

When it came time to polish my shoes I spread newspaper out over the kitchen counter and first wiped the shoes clean with a dish-rag. The polish had a little wand attached to the cap, and at the end of the wand was a furry ball that absorbed the liquid polish. Polish-ing the shoes was like painting. I could never get the polish to really cover the black scuff marks, but each week I added another film of chalky white to my shoes as the liquid, which went on shiny, dried to a dull finish. Then the men came home to get us for Sunday school. My mother, who always had a lot of last-minute things to do, was the last one out of the house. By that time my father would be sitting in the car in the driveway, impatiently honking the horn.

When we were sick, the elders were sometimes called to perform a laying on of hands. My father always took part in this ritual, as the priesthood holder in our household. Usually three elders joined together to perform the blessing, one of whom was always my dad.

Once, when I had a bad case of the flu, I remember the elders came to administer to me. This was after we had moved to the new sub-division high up on the mountainside, into a big house with six bed-rooms. My sister and I shared a bedroom on the main floor with a window that looked out onto the street. My mother, an avid quilter, had made new matching quilts for our twin beds and when I first saw our new room, with the pretty lavender flowered quilts and the new white dresser trimmed in gold, I thought it was almost too beauti-ful to occupy. When I came down with the flu, I didn't really mind because I could stay home and lie in my new bed, in my new room, and look out the window at the view of the street and the mountains across the way.

It was late winter when the elders came, summoned by my father to perform the laying on of hands. My parents had become worried when I began to run a fever. The house was located in the foothills of the Wasatch Mountains where heavier snows always fell, and for several days it had been snowing hard. As I grew sicker and the fever overtook me, I watched the snow falling outside, thick and mesmerizing flakes, a swirling world of whiteness that left me feeling wrapped in a woolly silence. The long feverish days passed this way, watching the snowstorm, with my mother coming into the room occasionally to check on me and bring me liquids.

And then, as dusk fell one night, two elders arrived, called by my father to help him perform a healing. One was Brother Skanky, a small wiry bald man who taught art at a local school, and the other was Brother Wadman, who lived just up the street and whose son Ricky was one of my best friends.

I heard the elders assembling in the hallway outside my room. I knew they had come to administer to me because my mother had told me earlier they'd been called. They came into the room with my father, bringing with them the scent of men and men's lives and of power, carrying in the cold of the outside world, the smell of the world I'd been cut off from by my illness. They stood by my bed, pressing close in their woolen jackets and winter coats. The sharp, metallic odor of winter clung to their heavy clothes.

They were kind men, Brother Skanky and Brother Wadman. They both had a good sense of humor, especially Brother Skanky, and they talked playfully to me for a few minutes, asking me how I felt, if I thought I was going to live after all, patting my shoulder beneath the blankets and looking down tenderly at me. They said they had come to help me feel better, which they knew I would soon.

They grew more serious and gathered around my head and stood over me, looming above me in their largeness. My father took the small bottle of olive oil that had been consecrated earlier and placed a drop on my forehead and I closed my eyes. The elders placed their fingertips lightly on my head, over the spot where the oil had been spread, and then they closed their eyes and my father began to offer up a prayer.

He called upon the power of the priesthood that had been invested in him to make me well, as he uttered my full name, asking God to take away the sickness that had befallen me and restore me to health. He said other things, how grateful he was to belong to the one true church, restored here on earth in the latter days, and to hold the priesthood with all its powers, and he thanked God for giving me life, and asked that my body should be freed of any illness, and any suffering, and then he closed the blessing by saying he asked these things, on my behalf, in the name of Jesus Christ, Amen.

The prayer didn't last that long, and as soon as it ended the men lifted their fingertips from my brow and opened their eyes. When their hands were taken away, I too opened my eyes and looked up at them: it was as if a great dark weight had been lifted from me.

I felt as if a spell had been cast over me—a good but slightly disturbing spell. I felt as if I had just emerged from a deep, dark, quiet place, a realm where magic could be summoned if you knew the right words and if you had the right power. You could heal people with that magic. All I had to do was submit to the power and believe in it, and I knew I would be made well. Still, the experience left me slightly unsettled and just a bit frightened, as if I had to be very careful now not to do anything wrong that might disturb the blessing.

I also understood that women could not have this power I had just experienced, that only men who held the priesthood could perform a laying on of hands. From a young age I realized that men would always have powers unavailable to me and thus I would always be beholden to them, required to obey their dictates as bearers of the holy priesthood, and thus I would forever exist in a somewhat lower realm.

This was not the first time I had experienced the laying on of hands, nor would it be the last. Each time the feeling was more or less the same—the drop of warm oil on my forehead, the weight of the elders' hands, the descent into the dark and magical place with the large men looming over me. Each time I gave myself over to the elders and felt myself suspended in their priestly world where they could do with me as they wished, but somehow I remember this blessing on that winter night more vividly than others. Perhaps it was the fever, or the days enfolded by the storm, or the kindness of Brother Skanky and Brother Wadman. Or maybe it was simply that it all took place in that bedroom which did not yet feel mine.

Later, in that same room, when months had passed since the elders' visit, I sat on my bed one afternoon, alone, with the door closed and the light falling through the window onto my flowered quilt, and I felt the powerful nearness of God. He was so near it was as if I could reach up and take His hand, and this is what I did: I simply reached up and held the hand of God, just for one quick moment. And then I let go, and went back to what I was doing.

NINE

Explain the Mormons to me, someone once said.

This was when I was older, when I'd already become an adult and long since left the church.

People were always asking me these kinds of questions when they realized I'd grown up in Utah. Mormons were the *peculiar people* to them, secretive and unfathomable and therefore a subject of curiosity. In those days I often got asked about my background, whether I liked it or not. By then I had come to realize how inevitably I would always be tethered to my past.

What I don't like about them, this man went on to say, is how they think they're so exceptional. They like to make exceptions of themselves. They think they're special, don't they? Like they have something the rest of us don't have.

I wanted to tell him, No, it's not just that, it's not so simple.

I had one image, of a small green satin apron in the shape of a fig leaf, stitched into smooth scalloped leaves and worn over perfectly white clothing, but it was nothing I could speak about. A fig leaf, decorated with a fine embroidery of veins. Worn by both men and women, green and shiny and pretty.

When Mormons go to their temples—for washing and anointing, to do baptisms for the dead, to marry each other or take out endowments or prepare for their missions—every single piece of clothing they will wear once inside is carried in a little suitcase. And every piece of clothing is white.

For many Mormons, going through a "temple session" (as my grandmother did every day later in her life) becomes a way of life. It fulfills a spiritual obligation and need, and at the same time gives the faithful a chance to mingle with each other in a very holy setting. It also allows them to do "work for the dead"—very important work that can only be done in temples—where the names of people who have passed on without being baptized are assumed by the living and are baptized in absentia. Originally, in the early twentieth century, baptism for the dead was meant to be a means of baptizing one's ancestors who may not have had a chance to receive the gospel; but later, through genealogical work, at which Mormons became expert, great swaths of names were gathered indiscriminately across centuries, and Mormons began suffering a backlash, including from groups of Jews who did not want to see their dead ancestors baptized as Mormons.

To get inside a Mormon temple a recommend from a bishop must be shown that can be obtained only by submitting to a regular interview in which one is asked, Are you clean? Have you kept yourself pure? Abstained from liquor, cigarettes, coffee and tea? Attended your church meetings? Paid your tithes? Been faithful to your spouse? Avoided profanity?

Are you, in other words, *worthy* to enter the sacred space?

Only then, when one has shown the recommend, can you pass through the checkpoint and enter the temple. The women go to one dressing area, the men to another. The white clothes are taken out. The men put on white shirts and pants, white socks and shoes, even white ties and belts, and the women wear white dresses, white nylons, white shoes. Little white cloth caps, like the shape of baker's caps, are worn by the men while the women wear veils with which to cover their faces at a certain point in the ceremony. And of course, beneath these white clothes everyone will have on the holy white garments, thin and silky against the skin. White everything, head to toe. Like angels, really. White does that to people—makes them look pristine, ethereal, ready for the Second Coming.

After everyone has changed into the white clothing, the rituals begin, the enactment of scenes from the Bible, little plays performed in fantastically painted rooms, some replicating the Garden of Eden in lavishly beautiful scenes, through which all the people in white move quietly, serenely going from room to room, until the last and final moment when they pass through the veil, having knocked three times to summon God, played by a temple worker. To see a whole group dressed like this is like glimpsing the hosts of heaven. More white than you can imagine in one place. It looks holy, it really does. People seem pure with all that white on. All white . . . except the aprons . . . the small green apron that each person will be wearing, the shiny satin fig leaf, which restores original innocence, I guess, or rather original sin, and turns everyone into fallen Adams and Eves.

How could you not feel exceptional?

And yet, for the first nine years of my life, the years when my family lived on Orchard Avenue in the little white house with the fruit trees and chickens out back, I felt anything but exceptional. Only much later did I understand how singular my life was, how singular every life is, and how the uncommon and noteworthy can arrive so unexpectedly and cause a person to feel strange, as if the world they thought they knew were only a parallel option.

In those early days, I simply felt enfolded by the collective—the collective family, the collective congregation, the collective stories we told, and the collective teachings we received in all the meetings we were required to attend—Sunday school and sacrament meeting, Primary for the young kids, Mutual Improvement Association, or MIA, for teens, priesthood meetings for the men and boys, the Family Home Evenings held once a week, the monthly visits from the brethren assigned as our home teachers, and the visits from the sisters from the Relief Society, and also in the many activities that were constantly being organized for all of us: the ball games and picnics and hikes and dances and other church outings around which the life of my family revolved and which absorbed me and took me up from the moment of my birth.

I remember in particular a trip that was organized when I was about seven or eight, called the Fathers and Daughters Outing. Arrangements had been made for the fathers in our ward to take their young daughters on a special day-long hike to a cave located high up on Mount Timpanogos, a peak named after an Indian princess, located a couple of hours away by car. No boys would go on this trip. This was to be a special time, just for the fathers and their daughters who were all more or less the same age.

What I remember about that trip is the long hot hike to the cave with the girls hanging on to their fathers' hands, getting pulled along the steep trail and fed little bits of licorice as encouragement to keep going. My father held my hand for much of the climb, helping me along, until finally we reached the cave, a forbidding black hole high up on the mountainside.

As we entered the cave, it felt suddenly very cold after the long hot climb and we all stopped to put on the coats we'd been told to bring along. Then the fathers took their daughters by one hand, and in the other held their flashlights, and we began following a guide into the dark cavern, with the fantastic shapes of the stalagmites surrounding us. The beams of the flashlights played off the strange twisting forms, and water dripped everywhere, running beneath the wooden boards that had been laid down as a path for visitors to walk on, and oh how black it was! How utterly black, just beyond the flashlight beams!

After walking for some time through the dank, dark chambers, feeling cold in spite of our coats, the guide suddenly stopped and told the girls to hold tight to their fathers' hands because he was going to ask the fathers to turn off their flashlights.

When they did we were plunged into blackness, disoriented and unable to move for fear of dropping off into the unknown, and I felt amazed to discover that all previous darkness I had known was not really darkness at all. This was *darkness,* absolute and enveloping. And then I heard the guide say, Now you have come to the heart of Timpanogos Cave, and suddenly a large red heart was illuminated in front of us. A big heart, perfectly shaped, made of glass or perhaps plastic. It burned, it *blazed* in the darkness with such a ferocious red it was as if I had never seen red before. A black blacker than black. A red redder than red. All experienced in a wonderfully creepy dank cavern with my father's hand in mine.

It's a moment I've never forgotten.

Just as I have never understood how they made the heart glow so red, so deep in the middle of the black cave. But of course it must have been something that ran on batteries. An electrical heart, the heart of Timpanogos Cave, the highlight of the father-daughter outing.

My father's hand in mine.

He was not unaffectionate with me.

There is a picture of the fathers and daughters of our ward, taken just before the outing to Timpanogos Cave. It shows the daughters all lined up with their fathers, who are seated or standing behind them, except for me and my father and a few others.

I am standing some distance away from him, in the center of a row, third from the bottom, wearing a checked shirt, and my father is standing at the end of that row with a group of women in between us—sisters from the ward who must have helped organize the trip. In this picture, my father doesn't look like a Western man at all, nor does he look like the bohemian musician. He looks like a tense, balding, middle-aged businessman, wearing a suit and tie, with rimmed glasses and a serious expression on his face. He looks tired, or as if he's been caught in one of his bad moods (is this why I am not standing near him?). He looks like he does when my mother and I pull up in the car in front of the Quonset hut at Hill Air Force Base to find him waiting for us, looking spent and slightly irritated that we're *five minutes late* in picking him up. Every day he checks the odometer on the car in the morning when she drops him off and again in the

afternoon when she picks him up to see how many miles she's driven that day, and then he says something like, Nineteen miles? Where the hell have you been running around to today? He keeps careful tabs on her. Makes sure she isn't wasting gas with unnecessary trips, "gadding about," as he calls it. He watches things closely so he knows exactly what she's been up to during the day when he's been away.

In the picture of the fathers and daughters, I look out at the camera as if I'm searching for something. As if I hope to recognize somebody. I have a serious look, serious and slightly quizzical, not like most of the other girls, who appear happy to be there with their fathers. My curly brown hair is cut chin-length, with a few strands partly framing my inquiring eyes. I'm smaller than most of the girls—much smaller. But what I really notice is the little scarf I've tied around my neck. Tied just right, so that the ends drape nicely over my shoulder. None of the other girls have scarves. Looking at it now, I remember the pleasure that scarf gave me when I first discovered how I could tie it that way all by myself.

There's a line from a James Salter short story I've always loved. It comes from a dinner party scene where a wife who's had too much to drink begins telling a story about her husband, who is also at the table, about how, during his first marriage, he once had an affair with the babysitter. The wife goes on and on, embarrassing him, but the husband doesn't say anything, he just sits there, listening, until finally he does speak up, and says just one thing: *Some women have minds like cops.*

I don't know why I love this line so much but I do.

It isn't because my mother had a mind like a cop, because she certainly didn't. She had a mind like a maid, as in always ready to serve somebody—maid, as in never having completely shed a certain girlish innocence and love of fun.

No, it was my father who had the mind like a cop.

And in this picture with the fathers and daughters, that's how he looks to me.

TEN

When I think of the little white house on Orchard Avenue, with its red roof and red-and-white-striped awnings, and the empurpled, sheer face of the granite mountains rising up steeply behind it, it seems that nothing ever stopped, the activity never ceased, the house and yard were always filled with people, with visitors and children and relatives and neighbors stopping by, with the harvesting and canning of fruit, the endless children's games, the meals eaten at a big wooden table, the small kitchen where endless meals were prepared.

I picture myself sitting in the driveway of that house on a sunny day, cracking apricot seeds against the cement with a rock and eating the meaty piths.

I see myself playing house beneath the big elm next to the drive, mixing up a "stew" of parsley and water. I cannot smell parsley to this day without thinking of those stews.

I can picture my mother in her bedroom in that house, having just brought my new baby brother, Gregg, home from the hospital. Sitting on her bed and holding him like a prize she'd just won. Displaying him for us.

I can picture the closet in the hallway between the two bedrooms upstairs where my father kept a leather razor strop, only occasionally brought into play to discipline an errant child.

I see my mother mixing up mustard plasters to put on our chest, an old-timey recipe for colds. And I can picture my brother Jerry, still a bed-wetter at the age of five, being subjected to some kind of

therapy or device meant to be a last-ditch effort to cure his problem (was it an electrical device that would shock him if he wet the
bed? I remember it this way). What I see when I think of Jerry is a
deeply ashamed and humiliated little boy, being berated once again
by my father for something he couldn't control. Shaming, as it turned
out, was my father's forte, one of his favorite disciplinary tools, often
administered via the sarcastic or cutting remark.

Jerry, the brother I would feel closest to as an adult, who would
turn out to be gay. So close to me in age and coloring we could
almost have passed for twins when we were young. There is a photograph taken of us at perhaps the ages of five and six, standing on
the lawn in front of the white house, holding plump ripe peaches in
our hands. It's a picture taken by my father, who took many photographs of his children when we were young. "Freeman Peaches" he
has labeled the slide.

I can picture me in the upstairs bedroom, hiding beneath a dressing table after throwing the tip of a ski pole through Jerry's cheek as
he sat playing in the sandbox behind the garage. I didn't mean to hurt
him. I was simply spear chucking, practicing my throw, and for some

reason I threw the ski pole at him, never thinking I'd hit him. He carried a little round scar on his cheek for the rest of his life. I might have put his eye out, as my father later said when he dragged me out from underneath the dressing table and gave me a good thrashing. I might have thrown that metal tip right into his brain, he said, and caused him to be an idiot.

No question I was the wild girl, the child who always wanted to be outdoors, the lover of stray animals and the natural world. My older sister, Marcia, was the ladylike one. Always ready to help out, so well mannered and sweet, a perpetual favorite of adults.

But I was my mother's child in many ways—not her favorite daughter, most certainly not that, but the one who most resembled her as she had been as a child. Later, in the stories she wrote toward the end of her life which she collected into a little book she called *The Autobiography of Alice Little Paul,* my mother talked about what a high-spirited and rebellious child she had been and how she often exasperated her mother:

> The only spankings I really remember were when my mother would take a little willow and switch my legs or behind with it. I would pretend to feel much pain and cry loudly so that I only received one or two little whacks. One day I had been particularly incorrigible and obnoxious and my mother was at her wit's end. Her words are still ringing in my ears as she said: *There is only one thing I wish for you and that is that someday you will have a child exactly like yourself.* I believe her wish came true.

She did not have to say which child it was that fulfilled her mother's wish.

In her memoir, she also recorded how her mother used to sing a little song to her when she was a child, a song called "Pet Marie," about a favored older daughter who had claimed her mother's affection.

❖ ❖ ❖

When I was six years old my mother saw an announcement in the newspaper that a children's beauty contest was being held to choose the Queen of the Fourth Street Park, who would ride on her own float in the town's children's parade. My mother entered me in the contest, which took place on a Saturday in the local park. The children were lined up outside a covered pavilion and when your name was called you walked past the judges and climbed up on a picnic table and turned around once or twice so they could look at you, and then climbed down and walked away. As my turn came, I noticed that one of our closest family friends, Bim Moore, was one of the judges.

I won the contest and rode in the parade in my own float, which was really just a red wagon that had been decorated with crepe-paper streamers. I wore a white dress made of cotton eyelet with a blue silk sash, and a crown of flowers encircled my head. An older boy pulled my little float down Washington Boulevard in the hot July sun and I waved at the crowd that lined the street, feeling quite special. It was not the sort of feeling I had ever had before.

A few days later my father took me out to Hill Air Force Base on a Saturday to have my picture taken for the base's newspaper. This time I was to be dressed as a cowgirl, which in my mind was how I liked to think of myself. I took my leather vest and chaps and my cowboy boots and the belt with the double holsters and toy guns, planning to change into my outfit when I arrived. But I had forgotten to bring a shirt and this was very upsetting to me. How could I have my picture taken as a cowgirl without a shirt? But the editor of the paper quickly solved the problem. She took off her red scarf and tucked it down my front between the flaps of the vest so it looked like a shirt, and then my picture was taken, with me smiling and pointing a gun at the photographer. When the picture ran in the paper, the caption read:

> Judy Freeman, above, is starting out young to capture hearts. She was recently chosen to reign as queen in a children's parade and rode in regal splendor all decked out in royal attire. But little Judy

is just as charming in her cowboy outfit as in queenly robes, as the photo above proves. She is the daughter of Roy C. Freeman, chief of the employee services unit, civilian personnel.

Bim Moore, the contest judge, and his big loud wife, Annalee, whom I remember as a very funny woman, always laughing and kidding around. Billy Smith, outspoken, blunt Billy, and her gentle husband, Vernon. Verda and Al Heitz. Meda and Ed Carlson. Marvin and Zelpha Crawford. Hilda and Harold Goucher and Thelma and Lee Cain. All neighbors and friends of my parents, people who were kind to us kids in those early years. Everyone helped everyone else. No one was ever left to feel they had to face their problems alone—and there were problems: husbands who secretly drank, sons who'd taken up smoking, a daughter suddenly pregnant out of wedlock, marital arguments that caused lingering pain and confusion. The women shared these secrets as they sat around a quilting frame, often set up in our dining room, or spent afternoons making Christmas candy together, not always realizing that a child lingered nearby, quietly listening to their conversations. I came to understand that women talked to each other in ways that men did not: they told each other secrets, shared stories meant only for them. They made their own little groups, fed each other gossip, confidences, the latest news. The church supported our lives and gave us structure, but one of the ways it did so was by creating intimate circles of friends who could turn to each other for solace.

We were a community as much as a religion.

A culture unto itself.

We were a *tribe,* bound by clan, blood, and ritual. A tribe deeply embedded in the landscape of the American West, which we had been the first to settle if we didn't count the Natives, which we usually didn't, even though American Indians figured so prominently in our Book of Mormon story that we thought of them as our Lamanite brothers and sisters who only needed to be brought back into the fold before Jesus could appear again.

❖   ❖   ❖

The living room in the house on Orchard Avenue opened onto a dining room that in turn led to a small kitchen. These rooms are still
extraordinarily vivid to me, in part because of the riotous wallpaper
my parents had chosen to cover the walls, a pattern of huge inter-
locking white leaves against a bluish background, a wallpaper so bold
and outrageous it dominated everything in the living room. A curved
archway led to the small dining room and here the wallpaper changed
into blue and white stripes, more demure but still peppy. There is a
picture taken in that archway, showing my mother and other family
members clustered together—my great-aunt Fannie and my moth-

er's sister Leone and my mother in the back row, my siblings Lee and Ron and Marcia in the middle, and Leone's daughters Connie and Janis and my brother Jerry in front, with a corner of the large rectangular dining table that could accommodate ten people just visible behind them. On a little shelf, in an alcove built into the wall, one can see a black telephone with a clock above it, and it is here, one day when I was about seven or eight, that I had an epiphany.

I was standing in the dining room, talking on that black telephone to one of the Wangsgard girls, who lived across the street in the house where we sometimes slaughtered chickens in the backyard. There was a pad of paper and a pencil sitting next to the phone and I began doodling, drawing on the paper. I no longer remember what I drew

but in a sudden flash I realized that what I had drawn was *art*. This was what it meant to make art, and I knew in that instant that I had done something wonderful, that I could make art, that *I had just made art*.

In some ways it seems a preposterous notion—I knew nothing about art, it was never discussed in our household, and I had never been to a museum or even seen paintings in a book—but I have never forgotten the feeling I had at that moment. It was as if some possibility was illuminated for me in the most profound way. It was not a feeling I experienced again, nor was it anything I acted on. I didn't imagine I was some budding little artist, endowed with a great talent. No. It was simply that I felt a tremendous wonder and excitement at the discovery I had made.

How strange that in the great wash of memories that have flowed through me over the years this one has never diminished, never dulled or faded, but retains the sharp bright pinpoint of excitement I felt during that initial moment.

In another photograph taken around this time—a slide which my father later labeled "Kids"—I am standing with my sister, Marcia, and my brothers Lee and Jerry and another boy I don't recognize in front of the fireplace in our living room. On the mantel are three ceramic figurines I remember very well: in the middle, a sleek blank panther; on the right, an Arab girl in harem pants; on the left, colorful birds perched on a branch. Above the fireplace is a large painting, a still life of flowers, with two sconces on either side. In the photograph I am dressed as an Indian princess in an outfit my mother made for me, with my brother Jerry standing next to me. Marcia is dressed as a Gypsy girl. The boys are wearing their ordinary clothes, though Lee and Jerry have matching shirts. And on the wall, the extraordinary wallpaper.

This is the room where one morning I watch my parents say goodbye to my oldest brother, Bob. He is leaving home. At seventeen, he has joined the Navy, in part to escape my father, with whom he doesn't get along. As the firstborn son he has endured the hard edge of my father's personality, and he has had enough.

I am sitting near a heat vent on the living-room floor with a blanket spread over me to catch the heat coming up from the furnace, and the warm air fills the blanket and causes it to float slightly above me in a little tent. It must be winter, though I have no sense of the seasons, and obviously I have no idea, and no memory, of the tension between my father and Bob. I am too young to know about these things. I only know that Bob is leaving, he's going away on a long journey, and I have gotten up early with my parents while the rest of the household is asleep and now I sit beneath my blanket, in the tent of warm air, and watch my parents tell my oldest brother goodbye. They stand just inside the front door. My mother cries and hugs him; my father shakes his hand and shows no emotion. My mother is not yet pregnant with her last child, but she will be shortly. She does not know that Bob will never return to live in this house again. She and my father have no idea what's coming, what is going to happen to their firstborn son, and, of course, neither do I.

PART TWO

❖

A Death in the Family

ONE

When Bob left to join the Navy on that winter morning in 1953, I was seven years old.

When his emaciated body was returned to my family for burial in Ogden, I was eight.

This was the pivotal year of my childhood, 1954, the year that death and birth became intermingled in a series of tumultuous events. The year my mother lost a son, gave birth to one, and became a grandmother, all within a few months' time.

Sometime during his first year in the Navy, while on shore leave in the Bay Area, Bob met a dark-skinned Spanish-speaking woman from Colombia who was older than he by a number of years. Her name was Alicia Rodriguez: she worked as a beautician, and she became pregnant with his child.

My mother, at the age of forty-three, was also pregnant, carrying her eighth child.

He was such a handsome kid, my brother Bob: you can see this in every picture ever taken of him, from the time he was very young until just before he died. He had the cheekbones, the graceful features, the sensuous, sultry look of a James Dean.

Of all my brothers he was the most beautiful—not just handsome, but beautiful. Dark curly hair. Sensuous full lips. Tall and long and lean, his jeans riding low on his hips, often wearing a plain white

shirt in family photographs, carefully tucked in, his thumbs hooked
casually in the pockets of his Levi's.
He looks at the camera directly, so
unself-conscious. It seems to me
there's something almost challeng-
ing about his look. He never smiles
or mugs while being photographed
like we younger kids do, with our
goofy grins and missing teeth and
faces all bunched up against the
sun. Bob stands cool before the
camera.

Why had he joined the Navy at
such a young age, dropping out of
high school in his junior year to do so? Was it because he wanted to
escape the tension between him and my father? Did he simply wish
to get out of Ogden, Utah, and away from the closeness of the Mormon culture? Was he doing things teenage boys weren't supposed to
do, smoking and hanging out in pool halls and drinking beer? I don't
know the answers to these questions. I never have.

A couple of years ago I wrote away for his military service records,
hoping to learn more about what had happened to him during his time
in the Navy. I hoped they might help me answer one of the questions
that had troubled me over the years: Could my brother have possibly
served on one of the U.S. Navy ships in the South Pacific that had participated in the nuclear tests being conducted in that area in the early
1950s? Was he one of the sailors ordered to line up on a ship's deck
to witness an atomic test being carried out on one of the small islands
that had been cleared of inhabitants, sailors who were given nothing
for protection except a tiny pair of goggles to shield their eyes from
the blinding light when the mushroom clouds erupted? Young men

who must have stood there while the radioactive dust from the blasts rained down upon them? And might this have had anything to do with my brother developing bone cancer at the age of eighteen? How *does* a healthy Utah boy die of such a disease so young? I wondered. Some part of me suspected there might be a connection.

From his service records I learned the date and place of his entry into the Navy—November 4, 1953, which confirmed my memory of him leaving home on a cold winter morning.

During his physical examination at the time he entered the Navy he showed no health problems. He checks all the boxes on the medical forms *no*. No homosexual tendencies, he says. Never been a sleepwalker, or attempted suicide, or lived with anyone who had tuberculosis. Never worn glasses, or had an artificial eye, or been a bed-wetter. Never had a blood relation go insane, never had terrifying nightmares or gotten carsick or had a drug habit or a trick knee. And, most importantly, never had a tumor, or a growth, or cancer.

His plan was to serve in the Navy for three years. He signed a form acknowledging that he'd been given a pillow and two blankets upon induction and agreed to return them when he completed his service.

On another form he is asked, *How many jobs have you had in the past three years?* He answers *Six*—six jobs since just before he entered high school. And what was the longest period he'd held any of these jobs? *Six months,* he wrote. Six jobs in three years, the longest held for six months. But what were those jobs? He doesn't say.

Under *Usual Occupation,* he puts *Student.*

On the induction form he lists two of his favorite leisure-time activities: auto mechanics and singing baritone, which he says he has done for two years. He played sports in high school, excelling in both football and track, had perfect vision, was right-handed and a Class III qualified swimmer.

None of these things did I know about my brother before I read his service records. In truth I know so little about him. After his death nobody in our family spoke that much about him, though I know my older siblings who had been close to him in age must have talked about him often with each other. But for the younger children he got lost somehow, left behind, couldn't ever be properly remembered or honored or even discussed openly and freely. There was no joy around his memory, but rather always a faint aura of regret or remorse—not just sadness over his death at such a young age but something more layered and complex, something like guilt and shame. I found this very confusing as a child, and upsetting as an adult. I believe I know why this was the case, though I am loath even now to admit it.

The problem came down to two words: Alicia Rodriguez.

After receiving his basic training in San Diego, he was sent to the Bay Area and assigned to a ship, the USS *ARD-28*, which really wasn't a ship at all but a floating repair dock that depended on tugboats to maneuver it. The USS *ARD-28* plied the waters of the Pacific during the Korean War, servicing ships, and later made its way to the Philippines. At some point he was reassigned to a larger ship, the USS *F. C. Ainsworth*, a troop transport involved in trans-Pacific operations. It was while on this ship, six months after joining the Navy, that he checked into the ship's infirmary, complaining of a pain in his right clavicle. The area around his collarbone was found to be swollen and red and there appeared to be some kind of growth. He'd also begun to lose weight—twelve pounds in the last five months.

He was transferred to the infirmary at the U.S. Naval Station in Subic Bay and then taken to the U.S. Air Force Hospital at Clark Air Force Base in the Philippines for further tests.

This was on the 8th of April, 1953.

On the 16th he was sent to the U.S. Naval Hospital in Oakland, California, where he would remain, with short interruptions, for the rest of his life.

In the medical history that was taken from him at the Air Force

Hospital in the Philippines, he revealed that he had had pain in his clavicle even before he had entered the Navy but that it had been exacerbated when he'd banged that area with a rifle during basic training. He had seen a doctor back home about the pain two months before he even enlisted. An X-ray had been taken but it didn't show anything. Gradually, however, during the months at sea, the swelling had increased, and also the pain, and he had also become hoarse, almost losing his voice.

A large tumor was discovered and found to be so deep it extended into his neck and was pressing on his vocal cords, causing the hoarseness. The diagnosis was sarcoma, a fatal disease. Still, incredibly, he was pronounced fit for duty and recommended for return to active service—a recommendation that was quickly modified, and instead he was sent to the Navy "tumor board" for further evaluation.

The Navy tumor board found his tumor to be *highly destructive* and recommended *a full course of deep x-ray therapy to the point of skin toleration,* a treatment that was carried out and left his skin burned and permanently scarred. After a few weeks of recuperation, he was pronounced fit for duty, though it was noted that his *probable future duration* was only six months.

Probable future duration: Was this Navy-medical-speak for You have six months to live?

The lesion and tumor regressed, due to the intensive radiation, and the attending doctor wrote, *The patient reported to have no symptoms referable to his clavicle other than mild aching in the region on cold, foggy nights.*

Instead of going to sea again, Bob was kept in the Alameda Naval Hospital in Oakland, where the nights were often cold and foggy and where he seemed to hover in a medical netherworld. His pain soon returned, in spite of the treatments. Also the hoarseness and weight loss. By now he must have understood his condition was very serious. Did he understand he was dying? At eighteen? This might have been impossible for him to believe.

❖   ❖   ❖

By this time he would have met Alicia Rodriguez, though where they met—how a Mormon boy from Ogden, Utah, and an older Spanish-speaking Catholic beautician from Colombia got together—remains a mystery. Was she the reason he went AWOL from the hospital for a brief time a few weeks later? On May 5th he walked out of the hospital at 9 p.m. and did not return until 4:55 the next day. Where had he spent the night? Perhaps attending one of the dances in Oakland that he occasionally went to and which he had mentioned in a letter to my parents. Or maybe he had simply escaped the hospital in order to spend the night with Alicia Rodriguez.

For his unauthorized absence he received a court-martial summons and was charged with three violations: unauthorized absence from a U.S. naval hospital; wearing civilian clothes without having been issued a civilian clothes pass; and wrongfully communicating to another person in the naval service a threat to injure said person.

He may have understood how seriously ill he was and thought he had nothing to lose by going AWOL for a night and a day. And he must have been angry enough when he returned to threaten someone with bodily harm.

Two months earlier, in February, he'd made his first trip back home to see our family in Ogden and stayed for twelve days. In a letter to my parents, written after he'd returned to Oakland, he talked about not feeling well and also referred to the problems he and my father had during the time he spent at home on leave, as well as my mother's new pregnancy:

> I don't know ever sience I came back I haven't felt right. I just wish Dad and me could get along together. I'm probably all wrong I should have stayed home a little more when I was home. I didn't tell him how much I appreciated his car and all his help. I don't know what I can do to ever repay him for all the things he's done for me.

I never had said to his face about how much I love him and respect him but I feel it more than anything in the world. I will never be able to raise 7 healthy children and feed and cloth and take care of them like you and dad have done. And I think it's wonderful that Moms going to have another one. Just take care of yourself Mom and make the boys do the heavy work and the girls the housework. I love you all very much and can't wait to get home again.

Perhaps at this point my parents had no idea how serious his condition was, and even as his condition worsened they may have been kept somewhat in the dark. He may not even have told them about his medical problems for a while. His first letters to them upon entering the service had been full of the ordinary details of life, filled with a certain optimism (as well as misspellings):

This life is altogether different than what I've been used to . . . but I believe I'll like it. You learn something new everyday and get a little smarter everyday. You relize that theirs more people in the world than you . . . Tell the kids hello and tell them I love them.

From the time Bob was very young he'd been given the responsibility of taking care of his younger siblings. *Robert was always so dependable,* my mother later wrote in her memoir: *When he was only ten we decided that he was the best babysitter we could get so if we were going to a party or meeting anywhere within a few blocks, we left him in charge of the younger ones and he did such a good job. Only now I think what a responsibility we put on his young shoulders.*

The responsibility on his shoulders. One of which was now a blooming locus of festering pain.

In the fall of 1953, after months of hospitalization, Bob was pronounced unfit for duty and transferred to the retired list, though not formally discharged from the Navy. He was given $78.65 as severance pay. The Navy had finally admitted his ultimate prognosis was poor. A letter was sent to my parents on official naval stationery, explaining that their son was being released from active duty and that he had been diagnosed with sarcoma.

I remember that letter. My mother had no idea what sarcoma meant, so she took the letter from the Navy with her when she went for her next checkup with her obstetrician, Dr. Curtis.

I went to the doctor with her that day and sat in the waiting room while she saw him. When she came out she was crying. Dr. Curtis had read the letter and then shook his head and told my mother very frankly that her son was gravely ill. He had cancer of the bone, he said, and he was most likely dying.

By this time Alicia Rodriguez was pregnant as well. Bob called my parents and gave them the news and said that he and Alicia planned on getting married soon. My parents tried to talk him out of this. How did he know, they asked, that the baby was his? Alicia was older, more worldly, and she might have tricked him. My mother had a cousin living in the Bay Area, a lawyer named Heber Brown, and my parents suggested that Heber Brown might be able to help Bob get out of marrying Alicia. But Bob didn't want to get out of marrying Alicia. He believed the baby was his. What's more, he said, he loved her. And she loved him.

On December 20th, 1953, three weeks after he'd been released from the Navy, they were married in a civil ceremony with a small reception afterward, attended by a number of our relatives living in the Bay Area. There are photographs from this day—Bob looking very thin and somber in a white shirt and dark suit, and Alicia dressed like a proper bride with a veil and short white dress. Our Mormon relatives stand around in the background, looking happy and festive, while Bob gazes quietly at the camera and Alicia, holding his hand, glances down, away from the lens.

Bob brought his bride home to meet us. I remember my first glimpse of Alicia Rodriguez, with her smooth brown skin and black eyes, and her shiny hair styled in a sleek pageboy. Her pregnancy

didn't yet show and she wore a shiny red sheath that showed off her figure. She wasn't beautiful, I came to admit, in the photographs I saw of her later, but she was stylish and trim and, most strikingly, she was exceptionally vivacious. She wasn't shy with my parents. She didn't hesitate to call them Mom and Dad. Mom and Dad, she said, I'm so happy to meet you, and then she hugged them and smiled broadly.

Mawn and Dad.

She spoke with a singsongy accent and I had never heard anyone speak that way before. Bob introduced us to her one by one and she in turn embraced each of the siblings. When she came to me, I felt so shy and overwhelmed I fled to the basement before she could touch me and hid in the closet beneath the stairs next to the laundry room.

After a while she came down and found me. She was gentle and sweet and coaxed me out of the closet by telling me that I was very pretty—*muy bonita*, she said, taking my hand in hers. I believe those were the first words I ever heard in a foreign language.

Tú eres muy bonita.

She translated the words, kneeling beside me in her red dress as I stood in the open doorway of the closet, looking at her as she spoke. That she could talk in two languages seemed amazing to me. I felt she must be very smart to do this. Very smart and very different. She had something no one else I knew possessed.

She told me we were sisters now and she promised to give me a better haircut than the one I had, and the way she laughed and smiled, kneeling before me on the cement floor that day, I was easily won over.

And then before I knew it they were gone, headed back to Oakland, where they had rented an apartment for themselves and Alicia's mother, who moved in with them. The apartment was near the naval hospital. Sometimes Bob lived at home with Alicia and her mother, but most often, as his condition worsened, he was confined to the hospital, where Alicia visited him every day. There are pictures of them from this time: Bob in a wheelchair and Alicia standing behind him smiling; Bob and Alicia standing outside, on the narrow, steep stairway leading to their apartment; Bob standing next to a car in front of the hospital. In every picture she is smiling. In every picture he has the same sad look.

This is what I thought of when I looked at those pictures later: his heartbreaking youth and beauty . . . the way Alicia looks at him with such love.

She had married a dying man and she must have known it.

All he wanted to do, my father said later, was live to see his baby born.

My mother had her baby in March. A little boy.

Alicia had her baby in June. A little girl.

Bob died in September: September 8th, to be exact.

Several times during that summer before his death my parents got urgent calls from the hospital saying that Bob was critical and might

not live through the night, and they would fly down to California to be with him even though they could not really afford to do so, but then he would live through the night, and the next one, and the one after that, and eventually they'd have to return home, where their seven other children, including a newborn baby, awaited them.

Sometimes when these phone calls came they just got into the car, leaving on short notice, and drove down to California, hoping they would get there in time. They always left baby Gregg in the care of Hilda Goucher, a neighbor who also helped look after the rest of us.

But mostly we looked after ourselves, living alone in the house when they were gone. My older brothers, John, seventeen, and Ron, fifteen, took over the meals and the care of us, and Marcia, thirteen, helped out. For a little while we were like the Boxcar Children from the children's books I would later discover. In those stories a group of children, brothers and sisters, have lost their parents, and they find a boxcar in the woods and begin living there alone, making a life for themselves without adults, foraging in the woods for what they need.

We didn't forage but I do remember how often we ate outside at the big picnic table that summer, sitting behind the house on the lawn under the Satsuma plum tree in the backyard, and how the neighbors came by every day to bring food and see how we were doing. That was the summer my older brother Lee, who was eleven, broke both of his arms while trying to stand up and go down the slippery slide at Liberty Park. His arms were set in casts in such a way that he couldn't feed himself, so it often fell to me to sit next to him at dinnertime and help him eat.

We ate outside so often that summer it felt as if we were always outdoors, playing in the yard, staying close to home, waiting for our parents to return from another trip to California, waiting to see what would happen to Bob. Sometimes we even slept outdoors on the grass at night, rolling out our sleeping bags on the lawn. At one such slumber party Marcia broke her leg while jumping from a fence when her nightgown caught on a picket. And then Lee, whose arms were still in casts, cut his foot on a piece of glass and an infection developed and he had to stay in bed for a while. Each time my parents went off to California to see Bob they must have wondered if they'd arrive home to some fresh new disaster.

Finally, in early September, when another call came, my parents left and drove all night to reach Oakland but again Bob hung on, and after two days they had to leave. It was Monday the next day and my father could not miss work.

Bob died two days later, with my mother's sister Fannie in the room with him, and Alicia and baby Sherry.

My mother gave us the news of his death the next morning as we came upstairs for breakfast. The light was coming in from outside through the small glass pane in the back door and falling on the narrow landing. She greeted us one by one in this small entryway off the kitchen, saying simply, Your brother Bob died last night. She seemed to need to deliver this news in a very small space, as if to contain her sadness. Her eyes were swollen but her voice was calm.

❖ ❖ ❖

Bob had told my parents he wanted to be buried in his hometown, and his body was shipped back to Utah. The Navy would pay for his burial.

The funeral was held in the Lindquist and Sons Mortuary Chapel and filled with our friends and relatives, with the service conducted by the bishop of our ward. Everyone who attended the funeral that day was white, with the exception of Alicia Rodriguez, who with her newborn baby sat in the special section reserved for our family. It was the first time our friends and relatives had met Bob's wife (now widow) and she stood out, there was no mistaking her. She had requested that "Vaya con Dios" be sung as one of the musical numbers and the request was honored.

A viewing had been held the night before, with an open casket, and many people had come to see Bob and pay their respects.

It was an unforgettable feeling for me, as an eight-year-old, to approach the casket that night and stand next to it, peering over the edge at my dead brother whose face was only inches from mine. Emaciated as he was, even in death, he still managed to look beautiful, the flesh over his cheekbones more sunken now, his face narrower, his hands so bony and white. He had been dressed in a black suit and white shirt, though only his upper torso was visible. His lower half, covered with the same ruche white satin that lined his coffin, seemed to already be disappearing.

At the funeral the next day, when it came time to close the casket, a curtain was drawn around the area where our family had been seated so we could say our final goodbyes. People began crying as one by one we were allowed to approach the casket. I was crying too. My mother had provided all the children with tissues before the service began.

It was at this moment, when the family was curtained off with the body just before the casket was closed, that Alicia became distraught. She was overcome with grief as she stood and looked down at my brother.

She threw her body across his and began sobbing, holding on to him, and then she tried to force a ring onto his finger—or did she try to take one off? Force it on, take it off, I don't remember which. This detail is blurry, and I am reminded what a slippery thing memory is, how it creates its own indelibility, plucking a hazy moment from time, retaining the emotion and often dropping details, shaping, perhaps, by *feeling* more than fact. I do recall the queasy sensation that came over me as I watched Alicia take my brother's lifeless hand and do something with that ring. She should not be doing that, I thought; she should not be touching him, because *he is dead*. And then again she spread her body over his and wept, refusing to let him go, until finally my father took hold of her shoulders and gently but firmly guided her away so the casket could be closed.

All this remains very vivid for me, all these years later. Bob was buried with a military send-off. Navy servicemen played taps, and the flag that draped his coffin was ceremoniously removed and folded into a neat hard triangle and presented to his widow. This I found very impressive. The sharp sound of the taps in the quiet graveyard on a hill overlooking the valley. The flag so perfectly folded and handed over like a final gift. The way his casket was slowly lowered, with all our family and friends looking on—Alicia holding baby Sherry, sitting on a folding chair and wearing a little hat, my mother sitting next to her holding baby Gregg.

Alicia did not stay around for very long after the funeral but returned almost immediately to Oakland. My parents saw that she got any money due her as Bob's next of kin. Only after she had gone did they realize that she had done something they didn't like. Something impossible now to undo. She had ordered a tombstone with a cross on it for Bob, paid for by the Navy but chosen by her.

I don't think she could have known that Mormons don't believe in displaying crosses or religious iconography of any kind. That they consider it a form of idol worship. There are no crosses in Mormon churches, no crucifixions, no pictures of Mary on the walls, no statues of Christ or suffering saints. Mormon chapels are as free of these things as a Laundromat. How could she have been expected to understand this?

How could she have known she'd upset my parents with her action? As a practicing Catholic she would have seen nothing wrong with what she'd done, would see it as a holy final gesture. But the idea that their son would now forever lie beneath a headstone marked by a cross rankled my parents, and they discussed it openly in front of the children in the days following the funeral. I don't know why she had to do that, my father would mutter, and my mother would shake her head and frown and say, Well, I don't either. It was as if Alicia had somehow had the last word when it came to their son.

Over the years my parents would avoid having much to do with Alicia Rodriguez. My mother never forgot that Sherry was Bob's daughter—and there's no question that she was. She had Bob's eyes, his curly hair, and in her features there was also something of a resemblance. We ought to do something for her, my mother would say now and then, After all, she is Bob's daughter. The guilt and sadness she felt would be evident in the look that came over her face. But doing something for Sherry would also mean doing something for Alicia, if that meant only trusting her: how could they send money to a little girl without it going through her mother?

I don't believe they actually disliked Alicia. She simply remained the Other, a person they couldn't really know (and didn't want to). She wasn't shy about asking my parents for help and playing on their guilt. Help which they were reluctant to give since they struggled themselves to make ends meet—to take care of their own seven children, including the new little baby that now took up so much of my mother's time. In large part I think it was a case of out of sight, out of mind: it was so much simpler to just not think about it.

TWO

Alicia married an Oakland policeman a few years after Bob died and had two more children with him. And then, in an incredible stroke of bad luck, her new husband became ill. He was diagnosed with a serious kidney disease.

They traveled to Colorado in order for him to have a kidney transplant, which was then a rather new procedure. En route they stopped by Ogden to see us, bringing Sherry and their other two children. I was a teenager at the time. I remember Sherry as a somber, quiet child, something heavy and slow about her. Even then, at the age of six or seven, you could see something was wrong. She seemed dull; she didn't talk much. For most of the visit she just sat on the edge of the marble hearth in the upstairs living room and stared at us with the eyes she had inherited from her father. Alicia was still the vivacious person she'd always been and her new husband seemed okay, and my parents were nice to them during the visit, which lasted all afternoon, but they were also not sorry to see them go.

Alicia donated one of her kidneys to her husband but the transplant failed and he died. She now had three children, one kidney, had been widowed twice, and she could not have been more than thirty-five years old.

She returned to Oakland with her children and set up a beauty shop in the basement of her apartment in order to make a living and support her three kids. But when one of our Bay Area relatives visited her she reported that Alicia and her kids seemed to be living in poverty. Again my mother said, with that worried look on her face, We should do something for Sherry, she is Bob's daughter, after all. But Oakland was very far away, and there was so much to do at home, caring for her own children, keeping up with her church activities, all the responsibility she already shouldered.

I don't know how much contact my parents had with Alicia over the years, or whether they tried to help her. I know she occasionally wrote to them, giving them updates on Sherry, and sometimes sent a picture, and they wrote back, but as Sherry entered her teenage years things again took a turn for the worse.

By then Alicia had married a much older man, a not very nice man as it turned out, and moved into his house in a suburb near Oakland. Something untoward happened between Sherry and her stepfather. Something sexual. Alicia revealed this in a letter to my parents, and also said that Sherry wasn't normal. She was in some way retarded, Alicia said, which made the idea of a stepfather abusing her even more repugnant than it already was.

I don't know how she can stay married to someone like that, was my mother's response.

But somehow I could understand. I was old enough to know that women often cut deals to survive. I had watched an aunt, for instance, and also one of my mother's best friends, who both lived with alcoholic husbands, cover and lie for their men because they could not possibly think of leaving them. I had overheard them talking about this. It made sense to me that a woman like Alicia, a woman without means who'd endured terrible hardships, might feel as if she had no alternatives. If Alicia left her third husband, life might only get harder for her.

She wrote to my parents and asked if Sherry could come visit them for a while, to get her out of the house and away from her stepfather, and this time my parents agreed. To not agree would have no doubt ratcheted up their guilt to an intolerable level, and by that I mean the guilt they so evidently felt (especially my mother) about neglecting their granddaughter, their own flesh and blood. About leaving her, ignored, in a predatory situation, and disengaging so thoroughly it appeared as if they wanted no part of her. So they relented and Sherry came to Ogden. And the visit was a disaster.

She was a damaged child. I'll never know how damaged, or exactly where the damage had come from, but whatever the exact nature of her problems, they included displays of violence, inappropriate sexual references, and a mental slowness.

She used foul language around my parents, and talked about the things boys did to her and the things she wanted to do to them, things that could as easily have been based on fantasy as on reality, and my parents were not only shocked, they couldn't understand how she could have been raised this way.

At the time of her visit my parents were no longer young. My father had already suffered his first grand mal seizure and retired from his job. He now spent much of his time playing music with a little combo he'd formed, entertaining regularly at the senior center in Ogden. One day during Sherry's visit he decided to take her to the center with him and while he was busy playing music during the lunch hour, Sherry had gone into a room where the seniors were playing cards and found some lightbulbs in a supply closet and begun throwing them one by one against the wall, where they exploded like little bombs. The seniors were deeply alarmed and quickly summoned my father, who helped clean up the mess and then left with Sherry.

When my father told my mother what had happened, he said Sherry had to go back to Oakland immediately. He could no longer tolerate her being around. Arrangements were made for her return, and she was taken to the airport soon after. It was the last time my parents ever saw their granddaughter.

THREE

Many years later I tracked Alicia down. Why, I don't exactly know, except that I had always been troubled by all the guilt and shame that had seeped into our household in the years that followed Bob's death and perhaps more than anything I felt disturbed by the unfinished nature of the story.

To have shunned Alicia and Sherry the way we did went against everything we had been taught by our religion about the importance of family and the need for compassion and kindness. In some way, this story had become a story not only about the tragedy of a family losing a son but about a family's collective and enduring guilt and the dark little thread of racism that stitched it all together. The ugly and often unacknowledged strain of prejudice that was such an open and common feature of white America in the 1940s and '50s, and which could result, in the years before I was born, in my parents having named a little black family dog *Nigger,* and to have done so, I'm sure, while feeling a certain blameless innocence. It could make it all seem okay, and okay, too, to deny black men the priesthood in the church in which they so fervently believed. My father would never have considered himself a racist, in any shape or form. He'd had Mexican kids for playmates growing up in Snowflake and always talked of them fondly. And hadn't he even invited his black mechanic and his family to our house for dinner one Sunday? Surely no racist would do that. He could not see that when his son married a person of color, things were suddenly cast in a different light.

Alicia was still living with her third husband in the suburb of Oakland and she seemed happy to hear from me when, during a visit to the Bay Area in the 1980s, I located her number in a phone book and called her up. She invited me to come see her and gave me directions.

The house was on a street with many houses just like it—small 1950s brick one-levels with a patch of yard out front, often weedy and unkempt. Older cars were parked in the driveways along with a clutter of children's toys. Not a bad neighborhood by any means, just a little down at the heels. Sherry wasn't there when I arrived: she was in a special school, Alicia said, for the retarded. Nor was her third husband around.

There were pictures of Sherry, taken over the years, as well as Alicia's other children, clustered on a table in the living room where we sat down to talk. One photograph showed Alicia holding baby Sherry, taken outside on a bright day sometime during the summer before Bob died.

A picture of Bob in his naval uniform sat near the other photographs. At one point she went over and picked it up and held it up for me to see. It was a picture I knew well: one just like it had sat on top of our piano in the living room for years.

As she gazed at it, it seemed all the love she had felt for him and all the sadness she harbored rose to her face and this flood of feeling softened her features for just a moment, causing her to appear less worn.

Alicia was no longer the lively woman I had remembered. She looked tired and thin and old. She was nice enough to me but there was something strained between us, some tension lying there beneath the surface. It wasn't until I was about to leave that Alicia spoke up: she suddenly became serious, almost hostile.

Your parents? she said. You don't know what they did to us, do you?

I didn't think my parents had done anything except sometimes refuse her pleas for help.

You know that time Sherry went to visit them? she said. When they sent her home early? Well, they also did something so cruel, something that hurt Sherry so much she's never gotten over it, and I promised myself I would never let them see her again.

What did they do? I asked quietly, wondering what she could possibly say.

After she got home, they packaged up all the letters Sherry and I had ever written to them, she said. Every picture she'd ever drawn and every card we ever sent, and every photograph of her from the time she was little, and they put it all in a big envelope and sent it back to us. Everything. No note or nothing.

She looked away from me and stared out the big window that faced the street and then she turned back and stared at me with a furious look in her eyes.

I never saw Alicia again. Or Sherry. And I never mentioned to my parents that I had seen her, or that she had told me this story about them. It remains one of those mysteries I know I can never solve. My parents are gone now. There's no one to ask, Did this really happen? I'll never know.

FOUR

In my mother's memoir, *The Autobiography of Alice Little Paul,* there is
a section devoted to Bob—stories about how when Bob was born
my father was making fourteen dollars a week selling shoes at Thom
McAn, how when he was small she had made a little harness and
tethered him on a rope to a ring attached to the clothesline and left
him to play outside, until an "idiotic" neighbor threatened to report
her to the Humane Society—as if he were a neglected dog. How he
had always been such a helpful little boy, so close with his younger
brothers. There are two pages that deal with the end of his life, how
he had joined the Navy, been diagnosed with sarcoma, how she had
taken the letter from the Navy to her obstetrician and her description of the difficult summer when he was dying. Of his death, she
says only, *We were grateful that Bob was released from his suffering,* and
concludes:

> One of our greatest trials was the death of Robert, our firstborn.
> He was such a handsome, beautiful person with everything to live
> for but it was not to be. He died of cancer as he neared his twentieth
> birthday. That year, 1954, was a year of joy and much sorrow.

That's it. Her complete account of the end of his life. There is no
mention of Alicia or Sherry. It's as if they never existed.

In my father's memoir, *Reminiscences of LeRoy C. Freeman,* I find a
somewhat longer entry under the chapter titled "Robert," which
begins very much like my mother's account:

The greatest tragedy of our lives was the loss of our eldest son Robert. He enlisted in the army [he means Navy] served his training period and was assigned to duty in the Philippine Islands. Within a very short time, he became ill. The illness was diagnosed as sarcoma . . . a vicious type of bone cancer which cannot be arrested . . . We were given our choice of [having him treated] in navy facilities in Denver or Oakland. We chose Oakland and for the ensuing year we drove or flew there on numerous occasions. One of our reasons for choosing Oakland was that Alice had a number of relatives in that area and we felt that they could be of assistance. Little did we know how much help they would be. John and Flora Sears, Heber and Dottie Brown, and many others visited him and took food and gifts.

He goes on to write that Robert married Alicia Rodriguez before he was aware of his illness, but of course this isn't true: he was already gravely ill when he married her, as I now know from reading his service records. My father does acknowledge Alicia's devotion to Bob:

She proved to be a tremendous help in being with her husband and assisting him during his illness. She was pregnant and was to be delivered about the time the doctors had scheduled [he means predicted] her husband's death. Although Robert sank very low at times and we were called to rush to his side, he would not give up until the child was born. In fact, even though he may have known otherwise, he always seemed so sure he would live.

Such a happening is very difficult for anyone to understand, in fact impossible, particularly for a young man who is standing on the threshold of a life of which he rightly expects so much.

As frequently occurs, this tragic experience brought our family closer. The older sons, in fact all of the children, had to assume greater responsibility in performing duties in the absence of father or mother or both. We were so impressed of the necessity for faith and understanding. We prayed continually for his recovery, always committing ourselves to accepting what happened, attributing it to compliance with a divine plan which we could not be permitted to understand in detail.

Alice made most of the trips to Oakland. Gregg was a baby.

And so his entry ends.

At least my father took care to mention Alicia. He understood how this woman from Colombia, of whom initially he had so disapproved, had been devoted to his dying son.

Bob had been the first to leave home, to escape into that *different life* he spoke of in his letter, to *relize that theirs more people in the world than you.* And he was also the first to die, having only briefly glimpsed the world that lay beyond Ogden, Utah.

The ship my brother served on, the USS *ARD-28,* was decommissioned in the 1960s. It was sold to Colombia, renamed the *Capitán Rodriguez Zamora,* and is still in service today.

Colombia. The place Alicia Rodriguez had come from.

I am at a loss to explain, even to myself, why this small detail comforts me.

PART THREE

◆

The New World

ONE

In 1956, two years after Bob's death, my parents sold the little white house at 946 Orchard Avenue where I had spent the first ten years of my life and built a new house at 4135 College Drive, in a subdivision that had recently been laid out in the foothills high above the city. Ours was one of the first houses to be built in College Heights, then only a few dirt roads carved out of the oak brush at the foot of a steep mountain.

Funny to look at those two addresses now: Orchard Avenue and College Drive. They seem to contain, in a metaphorical sense, the very nature of the change that took place.

From the bucolic to the knowing.

From low to high.

From the Edenic to the worldly.

Innocence bleeding—in one sense literally—into knowledge as I prepared to enter puberty and make the transition from one world to another.

It must have been my parents' dream to build such a house from scratch. For months as the house was under construction we would make the trip from the old house at the north end of town to check on the progress of the new one at the opposite edge, driving down Washington Boulevard from 12th Street, heading south on the wide boulevard and passing beneath the big metal archway that spanned the entire road with the welcome sign that said: IT PAYS TO LIVE IN OGDEN HOME OF WEBER COLLEGE.

It pays to live in Ogden.

Weber College was where our new street got its name. The subdivision had been developed on land adjacent to the college, high up on the lower slopes of the mountain, just below the "bench"—the watermark left behind when the great prehistoric sea called Lake Bonneville had receded many millennia ago.

Lake Bonneville had once covered much of the Great Basin, a big sea that rolled over most of western Utah and small areas of eastern Nevada and southern Idaho, a prehistoric freshwater lake almost as big as Lake Michigan and far deeper. Woolly mammoths lived on its shores. Lush tropical plants grew where now there's only desert and scrub. For a time this great inland sea spilled over the rim of the Great Basin, north into the Snake River plain, but as the climate changed it shrank up on itself. Through thousands of dry years it receded, leaving higher and higher concentrations of mineral salts behind until all that remained was the body of water we now know as the Great Salt Lake.

It also left behind the evidence of how high its waters had once reached—a flat little shelf of land visible all along the mountainside, a horizontal crimp running across the sloping face and marking the ancient shoreline. During my adolescent years I would come to know a section of this old watermark well: it would become part of my new world.

When we first arrived at the site of our new house we found a lot covered in native oak brush and poison ivy, which grew everywhere in thick patches. A place in the oak brush had been cleared for the foundation and slowly a basement was poured—a basement that would become an important part of our new house. Oak brush was also cleared in the front and back for lawns, though wisely my father left stands of trees here and there, creating little leafy islands.

Soon a house topped the foundation—a house so much bigger than our previous one, with a large picture window in the living room that looked out toward the mountains, and another in the dining room that had a sweeping view out over the valley and the Great Salt Lake.

When I stood inside the unfinished house I could see far out over the city and even farther out to the lake directly to the west, to the sheeny surface of what has been called the deadest lake in America, with a salt content six times that of the ocean. A lake where nothing could live in the briny water except a tiny shrimp that in certain places combined with mineral sediment to give the water a reddish cast. A lake that was mostly inhospitable to humans, even though humans had, over the years, attempted to make it into a playground and resort destination.

When I was small my family would occasionally go on outings to an old resort called Saltair, a grand Victorian-style pavilion and amusement park built in the late nineteenth century at the south end of the Great Salt Lake. There was a roller coaster at Saltair and a restaurant overlooking the water as well as a huge ballroom where dances were held. A beach had been created out of salty sand, but neither the beach nor the roller coaster nor the ballroom could make up for the experience of actually getting into the lake, of entering that intensely salty water, which initially might seem okay, might seem novel and fun, in fact, the way you could float so easily, but the moment you put your head underwater the salt stung your eyes and filled your nose and mouth and you came up gagging, and then the lake wasn't so fun, it was something to get out of as quickly as you could, and as you sat on the sand and the sun dried the salt on your skin, it began to sting, the drying saltwater creating a terrible itching, and then the tiny black flies began swarming over you, and all you wanted then was a shower, anything to wash off the stinging salt, anything to escape the swarms of black flies. I remember once standing on the beach at Saltair and puking after accidentally swallowing a mouthful of the Great Salt Lake and thinking, I'll never get in that water again.

At least there was a beach there at the old Saltair. In most other places a kind of sticky green gumbo-like mud or mushy salty sand made it hard to even reach the lake. All along the shoreline dried salt caked the rocks and weeds and willows, turning the landscape into a crusted world of briny white and trapping dragonflies and bees in the salt-soaked earth.

From the moment we moved into the new house on College Drive the lake took on a great presence: it became an inescapable element in our daily life. Not the lake as seen close-up by wading through the green gumbo mud or taking a plunge in the salty water but the lake as a kind of perpetual vision, iconic in its sheeny vastness, an ever-present and ever-changing mirror of weather and sky, a lake that looked like liquid mercury when the sky was gray and turned blood red when the sun began to set at the same time every evening as my family sat down to dinner at the table before the window that looked west, out over the distant water reflecting the lurid color. It was as if the mainland oscillated in the setting sun, shimmering with waves and pulsations, while the lake itself remained still in its crimson glow.

On certain evenings, sitting at the dinner table, it seemed this way to me: the lake was quiet, permanent in its antediluvian vastness, and it was the Freeman family, huddled around their pot roast and mashed potatoes, who shimmered and quaked uncertainly in the wavering light.

The new house on College Drive had six bedrooms and two bathrooms—one up and one down—as well as a fireplace on both levels. More room than my family had ever had. A large recreation or "rumpus" room ran almost the whole length of the basement. There was a walk-in fruit room for our two-year supply of food, and a big laundry room with a huge chest-style freezer where many bags of frozen laundry could be kept until the moment of ironing, and where the many packages of venison from the deer my brothers would soon begin shooting could be stored. It had a two-car garage where not only could cars be parked but also the carcasses of deer could be hung upside down each fall from the rafters so the meat could cure in the cool air. It even had a separate room in the basement where wood could be kept for the fireplace to avoid having to go outside in the winter.

I did not think of this then, as a child, because such things never entered my mind, but the thing I wondered later was, How did my parents ever manage to build this new house? How could they afford it? But the answer is clear to me: they did it by saving, by scrimping and scraping up every bit of extra money, by being the frugal, careful, responsible people they were, and by holding a continuing vision of bettering our lives.

In this new world, we were surrounded by wilderness—the wilderness of the foothills of the Wasatch Mountains.

Not long after moving in my father killed a large rattlesnake in our front yard. He cut its head off with a shovel, and then he wound an elastic band around one end and hung it from the mailbox as a surprise for the mailman.

The first day of school I picked some pretty red leaves for my teacher and brought them into the house so my mother could wrap them up for me. I didn't know I had picked a bouquet of poison ivy until my mother looked at my "present" in horror and told me to ditch it.

The new world was full of dangers—snakes and spiders and noxious plants I hadn't encountered in the old one. The neighborhood felt adventurous and exciting. To a girl like me, one who had always loved being outdoors and who longed for a dog and a horse of her own, this was a world filled with happy possibilities.

For a while we couldn't see another house because there wasn't another house to be seen. Only the dirt road out front, recently cut through the oak brush, and the steep mountain face, and in the other direction the eerie remnants of an ancient salt-laden lake.

Here, on College Drive, I would first begin to sense the clear delineating boundary of wealth and privilege, a world to which we did not belong and of which I had been completely unaware before. It was the place where I would begin to feel that the only way I could be myself was in fact not to be myself at all.

TWO

On College Drive, even our family seemed to undergo a change. We attended a different ward, where the meetings were held in a new, modern building, not at all like the old church we'd gone to before. The new church looked like many structures being built in the fifties, modern yet somehow blandly institutional, all appearing rather alike, so it seemed like a church could almost pass for an insurance office, or a library for a medical building.

The houses around us were new and the people were new, the church was new, and the school and all the students too. We might as well have moved to a different city for all the connection to the old life I felt. My parents made new friends and so did we kids, but mostly we just met people at church who very quickly came to feel like friends.

Even my parents began to seem different to me.

My father was called to a high position in the local church, as first counselor to the bishop of our new ward. This meant he was much busier and often gone at night, called away on church business. It was as if he'd suddenly gotten two jobs, one a day job working for the Air Force, the other a night job working for the church. Lay clergy in the Mormon Church are not paid: when you are called to a high position, like bishop or bishop's counselor, you serve without compensation, sometimes for five or six years, before a new bishopric is formed to take over.

I think he liked the authority and power the church position gave him and he also liked the men he served with, in particular Norm Skanky, the other bishop's counselor. Brother Skanky was an art teacher and principal at a local school and a very funny man who loved to play practical jokes. He wasn't just funny, he was witty and droll and clever, and this made him the perfect foil for my father, who was never known for his humor. Norm Skanky helped make the job of serving in the bishopric a much livelier experience for him.

Part of their job was visiting church members who were sick or in the hospital. One time Norm Skanky and my father went to the local hospital to visit some ward members, but instead of telling the receptionist they were there to visit Mormons, Brother Skanky passed himself off as a rabbi and asked if there were any Jews receiving treatment in the hospital they might visit. The funny thing is, Norm Skanky looked like a rabbi.

Sometimes my father and Norm Skanky would make prank calls to other ward members and pretend to be someone else. One time they called up Sister Marge Henderson and disguised their voices, pretending to be from the local chapter of the National Association for the Advancement of Colored People. They said one of their members, a black cleaning lady, had been walking by Sister Henderson's house that afternoon and had been nipped by her dog and they were calling to lodge a complaint on her behalf. They kept up this act for some time, going on about this black woman who'd been bitten by her dog, until Sister Henderson finally recognized who it was on the other end of the line and called them out for tricking her.

It's strange to think of my father participating in such larky behavior as a religious leader. But something happened to him after he'd been called to his position as first counselor to the bishop. He seemed to have found his place, as a leader, among men he liked. He drifted from us, both because his time was no longer his own, let alone ours, and also because he entered a more inclusive brotherhood, the high priests of the Melchizedek Priesthood, the highest priesthood level in the church. And among those elders he must have felt a kind of bonhomie, and he began making close alliances outside our family.

My mother, too, seemed to undergo a subtle change. She accepted a position in the Relief Society as a counselor to the president, a woman named Mary Miller. Mary Miller was the wife of the college president, a graceful, tall, educated woman who lived in a large lovely house provided by the college. The house was surrounded by beautiful trees and gardens, all maintained by a gardener, and the Millers also had a maid to clean their house. Just as Brother Skanky provided my father with something that might have been missing in his life, so did Sister Miller offer my mother a different kind of female friendship. All of my mother's friends had been housewives, or homemakers, as they no doubt preferred to be called, for there was a difference between a simple housewife and a good Mormon homemaker.

Mary Miller was also a homemaker but she was more than that: as wife of the college president, she was a hostess. She was part of welcoming and entertaining professors and students and she was also involved in local cultural events. She was educated and promoted a Great Books reading program for the Relief Society women. My mother admired her. She had different taste in clothes and always appeared refined and perfectly dressed and because she was slim and tall she wore her clothes well. She owned nice things. Her home was decorated with lovely furniture and objects. Mary Miller was a completely unpretentious person but no one could mistake her class when she entered a room or opened her mouth to speak. In many ways she could not have been more different from my mother, who had no education, did not own lovely things, and by and large had not come from a background that had cultivated good taste. And at five foot three she was neither willowy nor tall. But she and Mary shared something much more important: they were both very intelligent women, and both devoted to their religion.

Mary Miller and my mother became fast friends in this new world. Together they coordinated Relief Society events. They established programs, collaborated on socials, led the ladies' organization, seeing to it that the Relief Society home teachers visited every sister regularly once a month and that the uniform, prepared lessons that came from church headquarters were delivered at that time. They came to both love and admire each other and later, much later, when my mother was in the hospital and dying, I realized how profoundly deep their affection really was. Mary Miller came to see my mother one day while I was sitting alone in the hospital room, keeping watch over my semiconscious mother. She leaned over my mother and brought her face very close to hers and said, Oh, Alice, dear Alice, I have loved you for so many years.

She was a very smart woman, my mother, I mean naturally intelligent, and I think the people she met after we moved to College Drive helped nurture that side of her. The Mormon families who began to occupy the new houses being built in College Heights were headed by doctors and lawyers, professors and successful businessmen, people who didn't just have jobs but rather had careers. For my father, in many ways these men would become the *problematic people,* the brethren he'd begin comparing himself to, the more successful, wealthier men in the ward who could make him feel he wasn't quite as good as they were, hadn't achieved as much in life, when in reality how could they know what he might have become if he hadn't had so many kids? How could they know that for the most part he knew himself to be much smarter?

A year or two before leaving the old neighborhood, at the age of eight, I had been baptized for the remission of my sins. This happened the same year my brother died. According to Mormon doctrine, by being baptized I was given a clean slate and all the bad things I had done before I was eight were washed away in a complete remission of my offenses.

On the Sunday afternoon I was baptized, I was taken to the church with several other children my age. We were dressed all in white, as was the elder who baptized us. The baptismal font was in the basement of the church, a square pool with waist-deep water large enough to hold several people. The elder stood in the middle of the font with the water rising to his hips. One by one he led us into the cold water, and holding both our hands in his as he tipped us backward, he submerged us briefly and baptized us in the name of the Father, the Son, and the Holy Ghost.

What I remember is how our white clothes turned translucent after they got wet that day, so that as we emerged from the pool and stood around shivering, waiting for the next person to get dunked, they clung to our bodies. They took on the pinkish hue of flesh, showing the outlines of tiny breasts and crotches, lending what should have been a purely holy ritual a faintly erotic air.

In some prescient fashion, that moment of innocence, of cleansing and redemption—a baptism so tinged with the duality of carnal awareness—would foreshadow the years to come, when nothing would ever again seem so simple.

THREE

Each summer, around the Fourth of July, my family took our annual vacation, traveling by car to visit my paternal grandmother in Snowflake, Arizona.

My grandmother Emma was the daughter of the polygamist William Jordan Flake, the founder of Snowflake, the small town in the northern part of the state. She lived in an older two-story brick house in the middle of town, just across from the Mormon church. This was the house in which my father had been raised as well as nineteen other children.

It took two days for us to reach Snowflake from Ogden. Our route took us down the old Highway 89, past Big Rock Candy Mountain with its little trading post and the roadside attraction that always included a caged rattlesnake or two and some sad-looking coyotes and bobcats hunched up in their pens. We passed through sections of two national parks, Bryce Canyon and Zion, weaving along a two-lane road through a landscape of extraordinary color. At the border of Arizona, we began climbing up through the Kaibab Forest, and crossed the Colorado River on the Navajo Bridge and then traversed a part of the Navajo reservation before skirting the rim of the Grand Canyon and joining Route 66 at Flagstaff. There are photographs from these trips, one showing a cluster of family, including my mother and Marcia and my brothers Lee, Jerry, and Gregg posing with me at the rim of the Grand Canyon. When I look at me in this photograph I see a girl, in striped T-shirt and rolled-up jeans and sneakers, who could almost have been mistaken for a boy.

These trips left me with a deep affection for the red-rock country of southern Utah and northern Arizona, the buttes and mesas and scarps composed of startling shapes and colors—red, yellow, purple, scarlet, and orange—rocks sometimes sculpted into fantastic anthropomorphic shapes, a vivid landscape of lurid, haunting beauty.

We passed through deserts with mirages shimmering in the distance—cool-looking lakes that glistened deliciously under the July sun only to reveal themselves as dry desert valleys the closer you came. It was a trickster world, this world where my ancestors had settled, huge and awesome and in many places still so empty and unpopulated you could almost believe no human had ever passed through. You felt very small in such spaces, traveling in a little car down a narrow black ribbon of road under an immense blue sky.

There was no shortage of places to stop during our two-day drive and the little trading posts along the way were a favorite. With so many children in the car, crowded onto the seats and floor and even sometimes stretched out on the shelf near the rear window, we looked forward to these breaks. The trading posts had beaded coin purses and rubber tomahawks and bins of pretty polished rocks you could buy for a nickel or dime and each kid was always given a little money to spend. We never stopped at cafés or restaurants. My mother always packed picnic food and a green metal jug of lemonade and we ate in the little leafy parks in the small Mormon towns we passed.

Highway 89 ran through many of these towns, all Mormon communities settled in the latter half of the nineteenth century and organized according to the same plan and "millennial order" devised by Joseph Smith in 1833 for his City of Zion. He hoped to create a uniformity that would *fill up the world in these last days*.

Mount Pleasant and Manti, Marysvale and Circleville, Panguitch and Orderville. They all had streets laid out according to cardinal points and arranged in a numbered grid. The main streets were dotted with old two-story brick homes built by pioneers, like the one my grandmother lived in. There were cafés with festive neon signs, and shops advertising Western wear, like Freeman's Men and Boys Wear had done. Each settler had originally been allotted a plot in town on a lot large enough to raise vegetables and build corrals and sheds for domestic animals, as well as given acreage in the country where crops could be grown. People still kept horses and farm animals in their backyards and grew lush gardens with tall stands of corn and tidy rows of vegetables.

In the center of every town stood a Mormon church, and if we were traveling on a Sunday we sometimes stopped and attended a meeting and were always made welcome as members of the same tribe.

Often we stopped overnight in Orderville, just north of Bryce Canyon, where my mother's cousin Orson Hanks and his wife, Marion, owned a motel. The motel was on Main Street, in the middle of the little town, and had a carport attached to every room. They always gave us a discount. We usually got only one room with two big beds and Orson and Marion would set up cots for the rest of the kids. The motel had a little swimming pool with a crude mural of a bathing beauty hand-painted on a nearby wall and after a long day's drive the pool was always inviting.

Orderville was named after the United Order, a rudimentary form of communalism established by Brigham Young and practiced by the early settlers in pioneer towns.

During those early days, when poverty was rife and the settlers struggled to make a go of it in the harsh new world, all crops and goods were brought to the bishop's storehouse in each little community and then distributed by the bishop according to need. This system allowed for the survival of all members of the sect at a time when resources were very scarce, but eventually, as some settlers became more prosperous, the system fell apart, though the United Order continued to be practiced in Orderville long after other Mormon communities had abandoned it.

Our route took us across the Arizona Strip where the polygamist town of Colorado City was located. It did not seem strange to us that in this remote place, set against spectacular red cliffs, everyone was a polygamist. Even the local sheriff had multiple wives.

As my father explained, Colorado City had once been known as Short Creek. It had been a polygamist enclave for as long as anyone could remember, a place largely ignored by the rest of the world except during an ill-fated raid in the 1950s when government agents swarmed over the town and "rescued" the children of polygamists only to have their actions backfire when the nation at large reacted badly to front-page pictures of children crying for their jailed parents. The children had been returned, the name of the town had been changed, and the polygamists went back to doing whatever they wanted to under the direction of a prophet they called Uncle LeRoy, and everyone again turned a blind eye.

We were not shocked by polygamy. It was in our genes, the history we had grown up with. And just because the church was forced to formally renounce polygamy in 1890, in a proclamation known as the Manifesto, in order for Utah to gain statehood, that didn't mean there was anything *wrong* with it. The world simply wasn't ready for the Divine Principle.

When the world became more perfect again, we were told, it would be restored.

In the meantime there were those who never did give it up, like the saints who broke away from the church after the Manifesto was issued and formed their own sect—the Reorganized Church of Jesus Christ of Latter-day Saints. They refused to stop practicing polygamy: they believed you could not take back the Divine Principle once it had been given by the Lord.

The Reorganized Saints moved out to remote places like Colorado City where they could have as many wives as they wanted and nobody would care. They could marry women of any age, including girls who were still children. They could force young boys out of the community when there was a shortage of girls for the older men, who were sometimes disparagingly called Old Bulls. They could even marry off relatives to each other if Uncle LeRoy gave the okay.

A century after the Manifesto was issued in 1890, it was estimated that as many as fifty thousand people were living in polygamous households scattered throughout the American West. And then came the cable TV show *Big Love* that made it all look so sexy.

❖ ❖ ❖

From the time of the Manifesto the Mormon Church had begun working to transform itself bit by bit, attempting to become ever more mainstream, shedding the less reputable parts of its past, playing down the more mystical and strange aspects of the religion in an attempt to appear less peculiar to outsiders, hoping to seem less "cultish" and more "Christian." They had shed, or in some cases simply buried from public sight, much of the mystical thinking of the nineteenth century, the thinking that saw magic everywhere, in rocks and trees and all living things, beliefs that meshed well with those of the native tribes among whom they settled. Talking in tongues was banned, though it had been practiced by many prominent women in the early church and even in my lifetime by one of my aunts. Nor did they speak anymore about the Deseret Alphabet, the strange system of writing using characters adapted from shorthand that Brigham Young's clerks had come up with and ordered to be taught to all pioneer children as a means of excluding outsiders. And of course the violence embedded in the early church, which erupted in tragedies like the Mountain Meadows Massacre, when an entire wagon train of emigrants—120 people, including 70 women and children—were killed in 1857 by a group of Mormon settlers and the Indians they incited, was absolutely buried as deeply as possible in an attempt to eradicate it from history.

Church leaders would also eventually stop talking publicly about how in the future the Constitution would hang by a thread and one day a Mormon would save the nation, even though privately it was something they continued to believe.

They learned, in other words, how to appear more and more like the mainstream red-blooded Americans they really were.

No question, the Mormon Church became a different church in the latter half of the twentieth century, less open about its beliefs and practices, more concerned with public image. It lost a part of what once made it unique and became much more a corporate entity, investing part of its massive wealth in urban development, creating shopping and apartment complexes and movie theaters, like the development recently completed in downtown Salt Lake City, estimated to have cost the church five billion dollars. The church is planning to develop an entirely new city in Florida, on its 300,000-acre Deseret Cattle Ranch, a metropolis that will accommodate half a million residents. They are building churches and temples all over the world, investing their wealth in real estate in order to generate even more wealth. I never thought about any of these things when I was a child, making those long drives with my family through the Southwest. It became apparent to me only later, when I had long since left the fold, that these changes were already occurring during those years.

When we arrived in Snowflake after our long drive, our first stop was often a ranch owned by a cousin of my father's and his wife, LaVon and Verna Turley. Verna would make fresh donuts to celebrate our arrival and then all the Turley kids and the Freeman kids would head outside to play.

To be loosed upon the Turley ranch after two days of traveling in a car was to be set free in a world of wonders. Located at the edge of town, the ranch spread out over the high desert landscape where there were strange horned toads of a vivid turquoise color, and rattlesnakes and scorpions lurking under bushes. A creek lined with old cottonwoods flowed cool in the summer and had a deep swimming hole. There were riding horses, milk cows and bawling calves, and a big barn with a hayloft.

The Turleys had a boy my age nicknamed Sweego—a fresh-faced farm boy who loved horses and working on the family ranch. Over time we developed a crush on each other, even though he was my cousin, or second cousin—something that didn't seem to matter to us anyway.

We flirted, sought each other out at family gatherings—the barbecues and brandings hosted by his family. I learned to ride on the Turley ranch. Sweego's father, LaVon, was the livestock inspector in town and there was always an assortment of horses and cattle and various other animals in their corrals. I spent as much time as I could there, riding horses, playing in the hayloft, exploring the ranch. I gained a reputation for trying to ride anything, including the big calves kept in corrals next to the barn. There wasn't a horse on the place I wouldn't try.

I rode out into the desert with Sweego. He was a polite boy, with a shyness that made his country manners seem even more unusual to me, as if his knowledge of animals and ranching had given him some extra gravitas. It was the horses I loved, and Sweego knew horses. The combination of riding and being with him seemed doubly wonderful. Riding a horse full speed was like finding that vehicle I had imagined one day would let me race across the earth, but unlike the *Mormon Meteor* it turned out to have four legs and a big heart and a keen intelligence that could read the world.

Later, my mother would say to me, You know what you are? You're boy crazy. That's what you are. Boy crazy.

This was when I was fifteen, long after my crush on Sweego Turley had ended, but I believe he might have been the first. My cousin Sweego.

When my mother accused me of being boy crazy I couldn't deny it, but even then it seemed to me the story was somehow much larger than me, and much, much older. It was connected to the other thing I was, which was a Mormon girl, descended from a people who had once married such girls off at the age of thirteen.

Running beneath my childhood was a charged current of sexuality that I later came to see was endemic to both the culture and the religion and which found a kind of legitimized outlet in the Mormon love of dancing and the social events and parties that resulted in the early pairing up of youths, practices which had existed since pioneer times. That had been there since the prophet Joseph claimed the Lord appeared to him and gave him a revelation concerning polygamy, instructing the faithful, worthy men of the church to take multiple wives. And the prophet *had* taken many wives: he'd married girls and women of all ages, teenage maids who worked in his household, even women who were already married to his friends. He took widows for wives and sets of sisters. He took his wives in secret, never publicly admitting to his polygamous practices. The exact number of Joseph's wives varies but most estimates fall somewhere between thirty and forty.

Polygamy may have been outlawed by the church in the 1890s but many Mormon men continued to practice it in secret, including church leaders, while others, like Miles Romney, fled to Mexico and set up a polygamist colony across the border. The emphasis on preparing girls from early youth to become wives and mothers was never lost. Nor was the urgency for boys to find wives as soon as they returned from their missions, and this they were happy to do, having been celibate for two years and knowing they must not have sex until after marriage.

All this contributed to a charged atmosphere for boys and girls. From the time I was very young I felt a freewheeling interest older men seemed to take in younger girls, as if the polygamous gene, once implanted, had never been fully erased. Inculcated within the history of the people was the notion that a man needn't completely give up the idea of flirting with a young girl, if only innocently, to spice up what had perhaps become a sexually lackluster marriage or maybe just to make him feel, even for a brief time, like one of those old bulls from the polygamy era.

In my grandmother's house the children always slept upstairs, in two large rooms with ancestral portraits leaning out from the walls— stern-looking pioneers, women with their hair pulled back into tight buns, their unsmiling faces as hard and round and inscrutable as old coins, and men with heavily bearded faces and intense black eyes. The old wooden floors creaked in these rooms and it felt rather scary at night, with the house creaking and the large ancestral pictures look-ing so ghostly on the walls. Grandma warned us every year that we mustn't open the doors that led to the second-story balcony because it was old, the wooden floor rotten, and it might collapse under our weight, but we ventured out there anyway when no one was look-ing. A trumpet vine grew along the railing with orange flowers. We'd pick the flowers and stick one on each finger, making trumpet-flower hands, like witchy paws, and chase each other around.

During those trips to Snowflake I got to know different relatives, aunts and uncles I didn't often see, girl cousins who visited at the same time that I might not encounter any other time of the year. Diane Shumway and Joan Freeman, cousins older than me by a few years, were more Marcia's age and closer to her, and yet I remember them vividly. All the girl cousins slept together in the upstairs rooms in my grandmother's house, in beds with sagging springs, covered in handmade quilts and pushed up against walls beneath the portraits in their heavy frames.

My cousin Diane seemed more worldly than the girls I knew in Ogden. Her mother, Marge (my father's sister), was a professional beautician and she had taught her daughter all sorts of ways to look more glamorous. They lived in Phoenix, had orange trees in their backyard; this seemed exotic to me. Diane always looked tan, liv-ing where it was so sunny all the time. She had honey-blond hair and wore fingernail polish and lipstick and the bright colors looked pretty against her browned skin.

Joan was a very different sort of girl—tall and ungainly, shy and awkward, a pale, quiet child with large protruding ears that turned pink and translucent in the sun. Her mother had been confined to a mental institution. It was said that her mother was crazy but later the true diagnosis came out: she had Huntington's Syndrome, a degen-erative disease of the brain. My grandmother was exceptionally kind to Joan, taking her under her wing, aware of just how fragile and lonely she was.

Later, as adults, Joan and I would become good friends. We shared a love of books and hiking and the outdoors. But the prospect of being diagnosed with Huntington's would haunt her as well—it being a disease that offspring have a fifty-fifty chance of inheriting—and one day when she was in her sixties, having recently been released from a psychiatric ward in Tucson after being treated for depression, she decided to take her life by hiking into the nearby mountains with a pocketful of sleeping pills and simply disappear. She had been a great hiker all her life and this is the way she'd chosen to go, before the Huntington's she feared was coming on could rob her of her senses as it had done her mother. Though searches were conducted for months, her body was never found. And then one day several years later a motorist spotted a skull lying in a ravine near the roadside outside Tucson. Forensic testing determined it was Cousin Joan, washed out of the mountains in heavy winter rains.

Both Joan and Diane grew up to be interesting, strong women, but when I think of them now I see us as girls, sharing a bed beneath the haunting ancestral portraits looming out from the walls in the upstairs room of my grandmother's house in Snowflake.

FOUR

Not long after we moved to College Drive I was given a horse to ride. The horse belonged to the father of a girl I became friends with named Marlene. The red roan mare was long past her prime, over twenty years old, but still sound and willing and rather spirited for her age. I took to caring for her with a passion. Her name was Lady.

Marlene had her own horse, a big bay gelding, and her father was happy to give me his old horse if I would take over paying for her pasture and upkeep.

He was a rough man, Marlene's father, an auto mechanic who worked at the local garage, thin and jittery, always smoking, moving around. He had a swaggering, cocky manner and dark good looks. Her mother was pretty in a sort of slatternly way, a woman who kept a dirty house and yelled at her children. They argued a lot, the mother and father. They were much younger than my own parents and they seemed dangerously unhappy, as if drawn to each other in alternating currents of love and dislike.

Needless to say, they weren't Mormons; they weren't anything I could recognize. Marlene was rude to her parents and spoke back to them, and they were rude to her, something that would never have been tolerated in my household. They lived in a dreary apartment and both worked full-time at blue-collar jobs, leaving Marlene to tend her younger siblings, children with runny noses, poorly dressed in soiled clothes.

I could barely stand to visit her home, the place felt so stressful to me, with people yelling at each other and dirty dishes piled up on counters, the little kids often crying. On the other hand I was grateful her father had given me his old horse, although I knew he had done so because he no longer wanted to pay for the mare's upkeep and she was too old to sell. I was glad that a mutual love of riding had led me to Marlene and resulted in this gift of the horse, and also in our becoming friends in spite of the fact that we were nothing at all alike. Aside from horses we had little in common. I found her to be abrasive and harsh. I didn't like the rough way she treated her horse. She whipped it angrily with the ends of the reins when it didn't do exactly what she wanted, and she was always jerking the bit harder than she needed to and raking the gelding's sides with the big spurs she'd inherited from her father.

Now, looking back, I see that she was a very unhappy girl, from a very unhappy family, and her unhappiness had made her mean.

It didn't take long for me to become part of a small group of kids in the neighborhood who kept their horses at the same pasture and spent hours each day riding into the foothills above our new house. We made our own little posse of twelve- and thirteen-year-olds. It was a time of great looseness, of exploration and independence. I began to drift away from my family and spend more time with my new friends. There was much to explore by horseback in the mountains and woods above College Heights, and long hot summer days in which to do so.

We rode our horses into the foothills, past Beus's Pond, galloping up the narrow Spring Trail to where it topped out on the bench—the little shelf of land left behind by the receding waters of Lake Bonneville. Sometimes we rode bareback, sometimes used a saddle if one could be borrowed or found. We took lunches and tied up our horses while we ate in the crude little "forts" we built out of sticks leaned together, like the Paiutes did to make their wickiup shelters.

We led secret lives in our forts, shared jokes, told stories, took afternoon naps and rested between rides. In the middle of the day in the summer it grew hot, even up in the hills, and it felt good to lie back against the cool loam beneath the canopy of sticks. Sometimes one of the boys would try to kiss us but it was all in a silly kind of fun. We were too young to know much about sex or care about it, though a girl I met not long after moving to the neighborhood had once told me how babies were made. She'd found a used condom in the parking lot of the college football stadium and put it in a jar and buried it. She dug it up and showed it to me one afternoon. This is how you can *not* make a baby, she said, shaking the bottle in front of me. You put this over his *thingy*. To me it looked like the milky-white skin a snake had shed.

I wasn't really interested in how babies were made. I was interested in freedom. In riding horses with my friends. I relished the feeling of being cut loose from adults. In discovering the secret beauty

that could be accessed by the narrow trails that led through thick woods into the mountains. I especially liked the view of the world from the back of a horse, the way it gave me a feeling of sublime loft and power, part of the power I shared with the horse. I liked knowing that horses had such big, giving hearts and you could win them over with patience and kindness and they would be your ally forever. They could also move so incredibly, so breathtakingly, so beautifully fast across the surface of the earth.

We rode in the summer when school was out and we rode in the winter after school, navigating the icy streets to reach the snowy foothills, the horses' unshod hooves skidding on the icy pavement, then heading home in the fading evening light with freezing fingers and toes.

We even rode on Sundays, when we weren't supposed to, until something happened.

One day my father came to me and said he had been getting a lot of complaints from certain members of the ward who'd seen me riding my horse on Sunday. How were they supposed to tell their children they had to keep the Sabbath holy and refrain from all work and activity when they could see the bishop's counselor's daughter riding her horse? Sunday was the day when you weren't supposed to do anything except go to church, or go visiting, or just stay home and read the funny papers and eat a big meal. They felt I set a bad example by being allowed to ride. They didn't think it was right. And they wanted my father to do something about it.

I hate to have to do this, my father said, adopting an unusually gentle tone, but I'm going to have to ask you to stop riding your horse on Sunday. If it were up to me, he added, I'd say go ahead and do it. But it's not up to me.

If it were up to me. Those were the words that struck me with an unsettling power.

He doesn't believe it either, I thought. He thinks it's as stupid as I do.

A chink in the armor began to crack open and I felt a certain empathy leaking in, a permission to go ahead and question it all. Whatever had made him say that—his sense of his difference, the musical side of him, the part that didn't want to obey rules—it suggested that, given his druthers, he wouldn't go along with everything the church said any more than I would.

I did what he said because I knew I had to. I stopped riding my horse on Sunday. But I also began to question many things and rebel against certain notions of right and wrong. I often felt I didn't want to be good, like I knew most of the other kids around me wanted to be good. Not good in that way. I knew I could earn the easy approval of adults by doing what I was told, but I often didn't want to do that. I didn't want that kind of approval. I wanted something else. I wanted for things to make sense to me, and when it came to religion and its rules and dictates they almost never did.

A sense of aloneness began to fill up the spaces in my consciousness. I understood it would be better to keep these things to myself, to refrain from questioning certain things in public. And yet I found this hard to do.

FIVE

My mother began taking in boarders. My older brothers had left home, one to join the Air Force, one to serve a mission in Mexico, and there was a room available downstairs, a room that could be let to students or teachers at the nearby college, and thus a bit of money could be made to supplement my father's income. As a government employee he climbed the paycheck ladder according to preset "grades," rising from G1 level to G2, and then G3, and so on. Each time he was bumped up to a new pay level it was announced with pride: Your father's become a G4, my mother would say, and the household would celebrate in its own modest way even though the actual difference in his pay could be quite small.

The work took a toll on him. He had many disagreements with the federal government, many reasons to feel crabby and complain, to be dismayed over the stupidity and waste, the cumbersome bureaucracy, and the hardened conservative and self-serving attitudes within the military-industrial complex. He often looked harried when he came home from work now. And the smell of him changed as well. On Orchard Avenue he had often smelled of burnt leaves, a smell I had come to love. He would come inside from clearing ditch banks in the fall, having burned away the weeds or piles of fallen leaves, and this smell would cling to him. It's the smell I associated with him when I was young, and the one I associate with him even now.

On College Drive he smelled of Sen-Sens, the little square licorice-flavored mouth fresheners that came in a small packet he always kept in his suit pocket and sometimes offered to me. He carpooled to work now with other people, and maybe he began using these breath fresheners because he spent so much time in cars, at close range with other people.

He also smelled of the wool suits he wore in the winter, which he would shed as fast as he could when he came home each evening in favor of the jaunty one-piece jumpsuits he began to favor as his casual outfit of choice.

The first boarder my mother took in was a farm boy named Veldon who was in his first year at Weber College. He not only paid for his room but also took his meals with us. It became hard for me to sit at the table and eat with him, not only because he was unattractive, with a ruddy complexion and a bad farm-boy haircut that accentuated his large ears, but because he was terribly shy and awkward and had nothing to say and he blushed easily and most of all because he had a hard time breathing through his nose and made odd noises at meals. He had something wrong with his sinuses. It was not easy to start a day at breakfast with him. He also wore heavy black work boots with hard rubber heels that left black marks on the linoleum kitchen floor—a floor my mother kept not only mopped but waxed by hand, and she soon had to admonish him. I remember him coming upstairs one morning and her intercepting him in the kitchen and saying in an even voice, If you continue to wear those boots in this house and leave black marks on my floor I don't think it's going to work out for you to stay here. Also, I wanted you to know I can't do your laundry anymore if you don't change your underclothes more frequently.

He did not stay long. He left after a year. But soon a new boarder would arrive. His name was Roland. Roland Green. He was in his late twenties or early thirties, trim and healthy-looking, attractive in a certain über-Nordic way. He taught religion at a local school. He had served a mission for the church but unlike other missionaries he hadn't gotten married as soon as he returned. It was unusual to find a Mormon bachelor Roland's age. Men didn't wait until thirty to get married and start a family. This made Roland unusual—more unusual maybe than I could have guessed.

He quickly ingratiated himself with the family. Unlike Veldon, he wasn't shy. He had a strong, forceful personality and because he was so handsome and such an extrovert, and because he taught a religion class, he easily won over my mother and older siblings.

But he made me nervous. He seemed self-righteous and arrogant. There was something about him I didn't trust. From the beginning he singled me out for teasing, and the teasing didn't feel fun. He teased me about the cutoff jeans I wore, about being a tomboy, about always riding a horse. And then one day—a particular Sunday after church—he went even further and he didn't just tease me, he terrified me.

I was standing in the kitchen in front of the window that looked out over the lake when he came in and accosted me. No one else was in the room. He had a rather sly, expectant look on his face, and I felt he was going to begin teasing me again, but instead he said, I heard the boys in priesthood talking about you this morning. About what you let them do to you up in the hills.

It's hard to describe how stunned I felt at the moment, and how afraid, both of his words and of the way he'd delivered them. He seemed to relish cornering me this way. And I did feel suddenly cornered, as if I'd become his prey.

What? I said. My heart was beating hard. I don't know what you're talking about, I added.

Oh, I think you do, he said. I think you know what you've been doing.

I haven't been doing anything, I said. But now I felt more frightened, because I saw from the way he looked at me that he didn't believe me and he wasn't going to let me go. I felt suddenly guilty, thinking of the secret forts, the experimental kisses, the afternoon naps in the wickiups. I thought, What could the boys have said? I really hadn't done anything, but did they boast? Did they lie and make stuff up? Or was it Roland Green who was lying? It was all so confusing and upsetting. He stood there looking down at me, waiting, a sly grin on his face, and then he again pressed his point, saying I must have done something or the boys wouldn't have been talking about me the way they were. He wouldn't tell me what they said, just that he had overheard them saying that I'd let them do certain things I shouldn't have.

I tried to defend myself again. I said I didn't believe anyone had said anything bad because nothing bad had happened, and that was the truth.

Then why are they talking about you? he said.

He was still smiling at me, as if he were enjoying what was happening. He must have seen I was close to tears. I felt overpowered and shamed by him, deeply shamed. Again I told him I hadn't done anything and again he said he didn't think I was telling the truth.

I began to cry. I hated doing it but I couldn't stop.

It's okay, he said, adopting a tone that made his voice sound creepy and evil, I'm not going to tell your parents if that's what you're afraid of. But I think you'd better think about what you're doing. You might pray about it. Ask for the Lord's guidance. And stop doing these things.

He left me standing in the kitchen, still crying.

I asked the boys who were my riding friends what they'd said the next time I saw them. They said they hadn't said anything. They said Roland Green must have made that stuff up because they hadn't even seen him at priesthood meeting, so how could he have seen them?

Only later—much later, when I thought about this episode as an adult—did it occur to me that Roland Green might have had his own secret. He might have been jealous of me. He might have liked those boys himself. Or perhaps it was me he liked. One of those older men, perverse and deceptive, interested in young girls, in trying to pry out their secrets and gain power over them by making them afraid.

I don't think he ever said anything to my parents, though for a long time I worried he might. It seemed he liked keeping me in a suspended state of fear. I do think he said something to the bishop, who one day following church offered to give me a ride home in his car, and since it was the middle of winter, I accepted.

But instead of going directly home he drove me up into the foothills near Beus's Pond because, he said, he wanted to have a talk with me. He parked the car but left the engine running because it was so cold and we needed the heater. I was sitting in the passenger seat, trying to figure out why he'd brought me to this place, why he couldn't have talked to me at church, in his office.

He turned to me and said, I understand some of the boys have been talking about you in priesthood meeting. About the things you've been doing with them.

The bishop did not scare me the way Roland Green did. But still, when he said this, I felt a familiar fear and shame. But I also felt angry and more defiant. What was going on? And why was I sitting with the bishop parked in his car in the foothills?

I don't know who told you this stuff, I said, but it's not true.

I think it would be better, he said, if you just told me what you've done with the boys. If you could just describe it for me . . .

I shook my head. I wasn't going to say anything.

The bishop was a pasty-faced man. A bit fat and soft and white. He looked like if you poked his face it would retain the imprint of your finger. He had a plump wife and several lackluster children. He took in a Navajo boy one winter, a boy who sat next to the bishop's wife and children in church and made them look overly pale and sickly.

I stared out the window at the pond. It was snowing lightly. Sometimes we ice-skated here—the girls from church or a group of friends. We'd build a fire and shovel the snow off the ice and skate around the bonfire. In the summer we made rafts out of logs tied together and poled our way out to the middle of the pond. We rode our horses along the path that circled the water, winding through the willows. It was a small pond but a lovely one, until one of the members of the ward who raised turkeys started dumping the refuse from his pens in the water. Then it was full of turkey shit and feathers. Somebody suggested he stop doing this, and eventually he did, but the pond never felt quite the same.

I'd like to know what sorts of things you've done with the boys, the bishop said. That way I might be able to help you.

I looked at him, and suddenly it became clear to me: He didn't want to help me. He just wanted to know. He wanted details. He wanted stories, and images. He wanted to sit there in his parked car in the foothills above the church and hear *descriptions*.

I thought of another man in the ward. A big, cheery, pink-cheeked man who used to come out on his porch and wave to me whenever I rode by on my horse en route to the foothills. Who always seemed to be there, waiting for me. Who would sometimes say to me when he saw me in church, I bet you've got those little Levi cutoffs on under your dress, don't you? I bet you never take them off!

His wife played the piano in church. She always looked to me like the unhappiest person in the world, but what did I know? She just looked like it was painful to even have to go out in public. She was a big, overweight woman. The flesh of her hips spilled over the bench when she sat at the piano. When my father became the choir director, she was one of his accompanists. I thought he always made an effort to be exceptionally gentle and kind with her because she seemed so awkward and shy, trapped in her big body. To me she always looked like she was blushing.

I didn't cry when the bishop grilled me that day in his car. And I didn't tell him anything, either. I sat silent, just shaking my head when he asked me more questions. Finally I told him I didn't have anything to say, because there wasn't anything to tell, and then I asked to be taken home.

Afterward I became a slyer girl. I kept more of me to myself. Even when I thought I didn't have any reason to hide something, I often hid it anyway. I felt I had seen something. Learned something about men, especially self-righteous men who could be a danger in ways that seemed twisted and unpredictable. These brethren, these elders— they were not like the women in the ward. Even the most religious and stern of the sisters didn't really scare me that much, not the way the men did. There was something specific to men and their over-bearing ways that was disturbing because it reminded you of who held the power to make your life either miserable or good.

SIX

Roland Green stayed with us for what seemed like a long time—maybe only a year or a little more, I'm no longer sure, but when he left I felt relieved. I didn't have to try and avoid him anymore and the house felt calmer and safer to me.

After he left, my great-aunt Fannie moved in and took over an upstairs bedroom. Like many of my Mormon relatives who had never drunk alcohol or smoked or indulged in other bad habits, she had lived to a great age. At ninety-five she was still a very spry woman, and also very sweet: she suffered only from poor hearing and failing eyesight.

She loved to listen to the Book of Mormon read aloud on records for the blind which were sent to her by mail and arrived in hard khaki-colored boxes. Due to her poor hearing she had to listen to these records at top volume.

For hours at a time, the inescapable sound of the Book of Mormon filled the house as readers droned on in rather monotonous, loud voices: *And it came to pass . . . And the angel said unto me . . . And behold, I, Nephi . . . And it came to pass . . .*

Again and again, it came to pass . . .

The sound of the Book of Mormon played at top volume became the strange background noise in the house. Most often it was just that, noise washing over me, but occasionally as I stood in nearby rooms ironing or doing homework or setting the table for dinner, I would catch a passage that actually interested me, usually about harlots or sinners or how the earth would wax old like a garment and everybody would die or the mighty Lord would feed people who oppressed him with their own flesh and they would be drunk on their own blood like sweet wine, and at these moments, suddenly leaping out from the monotony of the thus-sayeths and it-came-to-passes, I felt a kind of vivid and fearsome story leaking through.

In the summers, along with other girls from my ward, I was sent for a week to a church-owned camp in a high valley at the base of a towering mountain called Ben Lomond.

I loved this camp. I loved the older married couple who ran it, whom we called Uncle Leo and Aunt Ione. I loved the sports we played, the softball and volleyball games, and the way the girls all slept together in a big dorm at night. The camp had a beautiful setting in the woods near a stream. We spent all day outdoors. In the afternoon we made crafts, and put on little plays in the evening.

I loved the place called the Sacred Grove, which was supposed to be like the other Sacred Grove where the angel Moroni appeared to the prophet Joseph. It felt holy, this circular opening among tall trees, with a fire pit in the middle and beautiful light falling through the leafy branches onto the circle of logs where we gathered for prayers. It smelled beautiful in those woods early in the morning. At night we met in the same place, around a campfire, to toast marshmallows and listen to the excellent ghost stories Aunt Ione and Uncle Leo told.

They were a very theatrical couple, much taken with dramatics. On one special night every year they dressed up as Indians and put on a pageant. Aunt Ione darkened her face and wore a dress with Native designs and a beaded headband and a dark wig with braids. Uncle Leo dressed in his buckskin outfit and moccasins. And then they climbed to a special spot on a hillside above the Sacred Grove and waited in the dark for the pageant to begin.

When all was ready one of the camp counselors would lead us with a flashlight through the dark to the Sacred Grove and seat us around the campfire, which had not yet been lit. Suddenly a spotlight would illuminate the place on the hillside above us where Aunt Ione and Uncle Leo stood, dressed in their Native garb and frozen like statues, and then slowly they would come to life and begin to sing "Indian Love Call" to each other in warbling voices: first she would sing a line, and then he would answer, drawing out the *ooo* sound at the end of each line:

AUNT IONE: *When I'm calling you—ooo-ooo-ooo . . .*
UNCLE LEO: *I will answer too—ooo-ooo-ooo . . .*

On it would go, back and forth, their voices alternating. "Indian Love Call" was a famous song from the 1924 operetta *Rose-Marie,* with music by Rudolf Friml and lyrics by Oscar Hammerstein II. It was supposedly based on a Native legend about how men would call out to the girls they wished to marry, a song made famous by Jeanette MacDonald and Nelson Eddy. Uncle Leo and Aunt Ione didn't have good voices like Jeanette MacDonald and Nelson Eddy, but they sang as if they believed they did, and the sight of them standing up high on the dark hillside, illuminated only by a spotlight, made it seem as if they were suspended in the night sky, magically levitating above us.

Their performance had a very dramatic ending, one we came to look forward to each year. When they finished singing, Uncle Leo would light something—perhaps a ball of rags dipped in lighter fluid—that was attached by a clip to a metal line running down to the campfire, and a ball of fire would whoosh down through the darkness on the unseen line and crash into the fire pit and ignite the kerosene-soaked wood that had been stacked there, erupting into flames. It was inevitably a thrilling spectacle for us girls, and one I think now might have gone spectacularly wrong. But it never did.

The Mormons of my childhood were as enamored of entertainments and dramas as their pioneer ancestors had been. For those early settlers, holding regular dances and playing music together and dressing up and staging theatricals were how they buoyed their spirits and made it through harsh times.

Every Mormon meetinghouse had not only a chapel and a Relief Society room and classrooms for Sunday school as well as offices for the bishop, but also a large "cultural hall" where dances could be held and sports played. At one end of the room there was always a stage for theatricals.

Each year, in every ward, a special Gold and Green Ball was held in the cultural hall. This was a dance for all ages. Everyone dressed in their best clothes, a band was hired, and the cultural hall was decorated in gold and green. The gold represented the elders, the green the youngsters.

There we would all be. The portly ward patriarch, Brother Stromberg, dancing with his granddaughter. June Wadman waltzing with her son Ricky. My father taking a turn with me, while Helen Plowgian, a tall, imposing woman with braids wound around her ears, led her faintly mustachioed son across the floor.

Couples who had been married for many years often danced beautifully together. Teenagers paired up and relished the chance to hold each other close. Later in life I would meet people who imagined that Mormons were repressed, strict people, humorless and averse to cutting loose, and I would think of these Gold and Green Balls, of how fun they were, how much laughter and goodwill filled those evenings, and how much people of all ages had loved to dance.

Every ward also put on an annual "road show," often staging adaptations of popular Broadway shows like *Oklahoma!* or *South Pacific* or another perennial favorite, *The Music Man*. Upbeat musicals, in other words, with faith-promoting or virtuous themes. The Mutual Improvement Association—the church organization for teens— played a big role in these productions. A director would be chosen from among interested adults, and a play cast with an attempt made to select the kids with the best voices and acting ability. Other kids were assigned jobs of costuming or lighting or making props, and adults pitched in and took roles themselves. A competition was held every year among the wards within a "stake"—the term for a collection of four or five wards—to see who could stage the best roadshow, and people went all out to make sure their ward stood a chance of being chosen the winner.

My sister, Marcia, had a very good singing voice. She often took part in these theatricals, but I did not. She was the daughter who had inherited my father's musical gifts. He had a beautiful tenor voice; she sang alto with perfect pitch. They began singing duets together while she was still a teenager. She also sang in the choir he directed in church, and for the special Christmas program he conducted of Handel's *Messiah*.

Music became one of the things over which they could bond: Marcia played the piano and could accompany him when he sang solos or duets with her. They practiced at home, worked up numbers, hymns and popular songs they could perform together in church or for special occasions. They sang at funerals, celebrations, family gatherings. They appeared happy singing together, with Marcia sitting at the piano, my father standing behind her, stopping her to correct something if needed—always ready with a suggestion, eager to show off his musical knowledge and skills. Sometimes they sang a cappella, standing close to each other, sharing a sheet of music. Blending their voices and finding the harmony. Father and daughter doing something they both loved, together. I think I always understood this gave them a closeness that I would never have with either of them.

I had not inherited my father's singing ability. I hadn't even much enjoyed the piano lessons I had been forced to take from a large, elderly woman named Mabel Ridges, and had quit after a year or two, though later, as an adult, I recalled these lessons more fondly, and wondered if I might take up the piano again. In truth I had some musical talent, but I could not sing with my father. I wavered unsteadily between soprano and alto, couldn't really carry a tune. Still, I sometimes sang in his choir, recruited by him to fill a chair at Christmastime or some other occasion, though I always struggled to keep up. I couldn't take the parts in the roadshows as my sister did because I didn't have her voice, and in any case I preferred to be outdoors.

Instead of participating in roadshows I played on the girls' softball team, coached by a stocky, athletic woman who seemed to take a special interest in me. She was a single woman, in her thirties or perhaps early forties, and there weren't many of those in our church. A single woman was a great anomaly: it was presumed there was something slightly *off* about such a person. Only this could explain not having ever married.

This woman lived with her mother, just the two of them in a little house not far from the college. What had happened to her father? I didn't know, but it was almost as if the coach and her mother had become a couple of sorts. You hardly ever saw them apart. Like the man who used to wait on his porch for me to ride by, the one who had asked about my Levi's cutoffs, the coach, I felt, was strongly drawn to me. It didn't disturb me, because I liked her and everything was done in fun, the way she was always grabbing me and giving me hugs, catching my head in a hammerlock for a little joke, singling me out for special attention. But I think there was a reason for this that never occurred to me then.

The whole idea of homosexuality was something that really never entered our minds. It was never discussed, as if such a thing didn't exist. There must have been people among us who were gay but it would have been impossible for them to come out. To this day you cannot be accepted by the church if you are gay unless you've managed to keep your preference secret or agreed to lead a celibate life.

One of those people who would grow up leading a secret life was my younger brother Jerry, the one I was closest to in age. Later he would tell me that from the time he was quite young he knew he was gay, but not until he had accepted a mission call at nineteen did he finally face this fact.

Shortly before he was to leave for his mission—after my parents had already bought him the prescribed missionary outfit, the white shirts and dark suit with extra pants meant to last two years, the black brogues and dark socks—did he realize he couldn't do it. He saw that he could not serve a mission for the church, both because he was gay and because he didn't believe in it. He couldn't go knocking on doors in some foreign country trying to convert people to a religion he no longer believed in.

When he belatedly announced to my parents near the eve of his scheduled departure that he'd realized he couldn't go on a mission, it caused them a great deal of embarrassment. Now everyone in the ward would know that their son had backed out, reneged on his mission call. My father was so angry he kicked Jerry out of the house and told him he could never come back. In a way this was good news, because Jerry found an apartment in an older neighborhood in Ogden, on the top floor of a house on Quincy Avenue where he could live by himself—where he could finally *be* himself. I remember visiting him not long after he'd moved in and thinking how nice it was. He had furnished the place with things he'd found at thrift stores, as he would do with every place he ever lived. He'd let loose his good taste, surrounded himself with things he loved, including the books and music that had begun to absorb him. I couldn't help feeling a bit jealous. I wouldn't have minded fixing up my own place and living alone for a while. Not that I thought this would ever be possible.

In high school Jerry had won a contest by writing an essay about the United Nations. The prize was a trip to New York City and a visit to the UN. The Queen City Rebekah Lodge of Ogden sponsored his trip, which took place in the summer of 1965. He traveled by bus from Utah to New York City and met other students from around the

country, all of whom spent a few days at the United Nations headquarters, observing the proceedings, and sightseeing in New York City. It was his first trip east of the Rockies, his first time in a large city, and it led to a second trip six months later, when another essay he wrote about his interest in the UN led to an invitation to attend a United Nations Youth Conference in London.

His host during his stay in England was Nigel Nicolson, the author, publisher, and politician—son of Vita Sackville-West and Sir Harold Nicolson. Nigel Nicolson had grown up in Sissinghurst Castle, the crumbling estate his parents had bought in 1930 in order to restore it and create a visionary garden. In a letter to Jerry, sent to him before his trip began, Nigel Nicolson introduced himself and told Jerry what he could expect upon his arrival in England:

December 6, 1965

Dear Jerry:

You will be surprised to hear from me, whose name will mean nothing to you yet, but I am chairman of the British United Nations Association and I will also be your host during part of the time that you are over here. When I was recently in New York I called on the UNA of the U.S., who are arranging the trip, and I looked at the very careful brochure which you sent them describing your interests and your life. I was much impressed by the keenness you have always shown in the United Nations, and I was delighted that the association will be able to help you with the fare.

During the first week in London, while you are attending the lectures, you will be the guest of Mr. Albury, who lives in Princes Gate, near Hyde Park. I don't know him personally, but I expect that he will be writing to you soon. In the second week, after the lectures are over, you will be staying with my family down in Kent, about fifty miles from London. We live in a place called Sissinghurst Castle. This is not a castle in the ordinary sense (with battlements and drawbridges) but a brick house with a tall central tower, constructed between 1485 and 1560. It has one of the most famous gardens in England, although there will not be much to see by way of flowers at this time of year, and it has recently been modernized, with central heating and five bathrooms. It is a comfortable house, in spite of its age, and it is among the historic buildings of Britain. There is a large farm attached to it, a moat, a lake and 100 acres of woodland. It lies at the heart of the fruit and hop growing district of England, and is very rural, with the village a mile away and the nearest town (Canterbury) about twenty miles further on. You had better bring some warm clothing, for in January there is very often a heavy snow fall in that part of England.

By profession I am a book-publisher and a writer (mostly on politics and history), and I give my spare time to directing the affairs of this Association. I am 48 years old. My wife, Philippa, is 36. We have three children—two daughters of 10 and 2 and a son aged 9. Although they are much younger than you, I am sure we shall all get on well together. In addition to yourself, I have also invited Miss Macdonald from your party. She is a young teacher whom you will get to know on your way over, as she is in charge of the whole group. I met her in New York, and I am sure that you will like her. We won't stay at Sissinghurst all the time, because I plan to take you with me when I travel to other parts of the country on various speaking engagements. In this way you will be able to see quite a lot of the country and meet new people.

I hope this gives you some idea of what you may expect over

here. At least I can promise you a very warm welcome. I will get
in touch with you at some time during the conference.

Yours Sincerely,
Nigel Nicolson

In England, Jerry spent a week at Sissinghurst Castle with Nicolson and his wife and children. He explored the house and gardens,
took his meals with the family each night, and made short trips by
car with his host.

Nicolson was fascinated by Jerry. He was especially interested in
the fact that Jerry had grown up as a Mormon. Jerry later told me
that during his first evening at Sissinghurt, Nicolson had spent the
entire dinner asking him questions about himself: he particularly
wanted to know more about Mormons, what their beliefs were, what
it was like for him to be raised in this way.

By this time Jerry knew he was gay. He was a gay teenage boy living
a completely closeted life in Ogden, Utah, within a family who knew
he was somehow different—gentler and quieter than other boys,
more introspective and thoughtful, not at all interested in sports or
hunting or other manly pursuits—but just how different we couldn't
have guessed. How ironic that at this point in his life he should have
found himself in a domicile—a very grand domicile—that had been
restored and inhabited by Nigel's parents, both of whom had homosexual affairs.

He could not at the time have known the story of Harold Nicolson—
how he'd had male lovers before he met Vita Sackville-West, how
Vita had been the passionate lover of, among other women, Virginia
Woolf. How their affairs continued during their married life. That
story, told by Nigel Nicolson in his book *Portrait of a Marriage,* had not
yet been published. But he understood that the world of Sissinghurst
Castle was very far away in every imaginable sense from the life he
had known growing up in Mormon Utah. At Sissinghurst, he had
been exposed to a very sophisticated, aristocratic life and a high level
of intellectual thought.

After returning from Sissinghurst, Jerry changed in several important ways.

He decided he could not serve a mission, and he left the church.

He came out as an openly gay man.

And he announced his intention to become a writer, influenced
perhaps by Nicolson—the noted author who had praised Jerry's
prize-winning essay and perhaps even encouraged him, as the founder
of the publishing house of Weidenfeld & Nicolson.

Jerry told me that when he later announced to our father that he
intended to become a writer his reaction had been to tell him, That's
fine if that's what you want to do, but I forbid you to write about two
things—family and religion.

Jerry kept in touch with Nigel Nicolson for a few years following
his return, after he had been banished from my parents' house and
while he was living alone in the upstairs apartment on Quincy Street.
He received one more letter from Nicolson, written on Sissinghurst
Castle stationery, in June of 1967, a year and a half after his visit to
England.

Dear Jerry,

I have just got home after six weeks abroad, writing a new
book about architecture. Among the letters awaiting me was
your very welcome letter of the 18th May together with the
colored photographs which you took at Sissinghurst. I like them
very much indeed and they will make a useful addition to my
album.

Kit McDonald was with us when we toured Europe and she
told me some of your news. I am glad that you are working in
journalism now. I received from the Peace Corps a form to fill
up on your behalf. I have done this and I hope you will get the
appointment.

Yours Sincerely,
Nigel Nicolson

Until this letter surfaced recently, I had never known that Jerry had represented himself as "working in journalism" during this period. He must have been describing an inner longing more than the outer reality, or maybe he was trying to sell articles I hadn't known about. I also had not known that he, like me, had harbored dreams of entering the Peace Corps.

In the end, Jerry didn't become a writer, nor did he serve in the Peace Corps. He moved to San Francisco in the early 1970s and met his longtime companion, Daniel Gundlach, a musician and artist. They bought a house in the Mission District and lived the exuberantly free gay life. Collectively they were known for their exquisite good taste: their apartment was featured in West Coast magazines. At one point they opened up a little store called Readymade where they sold mid-century designer furniture they discovered in thrift stores and rehabilitated. They had an eye for modernist designs, were very inventive, and led a very creative life.

In his thirties, after their store had closed, Jerry became a bus driver for the city of San Francisco, a job he held for many years. He said he liked the regular hours, the way it brought him into contact with an assortment of people and got him out into the world. He made a very sophisticated, literary bus driver, with his eye for art and design, his deep passion for James Joyce, his love of William Blake and devotion to Gertrude Stein. He was naturally kind and empathetic, treating his passengers with warmth and consideration, especially the elderly and poor, and he became a favorite driver on his routes.

Later he almost never spoke about his time at Sissinghurst, though he kept copies of several of Nigel Nicolson's books in his library along with other volumes he treasured, which included Blake's *Songs of Innocence and of Experience,* Gertrude Stein's *Autobiography of Alice B. Toklas,* and Julia Child's *Mastering the Art of French Cooking.*

He was a subtle man, not given to boasting. Maybe that's why he very rarely talked about his time at Sissinghurst, that experience which had had such a profound effect on him. Or maybe he didn't mention it because it brought him a little sadness when he thought of it: he had not managed to realize the promise of that time. He had not become a writer as he'd dreamed of being.

I'll never know how much my father's prohibition—his warning that Jerry must never write about two things, family and religion—might have played a part in his failure to do so. No doubt it troubled him. It troubled me when he told me about it later. But I know there were other factors that influenced this outcome, some of which I now understand, some of which I never will.

He never did come out to my parents. He didn't feel the need to do that. He probably understood it would have only made them uncomfortable to try and discuss his homosexuality with them. Of course they figured it out after a while and in their own way accepted it with considerable grace. They knew what a lovely person he was, the kindest man, so thoughtful and likable. Why would they ever take the chance of alienating him?

I have the feeling there are lots of openly gay Mormon kids out there now. Why this is I'm not quite sure but you see a lot of same-sex couples on the streets of Salt Lake City, holding hands and strolling along. Recently the city elected its first openly gay mayor, Jackie Biskupski. This could not have happened when I was growing up. It could not have happened when Jerry was coming out. And yet just days before Biskupski was elected the church issued a new policy, banning baptism for children of gay parents until they turn eighteen and agree to leave their parents' household and disavow homosexuality.

Later, when we were grown, and my parents would summon their children and grandchildren home for the annual family reunion, Jerry and Daniel were always invited. By then he was living in San Francisco, working as a bus driver. Dan was welcomed to the reunions like a family member, which is what we felt he really was. Occasionally my father might say something to me that would indicate he wanted to finally openly acknowledge Jerry was gay or somehow discuss it with me but it was always done with a kind of winking humor. He'd say, Do you think Jerry is going to bring his wife to the reunion this year? and I'd say, I don't know but I hope so.

Once he said to me, I can understand two men wanting to live together. I get that part. I just can't imagine what they do with each other.

I wouldn't try, then, I said.

SEVEN

The summer I turned fourteen I got a job working for a man who lived in our neighborhood named Harry Martin.

Harry Martin was rich and white and good-looking, a devout Mormon with an adoring wife who lived with his family in a big new house in the mountains above town. It was the kind of house everyone talked about, larger and grander than its neighbors. The Martins attended church every Sunday and referred to their fellow Mormons as "brother" and "sister," as we all did. They belonged to the same ward as my family and that's how I got to know them.

Brother and Sister Martin made a vibrant, attractive couple, popular and well liked. When I met them they were in their late thirties and already had eleven children. Sister Martin was a remarkably slender woman considering her many pregnancies; she had bright red hair and freckled skin and though she could not in any real sense be considered pretty she still managed to be attractive, in part because she dressed and carried herself well. She had both the money and the good taste to do so. She cared for her eleven children herself with the help of occasional babysitters. When I think of her now I see a quiet, somewhat harried woman surrounded by many kids, submissive, rather shy, and very sweet. I never understood how Harry Martin made his money. I just knew he made a lot of it.

I was initially hired to help with child care over one summer but I was soon given another job, that of helping Harry Martin organize his library in a very large room in the basement of his very large house.

Because the house was new the library was being built from scratch to Harry Martin's specifications. It had a walk-in security vault at one end and several large wooden tables in the center of the room for looking at the books and manuscripts in his collection. The room had just been finished when he asked me one day if I'd like the job of helping him organize his library and catalogue his books. All the books were still in cardboard boxes, sitting on the floor of the room that had been lined with new wooden shelves. It was my job over the course of that summer to unpack the books and place each one on the shelves according to a system Harry Martin had developed. I took deep pleasure in this job, in part because the whole idea of a library was something new to me, as was the notion of being allowed to handle such beautiful books. As teenage summer jobs go, it seemed vastly superior to babysitting.

Since there were so few books in the house where I grew up, I found it immensely exciting to discover that Harry Martin possessed so many. In truth I knew that even if we had more books in our house, there was really no time for reading. We were always busy going to church, or a meeting, some ward activity. I don't remember anyone reading a book for pleasure, unless it was maybe something to help prepare for a talk in church. But not real books. Not novels. Or poetry. Nor do I ever remember being taken to a library as a child or even owning a library card. I might have been forgiven for thinking there was no literature in the world.

Thus the great discovery I made over that summer working for Harry Martin: here was a real library, a treasury of books, each to be unpacked and catalogued by me.

Harry Martin owned many beautiful books. All hardcovers, editions of Shakespeare and the Harvard Classics, works by Dickens and other English and American novelists, books on history and the settlement of the American West, volumes of maps and books describing the world's cultures and religions. Of course he also had many books on Mormon history and volumes by contemporary Mormon writers.

Some days Harry Martin and I worked alongside each other in the library and he would tell me the story of how he acquired a certain book. Some were quite rare, he said, and he'd name a price he paid. As he talked about his books I came to see he was concerned with their value more than their contents. He rarely discussed why he'd chosen to buy a certain book, only what it had cost.

Harry Martin wasn't a scholar and seemed to have no great interest in literature. He lived in a world of money and finance: it's how he'd made his fortune, as I later came to learn. He was very good at getting people to invest their money with him. Until suddenly he wasn't.

His fall from grace came not the summer I worked for him but a year or so later when people who had entrusted their savings to him began to lose their money in what had been risky investment schemes. Many local people, including some of rather modest means, had given money to him and when the news of his losses came out the feeling against him ran very high. Some felt they'd been scammed. In no time Harry Martin lost his big house on the hill, and his expensive library. He and his sweet, shy wife and eleven children were forced to move away to escape the scandal. I never knew what became of him, or of that extraordinary library of books.

When I think of him now, and of that summer I worked for him, one of the strongest memories I have of Harry Martin is this:

One day, while working in the library, he said he had something to show me, something very special that very few people had ever seen. He took me into the walk-in vault at the end of the long room, where we stood close together—the handsome and charismatic man and the curious teenager swiftly becoming such a knowing girl—and with great ceremony he took down a beautiful wooden case from the shelf. The case was locked. He opened it slowly to reveal three

objects nestled inside against the velvet lining. The objects were made
of gold—two gold chalices, and a larger piece, beautifully formed
and decorated. This was a breastplate, he said. Two gold chalices and
a breastplate. These were ancient objects, discovered in an archaeo-
logical dig in Guatemala, the same objects, he said, that had been
described in the Book of Mormon.

He closed the box and put it back on the shelf. And then he swore
me to secrecy, telling me I must never reveal what I just saw.

He then touched my face, like a lover might, and said, Now you
know that the Book of Mormon is true. You have seen the very objects
described in its pages.

Working for Harry Martin, I became more aware of how seductive
men could be. I had felt a kind of erotic current in him, a charge that
he could pass through me seemingly at will. Something he could turn
on or off according to his mood. When he turned it on, I couldn't
help paying attention: I knew *something was happening*.

I could feel a change happening in me. Not only the normal changes
that I knew occurred in girls my age and I had been expecting but
something far more subtle and surprising. Something had begun to
happen. I seemed to have become more attractive, if not overnight,
over that summer. I could tell this from the way people began to
react to me.

For years I had looked into the mirror and not cared much for
what I'd seen. From the time I was quite young my eyesight was
poor and I wore terrible-looking glasses, the kind of glasses old ladies
wore, shaped like cat's eyes and made out of pearly black-and-white
plastic with pointed tips. My hair had always looked a little funny,
mostly because my father cut it himself with the big electric clippers
he'd ordered by mail. During that period in our lives, he cut all his
children's hair, always short, both the boys and the girls, in order to
save money. The boys got buzz cuts, the girls ducktails. He had no
experience cutting hair and the results could be rather awful.

On haircutting day he'd set up a metal stool downstairs in the laundry room and call us in one by one. Big metal clippers the size of horse shears would be turned on, and then he'd get to work, starting at the back of the neck and running the clippers upward as if he were shearing sheep. The clippers made a terrifying noise and sometimes he'd nick my scalp or neck but if I flinched he'd cock a middle finger against his thumb and flip it hard against my head and tell me to hold still. It always surprised me how much this hurt.

During the summer I worked for Harry Martin, I began to refuse to let him cut my hair. I looked at the other girls around me and realized I, too, could look different. I told my mother I wanted to go to a real hairdresser, and since I would pay for it out of the money I had saved from my summer job she couldn't really refuse me.

I let my hair grow longer, had it styled, and I also got my first pair of contact lenses, not because anyone cared how I looked but because my mother had been persuaded by the eye doctor that contacts might help keep my eyesight from deteriorating further. When I looked in the mirror, I saw a different girl. A becoming girl. A girl becoming something else.

I entered ninth grade that fall and began dating a boy who was four years older.

My mother didn't like this, the fact that at fourteen I was seeing an eighteen-year-old boy, but I ignored her complaints and went out with him anyway. Even though she tried to discourage me from dating him, she must have realized she couldn't stop me, and she quickly gave up.

I could feel myself growing into a more rebellious girl, one eager for experience. And Richard, the boy I had fallen for and who seemed equally taken with me, soon became a part of that experience I was seeking in ways I couldn't have predicted.

He was not only handsome but rich. He came from a well-to-do family that owned a chain of music stores and lived in a nice part of town. His parents belonged to clubs I had never heard of. They weren't Mormons, or if they were they weren't very good ones. Richard almost never had to go to church the way I did every Sunday, though on Tuesday nights he came to Mutual because that's where teens met and because there were often dances held after the classes, and dancing was something Richard and I liked to do, just as music was something we liked to listen to.

Richard played the trumpet, as did his best friends, Dave and Frank: together they had formed a trio. They had all been taking trumpet lessons for several years, going to summer music camps at Cripple Creek, Colorado, and they were serious about their music.

Richard had thick dark hair and pillowy soft lips, just right for playing the trumpet and also for kissing. Everything about him was sensuous. That's what I liked about him: he was so lushly sensuous, so unlike the other boys I knew, and he was also very funny, quick-witted and droll. He seemed more adult to me. He wore neatly pressed shirts, his black hair combed back into a sleek and shiny helmet.

Frank, on the other hand, was louche, a bad boy with lank dark hair. He wore rumpled clothes, smoked forbidden cigarettes, and stayed up all night listening to records, sometimes skipping school the next day.

Dave, the son of a judge, lived just up the street from my family. His mother was a good Mormon but unlike other mothers I knew she was very glamorous. She wore heavy makeup, including bright lipstick applied far outside the stingy contours of her mouth. Dave, handsome and blond, with an aquiline nose, was a romantic, though already a bit world-weary, like some slightly dissipated poet who regarded life with disdain.

Richard. Dave. Frank.

This was the thing about these boys: jazz was their passion, and they introduced me to this music at the age of fourteen. This opened up a new and very exciting world to me.

Jazz. A music of devilish complexity. This was not the music of the Mormon Tabernacle Choir, with which my father once sang. Nor was it the music he directed in church, waving his plastic baton. It wasn't the music I heard on Saturday night on TV as we gathered as a family downstairs to watch Lawrence Welk, nor was it the music we sang around the piano during Family Home Evenings. And it certainly wasn't the old Western favorites like "Home on the Range" that we crooned in the car to pass the time during family vacations. It was not music anyone in my family could have imagined I might be listening to, or even imagined at all.

This was *jazz,* crazy vibrant jazz, with its hint of wild goings-on and far-off places, a music that sounded as jumpy and unpredictable as its name, and to me it became an aural portal to another world.

For most of a year I listened to jazz with the trumpet-playing boys, lounging around with Richard and Frank and Dave in the hours after school while stretched out on the floor or nestled on a sofa with Richard, the music turned up loud. This was the year of Dave Brubeck and *Take Five,* a record we played over and over again.

We took five almost every day, often at Richard's house in the hardly lived-in living room with its fine stereo system and expensive brocade furniture and the baby grand piano sitting in the corner that I never saw anyone play. I remember how his perfectly coiffed mother used to occasionally wander into the living room when we were listening to music and how she would look at me with such a combination of knowingness and disapproval, as if she understood I might still look the child but something unmanageable was brewing in me and it did not bode well for her son.

The *Take Five* year was over almost before I knew it: Richard went off to college and Dave went on a mission to France and Frank simply disappeared from my life. And me? I went back to being the restless, questing teenager, held fast between the lake and the tall mountains in that place that once again seemed like the only world I would ever know. A period of my life had ended—the main part of my youth, and the sort of happiness and freedom that came to me then was never to be quite the same.

PART FOUR

◆

The Turquoise Notebook

ONE

There was a woman in our ward named Annabel Stone. She lived on a street at the very edge of the subdivision where the land sloped down to the valley in a series of gradual steps. She was tall and thin and middle-aged—a woman with something very intense about her. She always looked at you as if you'd just committed some sin you may have managed to hide from others but you couldn't hide from her. This look was made all the more unsettling by the fact that she always wore a faint smile on her face. It caused her to appear strangely scary.

Annabel Stone must have had a husband, but why can't I remember him? No picture forms when I try. Nor can I see her children, though I know she must have had some of those too, tucked away in her split-level house that overlooked the valley.

I see only Annabel Stone, with her faint knowing smile. And I hear her voice, that slow, deliberate way she had of speaking that seemed to contain warnings.

She took in unwed pregnant teenagers, Mormon girls who needed a place to live outside their own communities until they could deliver their babies and return home, hopefully with no one the wiser. The babies were taken from the girls at birth, put up for adoption through a church agency and placed with Mormon families.

Sister Stone was fanatically religious. There was something malevolent about her fervor. Even my parents could feel this: I knew that from the way they talked about her. "Crazy" was a word that sometimes got used to describe her. But if she was crazy, she was crazy like a fox. Her cunning rose off her in an almost perceptible miasma.

I pitied the young girls who were sent to live with her, many of whom were my own age—just fifteen or so. They couldn't possibly have known what they were getting into. But I knew, having had Sister Stone for a teacher in a Mutual class. Running beneath everything she said was some faint threat of hell, flames that licked up around her words and sent out warnings to anyone within range.

When I think of her now, I think of one particular Sunday, a fast and testimony day. On the first Sunday of every month the main sacrament meeting was given over to the congregation for the bearing of testimonies. On this day people were expected to fast until late afternoon when the meeting had finished. Technically you weren't even supposed to take a sip of water, though I don't remember our family being strict about this.

Fast and testimony meetings were always rather intense and unpredictable affairs. During the hour and a half in which they took place, people stood up spontaneously as the spirit moved them in order to bear their testimonies. There was always a certain frisson in the room: Who would stand up next? And what would they say?

Kids of all ages, as well as the adults, rose up suddenly and bore their nascent little testimonies, although there was always something rote about the words you were hearing, the beliefs the children claimed to have at the age of seven or eight or ten or eleven. I see this now as an adult, though I did not at the time when I was that child getting to her feet to say how grateful I was for the gospel in my life. How glad I was that I belonged to the only true church. How much I loved Jesus and hoped he'd come back soon when we were ready for him.

Sometimes kids said things that were completely hilarious and the congregation couldn't help laughing, because there was no censoring anybody, there was nobody telling you what you could or couldn't say, and in general the meetings were never stiff but heartfelt and full of emotion. Adults of all ages stood up and often spoke about their feelings for the church. How it had made such a difference to their lives and their families. The idea was to bear witness to the truthfulness of the gospel, to perhaps say something about its beneficial role in one's life, though often people used the occasion to tell very personal, faith-promoting stories.

On this particular fast and testimony day, I remember Annabel Stone getting to her feet, rising slowly and deliberately, as if she were in no hurry to rush what she had to say, taking her time because what she had to say was so important. She was thin, and slightly stooped, so that she stood slightly bent forward as she rose. A couple of young pregnant girls were sitting next to her on the bench, and they watched her as she stood up. She took a few moments to collect herself, and then she began speaking.

She opened with the usual kinds of remarks, saying how grateful she was to belong to the true church, restored on earth in these latter days. The Book of Mormon was true, and she knew it, because she had prayed about it and received certain revelations. She spoke like this for a while, saying things we had all more or less heard before. Then she looked over at the girls sitting nearby and began speaking about them.

Without naming them, she talked about the way they had sinned. They had defiled their bodies, she said, which were really the temples of the Lord. They'd made a terrible mistake, had sex out of wedlock, let the devil overcome them with his devious ways. But, she added, thanks to the gospel they could still be saved. If they prayed hard enough and led pure lives from now on, they might be forgiven their sins. But everyone should know, especially all the young girls who were listening, that this is what could happen if they strayed from the path of righteousness. The devil could take hold. They could end up like these poor souls.

She talked about the girls as if they weren't sitting there next to her. As if she weren't aware that she was causing them to feel even more humiliated than they already did, simply by having to appear in church each Sunday, with their growing bellies the undeniable evidence of their misdeeds.

As she spoke I looked over at the girls, sitting quietly with their eyes cast down. Their heads were bowed in shame, and I felt that shame with them. When Annabel Stone finally sat down, there was a long, uncomfortable silence and no one stood up for a while. I felt most people in the congregation knew she had gone too far this time in embarrassing those girls the way she had.

A few months later, at another fast and testimony meeting, I recall another woman in the ward stood up to bear her testimony. She was in her forties and had recently given birth to a Mongoloid baby (we did not use the name Down syndrome then). She said she knew the Lord had given her a Mongoloid child because of some sin she'd committed, and she accepted this punishment and vowed to lead a better life. I remember my parents discussing what she had said as we drove home in the car that day and my mother weeping in the front seat. She had given birth to a baby a few years earlier, when she was in her forties, and it must have crossed her mind that God might have given her a Mongoloid baby as well.

This was a woman we knew well, the sister who had borne her testimony that day, a righteous, good woman: what could she possibly have thought she'd done to deserve such a punishment?

I remember thinking about this later that day and wondering what sort of god would give a woman a deformed baby as punishment anyway. Wasn't it the innocent child who was really being punished? And yet this woman thought it was somehow her due, some sort of divine retribution. All around me I felt the righteousness of people who said things like this and believed in them and I knew I was not righteous because I did not believe.

And still, it seemed to me God could smash me if He wanted to.

My heart had stood still that day in church when Annabel Stone rose to her feet and shamed those girls sitting next to her. How did I know I wasn't the sort of girl who might be next?

When I was fifteen years old, I started to feel that you couldn't believe in something when you'd never had a chance *not* to believe. I felt there must be another way of looking at the world, of making sense of it. I began to push back against all the rules and restrictions. One day on a hike with the Mia Maids, a group of girls from Mutual, I took off my shirt and hiked in my bra because it was a hot summer day and it felt better to go shirtless. The Mia Maid leader, whose name I've forgotten but whose face I can still see, did not approve and she let me know. But I could see nothing wrong. We were on a little-used trail. The chance of running into other hikers was slim. What was wrong? What was wrong, she told me, was my way of thinking. What was wrong was not doing what I was told. Put your shirt back on, she said. I was setting a bad example.

I heard many variations of this argument when I went my own way. I needed to learn to obey, I was told. I needed to do what I was asked. I needed to understand that what my elders told me was in my best interest because they knew better than I did. It wasn't good to act so willfully. So *disrespectfully*. It would lead to a bad end.

My mother criticized me often now. About how I dressed. What I chose to wear to school. The boys I dated, the friends I'd made. She began having what she called heart-to-heart talks with me, drawing me aside to speak to me alone.

These heart-to-hearts were always uncomfortable for me. We would sit in the living room, on the three-piece sectional sofa where we gathered to kneel down for family prayers each night, and face each other. Sometimes she would take my hand. She would start out speaking very sweetly, telling me how much she loved me, and what a pretty girl I'd become, but inevitably the conversation would end up being about boys and how she was worried I might be doing things

I shouldn't with them. The sessions would turn into lectures about chastity. About keeping my body—which she, like Annabel Stone, referred to as *the temple of the Lord*—clean and pure so that when I met the right man I would be worthy of him and could be married in the temple as a virgin.

I'd get embarrassed at first, then angry. I didn't think I should have to listen to such talk. I had no plans to have sex with anybody. I did not want to discuss these things with my mother. It felt awkward and embarrassing. I reacted badly because I felt I was being accused of something again, just as I had been wrongly accused by Roland Green and the bishop. The result was that I began to push back, against everything—home, family, church—in an attempt to escape the feelings of oppression.

Once during this time we went on a family outing to a hot-springs resort and when I saw my father in the pool I felt shocked. It was as if I had never really realized how his arms and back were covered with black hair. From behind he looked like he was wearing an animal pelt, the way the water streamed down his back when he stood up and flattened the long black hair against his skin.

Everything began to feel strange to me, even the sight of my own father.

I lost Lady, the horse I had loved. She had somehow gotten out of her pasture one night and wandered into an old barn and fallen through a rotten wood floor. All night she had kicked, attempting to get out, and broken her leg. She was discovered in the morning by the man who owned the barn and had immediately been put out of her misery. I wasn't even told she'd been shot until it was all over and she had been taken away.

There would be many other horses in my life but she was the first and her death came at a time when I was beginning to feel I no longer knew where I belonged. It had a terrible effect on me: now I would no longer have that exquisite view of the world from the back of a

horse. I wouldn't be able to escape with her into the hills when I felt
I wanted to be alone. Some connection with the world had been broken, and I felt broken as well.

A certain period in my life had ended. The days of riding with
friends, of heading out to the field next to the Browning Armory
where we had practiced barrel racing with the Hill and Gully Riders,
the junior posse we had joined, were over and a part of my youth
was left behind. I wouldn't have the thrilling experience of riding
in the Grand Entry in the annual Ogden Rodeo anymore, wearing
the pink satin shirt and black cowboy hat that was the Hill and Gully
uniform, and later, after the rodeo had ended, heading home in the
dark with my friends, a little posse of raucous kids riding all the way
across town at midnight with the horses' hooves skittering on the city
pavement.

I no longer wanted to go to church but I knew I didn't have any
choice. It would have caused great unhappiness and upheaval in the
household if I'd refused. I did not know one young person who had
done this, who had simply said, I'm not going to go to church anymore, and gotten away with it. And the truth is had I not gone to
church, I wouldn't have had a social life. To refuse that place was in
some way to refuse the world.

When I went to church on Sundays now, I no longer listened to the
speakers. I played a little game instead: I sat in the pew and opened
the hymn book to a page with my eyes closed, letting my finger run
down the page to a place and stop. Then I'd open my eyes to see what
message I'd find waiting. Something that might presage my future,
reveal signs or portents, deliver a message. Words clustered in code,
just for me.

But there was never any message. Just the same old words to the
hymns.

TWO

I began spending more time alone, just sitting in the foothills after school, looking out over the city. I found I liked being alone. It began to seem like my natural condition.

One day I found a plump, waterlogged copy of *Peyton Place* lying in a thicket of oak brush just below Skyline Drive where lovers often came to park. Someone had left it there and it had become warped by the rain. Pages were missing but still I read the novel with great interest, turning the yellowed pages while sitting on a rock in the afternoon sun, hidden from sight. It felt like a transgressive act, to read the passages where sex was described. I hadn't realized that words could be so arousing, could make you feel such desire.

I entered ninth grade that year. I was not a good student. I didn't care about school. You could put a gun to my head now and say, Name a book you were assigned to read in your classes in junior high, and I'd have to say, Go ahead and shoot me.

But in ninth grade I discovered several books on my own, and these I remember very well. One was Pearl Buck's *The Good Earth*, which I liked because it took me into a foreign world, one I could never have imagined, and gave me a picture of that life, and because the women in the book seemed strong. The other was *Gone with the Wind*, which I read sitting in the hills after school. I could not understand how Scarlett would choose such a pallid weakling as Ashley over the manly Rhett. Still, the scope of the book swept me away, the soppy romanticism.

That year I discovered another book, *Alone* by Admiral Richard E. Byrd, the book that had the most profound impact on me. I have no idea how I came across it. In so many ways it seems like such an unlikely discovery.

Alone, first published in 1938, is the account of the months Byrd spent in a shack buried in the ice in Antarctica in order to take meteorological readings. It's the story of ultimate solitude. From the very first paragraph in the book I felt a voice speaking directly to me:

> This book is the account of a personal experience—so personal that for four years I could not bring myself to write it. It is different from anything else I have ever written. My other books have been factual, impersonal narratives of my expeditions and flights. This book, on the other hand, is the story of an experience which was in considerable part subjective. I very nearly died before it was over. And, since my sufferings bulked so large in it and since a man's instinct is to keep such things to himself, I did not see how I could write about Advance Base and still escape making an unseemly show of my feelings. Also, I was a long time recovering from the effects of my stay at Latitude 80°08' South, and the whole business was so intimate in memory that I doubted that I could approach it with the proper detachment.

Alone showed me what was possible for a human being to survive. The brutal, punishing cold Byrd endured, the ice building up on the inside of his shack, the poisoning from fumes emitted by a malfunctioning stove on which he relied for heat, the blizzards that sealed his trapdoor shut almost daily, and the failure of the radio he relied on for contact with home base—all this brought Byrd to the brink of death over and over, and yet each day, no matter how weak he felt, he forced his way out into the polar night to take his meteorological readings above ground. Standing in the darkness, feeble and ill, he could still marvel at his surroundings and witness the sublime spectacle of the aurora borealis, before the minus-seventy-degree cold sent him back into his subterranean, ice-bound shack.

It was an unlikely book for a teenage girl like myself to have discovered and one that I've never forgotten. I don't know what attracted me so. Was it the aloneness that mirrored the isolation I had begun to feel in my own life? The descriptions of the otherworldly polar landscape? The tale of survival? I believe it was all three, but especially I loved Byrd's descriptions of polar nights, as he stood outside in that deep dark exquisite cold, taking his instrument readings in spite of his weakness, while the sky flared, erupting in walking curtains of colored light.

I began hanging out with girls who were not Mormons. Girls who had an edge to them and none of the practiced niceness of the young women in my ward who'd been groomed by their parents to be obedient and deferential.

One day two of these girls hung a freshly used sanitary napkin tied to a wire hanger outside the window of the girls' bathroom so the boys would see it when they walked by. It was shocking to me. How could they do this? And yet I stood in the bathroom and laughed with them at the idea of this outrageous thing they had done.

They deserve it, one of them said, giving me a dark look. She was a plain, plump girl with lank brown hair and a round, bland face. None of the stuff that's happening to us, she added, is happening to them. They aren't the ones bleeding every month.

She made the idea of bleeding sound like a personal injury, as if menstruation were a wound.

I saw there were tough girls in the world. Girls much tougher than I was, tougher in fact than many of the boys I knew, and I wondered how you got that toughness. I knew I didn't have it, and I probably wouldn't ever acquire it. And yet I couldn't help admiring the way it made these girls seem strong and defiant.

I had few good friends. The edgy girls kept me at a distance and that was fine with me since I found them a bit scary. I'd lost the connection to my riding friends and also to the more religious kids in our ward. The bad girls didn't want me because I wasn't bad enough; the good girls didn't want me because I wasn't good enough.

The boys I had spent time with during my riding days had been inducted into the priesthood at the age of twelve and had begun rising slowly through the ranks. First they became deacons and were given the responsibility of passing the sacrament, standing at the ends of rows with solemn faces while they waited for the silver trays to be handed from person to person.

Later, at the age of sixteen, they were ordained priests and became responsible for preparing the sacrament as music was played and the congregation waited quietly. They tore slices of white bread into little pieces and put them on a tray and filled tiny pleated paper cups with water. Bread and water, this was the sacrament. Wonder Bread, which came in white plastic bags with brightly colored balloons, was the bread that was always used, the soft white—almost airily white—slices torn into small bits by the boy-priests. When the bread and water had been prepared and placed on the trays, they knelt down before the table and blessed it, and then the deacons, who had been waiting quietly, stepped forward to pass it around.

I knew you were not supposed to take the sacrament when it was offered if you didn't feel worthy but I never saw anyone refuse it and I certainly wasn't going to. Why call attention to yourself, announcing your sinfulness to the whole congregation?

This was the year I began smoking, picking up cigarette butts in the parking lot of the college stadium as I walked home from school. There were often half-smoked cigarettes, sometimes almost whole ones that had been discarded in haste as people hurried to leave the parking lot after a football game. I'd collect the best ones in my pocket and then climb up into the hills to one of my favorite spots and smoke them one by one while lying back and looking up at the sky. Of course I worried that my mother would begin to smell the smoke on my clothes, and of course she eventually did. It gave us one more thing to disagree about, one more item to add to our heart-to-heart chats. Why couldn't I be more like my sister? she'd ask me. Why did I have to keep doing things I knew I shouldn't?

Why did I? I wondered. It was a question I couldn't really answer, and so I never tried. I'd just shrug my shoulders and look away and wait for her to finish so I could go back to whatever I was doing. And increasingly, I knew what I was doing was wrong.

THREE

Ogden High was a remarkably beautiful old school, a yellow sandstone art deco building completed as a WPA project in the 1930s. It faced Harrison Boulevard, one of the main thoroughfares in town. The halls were lined with glossy marble, the classrooms large and well designed. Lovely old oil paintings hung in the wood-paneled library and the auditorium featured ornate art deco glass designs and beautiful wooden seats. In every way it felt as if I were entering a new world, in part because Ogden High had a large mixed student body. The district had been drawn in such a way that it encompassed a large swath of the black part of town as well as the more affluent east side.

I quickly discovered, however, that it really wouldn't be such a new experience when it came to race because the white students and the black students didn't much mix. They kept themselves separate, with the exception of a few black boys who became star athletes and won easy acceptance.

In high school I was no better a student than I'd been before. In spite of having discovered those few books on my own, I still took little interest in reading. But I began to make new and interesting friends, including a girl named Gail who would become an important part of my life.

That first year I also discovered two subjects that interested me—drama and debate. Both were taught by a woman named Portia Douglas: she was a gravely serious person, wore her hair in a helmet of stiff blond curls, assumed dramatic airs, and was easily given to emotional displays. When students in the class misbehaved she looked so disappointed it seemed as if she might cry, and sometimes she did. Girls and boys, girls and boys! she would say sharply, rapping her knuckles on her desk. How can you expect to be *thespians* if you have no discipline?

I remember one incident in particular that undid her for days. It occurred early on in the year. A boy in our class committed suicide by hanging himself in his closet. I didn't know this boy, and I no longer remember his name. He wasn't popular, in fact was so quiet and shy none of us knew anything about him. When news of his death was announced, we all felt bad but Portia Douglas was distraught. For days afterward she would suddenly start weeping in class: it was as if she felt we were all in some way personally responsible for his death. What could we have done? she kept asking us. What might we have done to help this poor boy? She insisted that the whole class attend his viewing at the funeral parlor as a way of paying our respects. I remember how we filed past his open coffin one by one, glancing down at him, and how afterward we became gruesome and talked about whether anyone had noticed any rope burns on his neck.

No one had. He looked so peaceful it was as if he'd died in his sleep.

The next year, I joined the debate team, coached by Portia Douglas. I found I liked arguing subjects, taking this view or that according to which side I'd been assigned.

There were often mixed debates, and one high school team traveled to another across the city, or participated in regional competitions. In this photo, our Ogden High School girls' team, the three girls seated bottom right (with me in the center), has been photographed for the local paper with the other co-winners of the Weber State College High School Forensic Tournament.

I liked gathering facts for a debate, doing the research, preparing my arguments, and I wasn't intimidated by public speaking, having already been groomed to give many talks in church. I was interested in current affairs and politics after years of listening to my father

hold forth about politics at dinnertime. At home now, when he began sounding off at dinner about those idiot Republicans or the shameful national debt or one of his other favorite subjects, I joined in the conversation, sometimes playing the devil's advocate and arguing with him, forcing him to defend his positions in ways he hadn't been required to before.

He began calling me "doll." As in, I don't know where you're getting your ideas from, doll, but they're a bit screwy.

In health class we were instructed by an older woman named Mrs. Torrey. One day she showed us a film about venereal disease that we found very embarrassing. The boys sat next to the girls, snickering in the darkened room as the sound of the projector hummed in the background and strange images flicked across the screen. No one had ever talked to us before about such things and everyone felt uncomfortable. In the movie a doctor holding a pointer indicated several places on a drawing of a body and said that the areas most frequently affected by VD were the genitals and the mouth. I didn't understand how this could be. After the movie was over I raised my hand and asked Mrs. Torrey, How do you get VD around the mouth? She never answered my question, instead looked momentarily flustered, and then simply moved on.

It was in Mrs. Torrey's class that we were told what to do if we ever felt as if we might get sick while listening to a concert. This really only applied to girls, she said. Don't try to leave in the middle of the music, she advised, disrupting other people in their seats, but instead just very quickly grab your handbag and empty the contents on your lap and throw up in your purse. This is advice, unfortunately, I've never been able to forget.

During my junior year, I signed up for a seminary class, one of the Latter-day Saints religion classes that most Mormon kids enroll in during their high school years. These classes were held in a low, shaded building across the street from the main campus of the high school, requiring a short walk down a leafy street. My class was taught by a man named Brother Gallup.

On the first day of class we were all given a turquoise notebook in which to keep handouts and class assignments. On the cover, made of cardboard covered in turquoise cloth, were stamped the words CHURCH OF JESUS CHRIST OF LATTER-DAY SAINTS SEMINARY, and below that, etched in gold, the angel Moroni stood atop a golden globe of the world, blowing his golden horn—the same figure that crowns most Mormon temples worldwide. By the end of the semester, this notebook would be stuffed with all the worksheets Brother Gallup had handed out, and all the assignments he had graded and handed back. Somehow this turquoise notebook survived over the years, saved by my parents, and it came back to me in the 1990s after their deaths. By this time the turquoise notebook had begun to fall apart: the metal prongs that once had threaded the pages and held them in place had become sprung and stuck out from the spine like tiny pliable swords.

For many years after the turquoise notebook was returned to me I avoided looking at it. But once or twice over the years I opened it up and flipped through a few pages, lingering over this or that passage, something I'd written in response to an assignment from Brother Gallup, and I always felt a kind of astonishment. Who *was* the girl who had owned this notebook? Who filled in these work-sheets, learned a scripture each week, made collages from pictures cut from magazines, extolling chastity and abstinence from sin? Who answered the questions on these tests, laid herself bare in little essays, made lists of things not to do on a Sunday, whose responses seem to reflect such ingenuousness and deference to authority? It seemed to me she was someone I never knew. At least someone I didn't remember being.

It's one thing when attempting to recall the past to rely on mem-ory, mysterious as it is in its workings, and quite another to discover hard facts in the form of written evidence. Whenever I thought about the turquoise notebook, I felt it contained such proof and I feared this book, what it might reveal to me.

One day I decided to take it out and really look at it. I had come to a point in my life where I wanted a firmer picture of me as I had been when I kept this book, though I also felt afraid of what I might unearth. A kind of dull dread loomed over the prospect of what lay ahead, what hadn't been admitted, or yet discovered. There was a sense of poor choices hanging over me. The old why-did-I-ever? feeling. The how-could-I-have? questions I'd never quite resolved, including the questions that had increasingly begun to trouble me and lay at the center of everything: How could I have gotten married at seventeen, becoming engaged in my senior year of high school? And how could I have thought it would work out to marry my sister's former boyfriend?

One of the first things I noticed when I opened the turquoise note-book was the names of the boys I'd inscribed on the inside cover, some encased in hearts, some with a big plus sign joining my name to theirs, just opposite the opening page listing Favorite Seminary Songs with a quote from the Doctrine and Covenants: *For my soul delighteth in the song of the heart; yea, the song of the righteous is a prayer unto me.*

But there they are, the names in which my soul truly delighted: Jay Gardner. Bob Stewart. Scott Waldren. David Parker. The boys then rotating through my life.

One hundred or so favorite seminary songs were spread over the next dozen pages and when I looked at these songs I remembered how we would sing one to start each class. "Come, Come, Ye Saints." "We Thank Thee, O God, for a Prophet." "I Stand All Amazed."

These were the hymns I grew up with in church, with my father often standing at the front of the room and leading the singing, urging us to pick up the tempo.

Brother Gallup, a wan man with watery eyes who always wore the same rumpled brown suit, now led us in the singing, standing at the front of the classroom flapping his bony white hands in the air.

One of the first pages in my own handwriting I came across was an essay written in response to the topic "How to Say No." Saying no, I wrote,

> is sometimes very easy and seems to be the only answer but sometimes it's hard. How do you say no to a drink of liquor when everyone else is drinking? How do you show affection for a boy and yet keep him in his place? How do you refuse a cigarette when you are the only one not smoking? All these problems face us all, and are you laughed at for being a baby or chicken or are you smart enough to think of a good answer and keep your friends? You have to have definite standards before you get into a situation where you have to use them.

I had chosen the great trilogy of Mormon teenage sin—smoking, drinking, and boys—to illustrate my thesis that one had to have *standards* about these things. I felt I knew what my so-called standards had been at that time. They were rather low, according to the Mormon model. But was my memory accurate?

I knew I was regularly smoking by this time, though I'd moved on from picking up butts in the stadium parking lot and was now cadging whole cigarettes, managing even to get a full pack now and then.

I had also begun drinking, raiding the liquor cabinet of my friend Gail's father, who had a fine assortment of booze we could filch.

And as for keeping boys in their place, what would that place have been anyway?

In spite of what I wrote in this essay, I felt I had been much more inclined at this point in my life to say yes than no. Saying yes represented curiosity, engagement, adventure. Saying no was simply what was expected of me, and this was what I had needed to write to please Brother Gallup. Could my memory, however, be flawed?

Gail had become my best friend and partner in pursuing good times and all sorts of illicit activities. She was very beautiful, with a long smooth pageboy, lovely eyes, and a terrific figure. She had great style. Other girls would come to her and ask her to do their hair or help them with their makeup because she understood these things in an effortless way. Her family was not wealthy but well-to-do, nominally Mormon though it seemed to me they didn't take religion that seriously, especially her father, a classic long-legged Westerner who liked to drink. Though they lived in town, her father owned large ranches to the north where he grazed bands of sheep and leased out land to oil and gas companies. He belonged to the Elks Club, and kept a jar of sheep testicles in the fridge, which he sometimes took down to the club and had the chef prepare as special fried delicacies to share with his friends.

Gail's house had a slot machine in the basement as well as the well-stocked liquor cabinet. It was here we spent a lot of time together, slipping coins into the one-armed bandit and sipping bourbon and water while plotting our evening activities. Her father had bought a new convertible and when she learned to drive, it was in this car that we cruised around after dark, stopping at the Blue Onion Drive-in for a burger and a shake. Sometimes our friend Trixie came with us. She came from the South, had a fetching Southern accent, a sweet heart-shaped face, and a large bouffant she kept lacquered in place. She was being groomed by her Southern-belle mother to be a debutante, even though we didn't really have those in Ogden. Still, she became a teen model at the local department store, strolling around and showing off clothes at lunchtime for people eating in the cafeteria.

Gail. Trixie. Me. We formed a trio of attractive girls who were not really wild so much as fun-loving, if you call fun driving around in a convertible at night, with the top down, smoking cigarettes and drinking bourbon, enjoying the fresh air and the boys who were out cruising in the same darkness.

When I read my little essay, "How to Say No," I wondered how I could have written it. I found I hardly knew this girl I was reading about.

In the turquoise notebook, I found more worksheets, more essays, more responses to assignments from Brother Gallup, as well as dozens of mimeographed handouts.

One was called "Plan of Salvation," delineating the Mormon concept of heaven and its four realms, the highest being Celestial, where the most righteous people ended up, followed by Terrestrial, which wasn't really much better than earth. Then came Telestial, which was lower than earth, followed by Perdition, which was frankly hell.

Everybody was going to end up in one of these realms, Brother Gallup said, and we'd better think about which one we wanted for ourselves.

He told us the most righteous men would end up as gods and rule over their own planets. They'd be able to have as many wives as they wanted, and as many children.

I had written in response, *Could a woman have her own planet if she led a very righteous life?*

No she cannot, he replied in the margin. *She will be the helpmate.*

❖   ❖   ❖

We were given a handout describing the life of Eliza R. Snow, who had been one of the prophet Joseph's wives and who after his death had married the next prophet, Brigham Young, and made the trip west to the new Zion, where she became known as the founder of the Relief Society and also as Utah's first "poetess." She was a mystic, could talk in tongues, and had written the words to a famous Mormon hymn called "O My Father," which proposed the idea that if she had a father in heaven she must also have a mother there. Reason, she said, told her this was the case, and her idea was embraced. God was married. There was a Mrs. God.

Brother Gallup discussed the role of the American Indian in Mormon history, how Native Americans were really descended from the people described in the Book of Mormon who had set out from Palestine around 600 BC in a little boat and crossed the ocean and arrived someplace on the shores of North or South America—perhaps near what is now Guatemala—following a perilous journey. But once they arrived some of the people had turned against others and they had been cursed with dark skin. These were the Lamanites—descendants of the evil brothers Laman and Lemuel.

We were descended from Nephi, the good brother, white people.

American Indians were Lamanites, the dark people.

I'd heard this story many times growing up. We no longer thought of them as bad, or cursed: in fact, according to scripture, Native Americans needed to be brought back into the fold and reunited with the faith before the Second Coming could occur, which is why we sent so many people to proselytize in Central and South America and why we also sent missionaries to the Navajos and other tribes.

Brother Gallup quoted one of the church authorities who had recently given a talk at General Conference, the great gathering of Saints that occurred at Temple Square in Salt Lake City twice a year, at the beginning of every April and October. People came from all over the country, all over the world, to hear the leaders of the church speak from the pulpit in the Tabernacle. The general authority quoted had talked about the Lamanites and the work that was being done to convert them. He said he had recently observed a Navajo family during one of his trips across the reservation and met a girl who had joined the church. Her skin, he said, was noticeably lighter than the rest of her family's. She was becoming whiter and whiter simply by embracing the gospel.

I came across an essay I'd written in a response to an assignment entitled "Describe a Faith-Promoting Incident."

> This summer I happened to be in the company of some very close friends up at Bear Lake. We were swimming and diving off a raft that the water skiers took off from. I dove off the raft, failing to see an outboard motor boat that was circling above. I went down deep and when I began to rise I noticed the water churning violently near my head. I suddenly realized I was beneath the boat and glanced to the left just in time to see the blades of the motor cut past my head, just above my shoulder. In panic, I was out of air but I didn't dare rise because I couldn't see the motor in the turbulent waters. I very quickly asked my Father in Heaven to help me find a safe way out. I could no longer stay underwater so I went upward, in doing so hitting my head on the bottom of the wooden raft. It was not hard to make the surface after that, and I realized how close to injury and perhaps death I came and knew it was only through the divine help of a power beyond ours that I survived.

As I read my account, I remembered that incident at Bear Lake. I recalled how terrified I'd been as the outboard motor cut close to my head. What I didn't recall was uttering any prayer in the middle of the chaos. I felt quite sure I hadn't done that. I felt this must be another embellishment, provided for the benefit of Brother Gallup. Or was this in some way really my younger self, one I'd conveniently refashioned in memory? Again I wondered, Did I know that girl? She seemed so foreign to me.

I came across another mimeographed page titled "Questions About Dating," posed by Brother Gallup for us to respond to:

What is love? Are we defacing God's property by kissing? What are we thinking when we kiss? Pet? Neck? Or make-out?

Have you ever been in a situation where you ask yourself, Why did we do this?

How does God feel when you destroy property?

At the bottom of the page I had scrawled, *I don't know*.

Defacing God's property? I thought, looking at this page. Is that how we were taught to think of our bodies, as God's *property*?

There were various clippings and bits of paper stuck between the pages of the turquoise notebook, some of which fell out: an old sales receipt from Wolpher's Distinctive Feminine Apparel for a three-dollar cash deposit on a layaway item. A snippet from a magazine, advertising a new pill that helped you quit smoking. A magazine illustration of boys and girls dancing wildly as if listening to rock and roll, with one couple holding each other chastely apart. I'd drawn an arrow to this couple and written *Be a conservative dancer*.

I came across a black-and-white clipping from a magazine showing a young woman, identified as a college sophomore, who is saying, *There will always be a double standard but I hope to teach my sons the value of sex with love and the lesser value of sex for its own sake.*

Yes, there would always be a double standard. I had already learned this much.

It took a long time to go through the turquoise notebook. There were sections on biblical history and the Book of Mormon, but the largest section by far was devoted to "Dating."

List some methods Satan has used on you this past week, Brother Gallup asked on one handout entitled "Questions of Free Agency," which included a "progress test" to name the methods you'd used to control the devil.

I listed Satan's techniques as *smoking, music, letters, stealing, drinking, books, and kissing.*

Books? Letters? Music? What nonsense was this? What could I have been thinking? What was I being *taught?*

As for the methods I'd used to resist Satan, I responded, *At times I didn't resist him but when I did—really truly I had no feeling—I just felt as if it was something natural. Maybe I didn't resist him enough.*

I had double-underlined the word "enough."

It takes time and practice to resist Satan, Brother Gallup responded. *Just keep trying.* He had underlined the word "trying" three times.

I came across an assignment titled "Draw Your Personality Profile," where we were asked to answer questions about ourselves by checking boxes marked "always," "sometimes," "rarely," and "never."

I had responded to only one question by marking "always," and this was the question "Are you depressed frequently?"

Here, for once, I may have told the truth. When I looked at my answer, I grew quiet.

I am *always* depressed, answered the sixteen-year-old me: it is the only thing I *always* am.

I confessed to *sometimes* having unclean thoughts. And *sometimes* being easily influenced by prevailing opinion. I outright lied about *never* drinking or smoking. I copped to *sometimes* feeling self-conscious about my appearance. And *sometimes* having feelings and opinions that were out of harmony with the church, *sometimes* even getting lonesome spells.

But I am *always* depressed.

Was this true? Did I actually feel that way? What could the word "depressed" have meant to me at that time? It wasn't one I remember being much used by my family and I don't remember my friends talking about such things. Mormons didn't get depressed: we had too much going for us.

Only later, much later, as an adult, did I read about the studies that showed Mormon women have one of the highest rates of depression in the country.

Yes, I think I could say it was true: I was depressed. Looking at my "personality profile," I remembered how once around this time when I'd been drinking after school with Gail in the room in her basement I somehow later ended up at the house of a girl I knew in our ward—not a girl I felt close to, in fact I no longer remember her name, only that she was a goody-goody, one of those girls who never did anything wrong. I locked myself in her bathroom downstairs and threatened to slit my wrists with a razor. The girl called her mother, Sister So-and-So, who came downstairs and pounded on the door until I opened it. And there I was, crying, half-drunk, sitting on the bathroom floor, feeling not just depressed but desperate. The mother was shocked and disgusted when she saw me: she wore a look of deep disapproval on her face, but I could also read the fear that registered there. What should she do with me? I didn't give her a chance to do anything. I simply got up and left the house and made my way home, just a few blocks away. For a long time I feared that she would tell my mother what had happened. But I don't think she ever did.

Chafing against the religion and all its strictures yet feeling the need to often pretend otherwise, I was developing a schism within me. Was this part of the reason I could not recognize the girl I discovered in the turquoise notebook? Because she wasn't really one girl but two?

The heart-to-heart chats with my mother became more unbearable. No longer did she take my hand when we sat down to talk and tell me what a pretty girl I was. Instead she launched right into enumerating the ways I was becoming a *disappointment* to her. Looming over every conversation was the idea of my older sister being some sort of model. The kind of girl it seemed to me I was constitutionally incapable of being.

My sister was not subjected to these chats. She didn't need them. She wasn't rebelling, pushing back against authority, chafing against all the things that troubled me. She didn't drink or smoke. Her behavior with boys was correct. She wasn't boy crazy. She was the girl, as my grandmother had noted in her diary, who could deliver an impressive family prayer, demonstrating that she had been raised up correctly, been *well trained*.

I grew angry over being compared to her. I felt jealous. I did not want my mother to love her in a way she could not love me, love her for a goodness I didn't possess, and yet increasingly I felt this was what was happening. I was losing my mother's love. I was becoming a *disappointment* to her.

A year or so earlier I had grown so tired of this comparison with my sister that I had taken my revenge. This was when she was in high school and dating a popular boy named Johnny Jones. She treasured her high school yearbook, which had many pictures of Johnny Jones. One day I took it down from the place where she kept it and put on thick red lipstick and kissed every picture of Johnny Jones in the yearbook—and there were many due to his popularity—defacing his image over and over with a big red lip print I knew would be impossible to get off. And then I took all her shoes out of the closet and wrote in ink on the bottom of every one, *I love Johnny Jones*.

Was it any mystery that she didn't much like me? That she considered me an annoyance, someone whom she could ignore if at all possible? A girl she might choose not to spend any time with?

After the incident with the yearbook things got worse. She tied a string down the center of the room we shared and forbade me to cross over to her side, and whatever thin bond of affection we shared was strained even further.

❖ ❖ ❖

Johnny Jones was replaced in her affections by another boy, named John Thorn, a handsome high school wrestling champ a couple of years older than her. She and John Thorn became pinned and she agreed to wait for him when he accepted an appointment to the Naval Academy and went off to Annapolis for his first year. But she did not wait for him. She enrolled at Weber College, taking secretarial courses. During that year she fell in love with a recently returned missionary, Dennis Garner. In December, she married him in the Salt Lake Temple.

As it turned out, I would be the one to marry John Thorn, just a few years later.

What I have never wanted to look at, what I have been loath to admit let alone try and understand, is what any of this might mean. What psychological insight might be buried here, in this complex little pas de deux I had engaged in with my older sister? Kissing her boyfriend's image in the yearbook the way I had, taking the boy she'd rejected? Feeling jealous of her for so easily winning my mother's affection in a way that I could not?

By this time in our lives, I don't think Marcia and I really felt that connected to each other much at all. We had grown apart, gone separate ways, led by the differences in our age and our personalities into occupying tangential worlds. Though we shared a room, we did not share much else. In the months before her wedding, she came and went, I came and went, we often didn't even meet at meals, and only at night, when we slept in our narrow beds, separated from each other by a dresser, could we be said to have inhabited the same space, and then only physically.

As I continued to work my way through the pages of the turquoise notebook, I made other discoveries. A questionnaire, for instance, where we were asked to *analyze the members of your peer group and come to an honest appraisal of whether they are seeking the PRAISE OF GOD or the PRAISE OF MEN.* We were urged to identify our friends by name and reveal the nature of their shortcomings, and either *drop them or lift them up to the level of your standards and lead them into activities which bring the Praise of the Lord.*

In the end I didn't drop anyone. The girls and boys I had listed as not being godly enough continued to be my friends.

We studied American politics in seminary. Mormon influence in national affairs had increased in the 1950s when President Eisenhower named a Mormon apostle, Ezra Taft Benson, to be his secretary of agriculture. Under Benson, American agriculture had undergone a great change. He believed corporations should be the future of the nation's farm policies, not family farms. His motto was "Get big or get out." Benson would go on to become the next prophet and president of the church and a proponent of the John Birch Society.

Brother Gallup taught us that America, as stated in the Book of Mormon, was a land choice above all others—an *exceptional* nation, just as we were an *exceptional* people. We were *the* American religion. It would be here in America that the Kingdom of God would again be established when Jesus returned to this earth.

Jesus had predicted this during the three days between his crucifixion and resurrection, when he had visited this continent and preached to the Nephites, his *other sheep* in the Americas.

When Jesus returned he would first appear in Jackson County, Missouri, near the town of Independence, which was also believed to be the site of the Garden of Eden. Brother Gallup told us a great temple would be built there during the millennium and Independence, Missouri, would become one of the two great world capitals, the other being Jerusalem.

I discovered a handout entitled "Social Disease Alarms Doctors," about communism and the brainwashing of American soldiers held captive during the Korean War. This, we were warned, was what could happen to all of us as America became more degenerate. Statistics were quoted showing a rise in juvenile delinquency and the fact that one third of all marriages now ended in divorce. There was an increase in illegitimate births as well, more dependence among the populace on alcohol, drugs, and tranquilizers, a flood of obscene literature, blood, and violence, and *dishonest fixing* of television quiz shows. Too much leisure time was making us soft, sloppy, and selfish. Man had to have a higher authority and learn to obey. And finally, both the government and the medical profession had an obligation to help relieve the fears of the people by making definite plans for protecting and caring for the population in the event of a nuclear war.

What was really most important, Brother Gallup told us, was to learn to be self-sacrificing. This was especially important for women. Motherhood was just another name for sacrifice, according to an essay written by David O. McKay, the white-haired prophet and president of the church, who was raised in a bucolic little valley in the mountains above Ogden.

In a few years' time, as I struggled to give birth to my son in a hospital in Salt Lake City, I would call out for President McKay just as I was being drugged into unconsciousness. *I would like to speak to President McKay!* I remember crying out loudly as I was being wheeled on a gurney down a hallway.

Motherhood, President McKay wrote in our handout, *is the one thing in all the world which most truly exemplifies the God-given virtues of creating and sacrificing. Though it carries the woman close to the brink of death* . . .

Is this why I cried out that day in the hospital as I entered that darkness? Because I felt myself approaching *the brink of death?*

Toward the end of the seminary year, our lessons turned again toward the subject of courtship, with an emphasis on marriage. It was time to think about marriage and how to prepare to be worthy of a temple ceremony. I was asked to make a list under the heading "What I Am Now Doing." Again, what I found when I looked at this list was an odd roster of behaviors, seemingly written by a stranger:

1. Trying not to kiss too promiscuously
2. Not swearing
3. Praying to get close to the Lord
4. Defending church standards
5. Preparing for Temple marriage
6. Watching my morals so they always keep high

Trying not to kiss *too* promiscuously? What sort of kissing would that be? Preparing for Temple marriage at the age of *sixteen*?

In the following pages I found something even more bizarre, a little essay I wrote entitled "The Wedding Ring," which began with the extraordinary line *A ring is just as useless as a rotten tomato.*

I wanted to laugh when I read that—I did laugh, a sort of barking, eruptive laugh that shook me—and then I read on:

> I would greatly desire a wedding ring as a symbol of my husband's love, many people would say this but for me I'd just as soon have a kiss as a wedding ring and it seems just as sensible! The greatest gift, greater than diamonds or rubies, that my future husband could give me on our wedding day would be a clean mind and body and the assurance that he is as chaste as I hope to be.

I closed the turquoise notebook for a moment. Surely I must have begun by this time to realize I did have choices—I didn't have to parrot this stuff. Or had I not seen this yet? Was I still entirely entrapped in a warped idea of how I could survive in the world, what would need to be said to pass by undisturbed? Was I simply working for a good grade? Or did this reflect something of who I really was at that age?

Brother Gallup called me in for a private conference. He wasn't convinced I was behaving correctly with boys, he said, or that I was truly as chaste as he knew I wanted to be. He said he had the sense I might be defiling my body by kissing and petting, spoiling God's property. We needed to have what he called a *chat* about this. Afterward he asked me to write one page in response to what he had said. My good grade depended on my response. And so I wrote:

> Through our discussion I think we realized the faults of my past dating experience. I wish to know [sic] end that someone had given me this advice three or four years ago. But wishing has never got anyone any place; after talking to you, I felt as though I'd never care to kiss a boy again in my life until I was married in the Temple to my husband. This isn't to [sic] realistic or probable though so perhaps I'd better take first things first and correct them. I have a sincere desire to accept your concept and I'm praying that the Lord will help me strive to keep the teachings thereof and sincerely thank Him for sending you to me to give me these teachings, for I truly feel that you will save me from a great deal of sorrow and depression. I really appreciate your efforts, Brother Gallup. May I make just one half that much in correcting myself.

At the bottom of this page, Brother Gallup had written in pencil, *Keep at it, it takes time,* with the last word underlined six times.

And then he gave me an A+ for the assignment.

Like a trained ape, I had performed for Brother Gallup with tricks pulled out of my dissembler's bag. Were they really tricks? Or did I in some way, in some fashion beyond my current ability to comprehend, actually believe in what I wrote? Was I caving in finally? Succumbing to the years of guilt and shame?

What I know for certain is these words and sentiments were offered up by a girl who in a little more than one year's time will have that wedding ring instead of the rotten tomato, though by then her chastity will have been fully compromised, her virginity lost.

During my senior year I had sex for the first time with a boy I'd been dating for some time. I liked him very much. We had fun when we went out: he could always make me laugh. It happened at his house one night when his parents were away. Johnny Carson's *Tonight Show* had just started to appear on late-night TV and we'd both become fans. My boyfriend hardly ever missed a night of Johnny Carson and I also watched it whenever I could, though I never watched it at home or as regularly as he did.

We watched Johnny Carson for a while that night and then we went into his room and had sex in his single bed. And then we came back out and watched Johnny Carson some more until the show ended. During sex I hadn't felt much pleasure but I did feel excitement. It all seemed to end so fast.

From then on, for the rest of my life, whenever I would think of that moment when I lost my virginity it would always, somehow, in the back of my mind, be connected to Johnny Carson and *The Tonight Show*. Because I liked this boy so much, and because he was so sweet to me, I remember that night of first sex with a certain lightness.

The remainder of the lessons on dating and marriage in the turquoise notebook included lectures on how to get a date (through church-sanctioned activities), whether blind dates could be recommended (no, they could not), the importance of starting a date with a prayer (totally necessary), why President McKay thought going steady was a bad idea (leads to dangerous intimacy), and the repeated singing of the hymn "Shall the Youth of Zion Falter?"

One of the last essays I had written contained the cri de coeur that seemed to summarize what I'd gone through, not only in the seminary class, but ever since that day in the kitchen with Roland Green. The point at which, broken in spirit, I seem ready to give in. Brother Gallup had asked me to respond to this question: *You should by now have analyzed your dating. Have you changed any?*

I offered up my handwritten reply:

I guess I have, but not much. If you mean have I necked or made out since we had our talk, the answer is no, but I still have a lot to improve on and you've given me a lot to think about. I'm about ready to just say to heck with dating because if I want to live up to your plan I've got to change completely. I don't know whether I'm strong enough to do this. I don't know whether your plan is really helping me at all. It probably is in the light of helping me to gain eternal life but it's making this one miserable. I get so depressed looking back on my past dating experience and then looking ahead to what I have to overcome. I wish dating was all over with and I was safely and happily married. I want to become better but it gives me a confused feeling inside.

To heck with dating. Why not proceed straight to that safe and happy port of marriage and be done with this miserable dating business? Especially if it leads to Eternal Life, even though it might make this one miserable?

I came to the end of the turquoise notebook and returned it to the box in which it had lain for so many years. I'd had a hard time reconciling the girl I discovered in its pages with my own memories of who I'd been at that age. I had imagined myself to be a rebel, so much more fiercely independent than this notebook seemed to indicate.

I still wanted to believe the girl I'd discovered in those pages, the one who'd written those banal little essays, wasn't really me. But she *was* me: I knew that. This was undeniable. I had unearthed a self I didn't recognize, one I didn't really wish to own, but a girl whom in the end I couldn't deny.

It's a good idea, Joan Didion once advised, *to keep on nodding terms with the people we used to be . . . We forget all too soon the things we thought we could never forget.*

To that long-forgotten self, that person I used to be, I could only nod. Earnest as she was, struggling so fiercely to reconcile her life, to that girl I made a humble bow. And then I spent a long time marveling at all the things I had forgotten, wondering how this ever could have happened.

FOUR

During our senior year, Gail got pregnant. She'd been dating one of the school's star athletes, a boy everybody liked for his sense of humor and his genial manner. Another of our girlfriends had gotten pregnant the year before and had been forced to drop out of school. So we knew this would happen to Gail as well, and we talked about what she should do.

She had to tell her parents, and of course the news upset them. But her father loved her very much, I think she was his favorite child, and as upset as he was he did want to help her somehow. For a while she and her parents discussed what she should do. Go away and have the baby and give it up for adoption? Marry her boyfriend and agree to drop out of school with the hope she could finish later? He was willing to go to any lengths to try and fix the situation she'd gotten herself in.

Gail was a really strong girl and she made it clear to her parents what she wanted to do. She loved her boyfriend, and he loved her. They wanted to get married. And that's what she did: quietly, and with no fuss, she accepted what had happened and began to make the best of it.

She and her husband moved into an apartment on the top floor of an older house, only a ten-minute walk from school. As long as her pregnancy didn't show she could continue going to classes but soon she got so big she had to stop. Then she began spending her days alone, sitting in the second-floor apartment while her husband went to school.

Often after school I would walk down to her apartment to see her. I'd climb the stairs to find her sitting on the sofa, reading magazines or making a list of what she had to get at the grocery store in order to fix dinner for her husband. It seemed so amazing to me that she was now married, that she had her own place, went to bed every night with a boy and had sex without guilt, then woke up with him and sent him off to high school and spent her days alone. She didn't seem depressed. In fact, she seemed rather happy. Her parents were helping them. She didn't have to worry about money. She knew she could rely on them because they loved her so much.

I knew this sort of scenario could not have been played out with my own parents. Very likely I would have been left to figure things out, or simply forced to get married—I could hear my father saying, You've made your bed, now you can lie in it. There wouldn't have been much financial help. Certainly I would have been made to feel ashamed. I'd have become an *embarrassment* to them, though in the end I knew they'd stand by me as best they could. I began to think about these things. If I weren't careful I could very well find myself in the same situation as Gail without the kind of parents who could help me out the way hers had.

Sometimes I envied her. I thought about what it would be like to live on my own with a husband, to furnish an apartment any way I wanted to. To be my own person, have long days all to myself during which I could do whatever I wanted, including not go to school. I wasn't a good student. I knew that. What was the point anyway?

College wasn't even on the radar. It wasn't a priority in my family. My parents expected their kids to go on missions or get married and start families, move out of the house, begin making their own money. Neither of them had gone to college. They figured by the time their children graduated from high school they'd supported them long enough and now it should be up to the kids to make their own way in the world. I didn't think of trying to go to college on my own. I didn't know girls who did that.

I couldn't see the future; most of the time I didn't even try. When I sat in Gail's living room with her after school and looked at her sitting on the sofa with her hands folded around her growing belly she seemed happy with her life in spite of everything that had happened. I wondered if I couldn't be happy with that sort of life as well. What else was there?

The feeling I had expressed in the last essay I'd written for Brother Gallup, the sense that marriage might represent some sort of safe place, a refuge from all the confusion, the depression, the sturm und drang of dating, seemed confirmed during those afternoons I spent with Gail. It began to seem to me the way I might eventually find my way out.

FIVE

One afternoon during my senior year I was taken to the ward patriarch to receive my patriarchal blessing, a special blessing all Mormons receive at some point in their lives. This is a highly personalized blessing, revealing your lineage from the time of the ancient patriarchs and foretelling in general terms what awaits you in life. Every congregation has its own patriarch: the office is handed down from father to son and the patriarchs are usually very old men. Brother Stromberg was our ward patriarch, and he was indeed very old.

My mother drove me to his house and dropped me off. It was the middle of summer and hot outside. Sister Stromberg met me at the front door and took me into a cool bedroom where the light was very dim: the curtains had been closed against the bright sunlight. She told me she would be acting as scribe, taping the blessing with a little recorder so I could be given a transcript, which I still have, an old carbon copy, the paper yellowed, the black print now grown fuzzy with age.

Brother Stromberg was waiting for me in the room, sitting quietly on a chair at the foot of a double bed with an empty chair beside him.

He was a quiet, calm man with a round face, bald head, and many dark spots on his face and hands. He indicated I should sit on the chair next to him. He explained he was going to give me a blessing, just as Abraham received blessings from the Lord. This blessing was just for me; no one else would get the same blessing. It was meant to help guide me in my life. Everything, of course, depended on my living a righteous life. He asked if I understood this and I said yes.

❖ ❖ ❖

The room smelled of old people. It felt musty, yet everything was clean and neat and spare. The walls were bare except for a picture hanging over the bed. The double bed had been carefully made. It seemed like an impersonal space—this room where this old couple slept. Or perhaps, I thought, it's an extra bedroom, a place where they take naps. I could see how one of the pillows still bore the imprint of someone's head.

His wife came back into the room with a tape recorder and sat on another chair in the opposite corner. Brother Stromberg told me she would record the session. Then he rose, taking time to steady himself, and placed his gnarled old hands on my head and closed his eyes. I also closed my eyes as he began speaking.

I felt a little afraid. I knew this moment was important. I might hear predictions about the future. Was I ready to learn what would be in store for me in the coming life?

He called me by my full name: Sister Judith Ann Freeman, he said, by the authority of the Holy Melchizedek Priesthood vested in me and in the name of the Lord Jesus Christ, I lay my hands upon your head and give you your patriarchal blessing, which will be sealed upon you for your benefit and welfare during your earthly sojourn.

He said this blessing would be a great inspiration to me if I was humble and prayerful and submissive before the Lord, if I listened to the promptings of the Holy Spirit who would be with me at all times if I had a receptive heart.

He told me I was faithful in the pre-existence and that with the sons and daughters of God I shouted for joy in the councils of heaven when it was revealed to me that I would be given the opportunity to come into mortality. It was made known to me that this earthly life would simply be another step toward exaltation and also that the Lord intended to test me here on earth to see if I could be faithful in all things.

I had been prepared for a very special mission on earth, he said, and I was held back to come forth in the evening of time.

I came through a noble lineage: I was of the family of Abraham, of Joseph through the loins of Ephraim, and the blessings pronounced upon the heads of the patriarchs of old would come to me here in mortal life. You, he said, will become a blessing and comfort to your fellow men. His hands felt heavy upon my head. I was aware of their weight and warmth, and in that weight and warmth I also imagined a splendid energy flowing into me. I felt as if I had entered a world laced with spirits. I could hear his voice and feel his plump, elderly body right next to me, feel the breath coming out of his mouth as he spoke, and yet his words came from far away, casting a powerful spirit. I couldn't quite grasp everything he was saying, though I knew it was important. I was waiting for him to tell me what my life would be like. I didn't know what it meant to say I'd become a blessing and comfort to others. How would that happen?

I opened my eyes just a little to let the light come in and see if anything in the room had changed. It hadn't. Sister Stromberg still sat in the corner holding the tape recorder in her lap, her eyes cast down. I could hear the buzz of a lawn mower engine coming from somewhere nearby, the noise drifting in loudly through an open window on a hot, still summer afternoon.

Brother Stromberg continued to speak in a steady voice. He told me I was going to search out the genealogy of my forefathers in order to baptize them in absentia. I must do this work for them that they could not do themselves.

He said I would become a mother in Israel and bring choice spirits into the world and I would go to the temple with one of the sons of God and be sealed by the Holy Spirit of Promise and the blessings of the new and everlasting covenant would be pronounced upon my life as I prepared myself for the great mission of mortality. I was going to receive the greatest blessings rearing children unto the Lord as Hannah of old did.

He advised me to be kind and loving to my fellow men and recognize that every individual was a child of God. The worth of souls was great, he said, in the sight of our Heavenly Father.

The Evil One, he said, and his emissaries were abroad in the land and they were going to sorely test me. We were living in a world of confusion. I had to remember the good and ennobling things which I saw and heard that would make of me a noble soul. I would be blessed with the gift of discernment. Confidence would radiate from me out to those whom I loved and this love and confidence would return to me again. I would be successful in my chosen vocation.

He ended the blessing with these words:

> I seal you up to come forth in the morning of the first resurrection crowned a queen and a priestess unto the Most High God. You will take your place and rule and reign in the House of Israel forever. These blessings I seal upon your head, through your faithfulness, in the name of the Lord Jesus Christ, Amen.

When he lifted his hands from my head, after a moment, I opened my eyes and the light flooded in, breaking the spell. Though the blessing was over, a strange feeling remained and this kept me from moving.

Brother Stromberg then looked down and patted my cheek and stepped away and with that gesture the feeling in the room suddenly changed. Everything returned to the way it had been before. I was there, with two old people in a sparsely furnished bedroom. I heard a *click*—his wife turning her tape recorder off. She placed it on the bed and then led me away and said goodbye at the front door and I walked home.

It didn't seem as if my life had really been foretold. Only the patriarch's last words stayed with me, the idea that when the resurrection came I would be crowned a queen and a priestess, which seemed like a good thing until I remembered that all of this would happen only after I was dead.

SIX

The school play was being cast, to be directed by my former debate and drama teacher, Portia Douglas, and when auditions were announced I decided to try out for a part.

I had never acted in a play before. Never even taken part in the church musical productions of *The Music Man* or *Oklahoma!* that were staged each year, but when I heard that the play that Mrs. Douglas had chosen was *The Diary of Anne Frank,* I became interested.

This was the fall of 1964, my last year of high school. I didn't know very much about Anne Frank but I knew that it was a story of survival, of a tragic end, featuring a high-spirited Jewish girl who had spent over two years in hiding in an attic in Amsterdam until she and her family and the others who had holed up together had been discovered by the occupying Germans and sent away to concentration camps. The diary Anne had kept during her time in hiding had been found after they were arrested, and saved by the woman who had helped them during these years—a former employee of Mr. Frank's named Miep—and was later returned to her father, the only member of the Frank family to have survived the death camps. It was published as a book and became the basis of the play, first produced in 1955. All of these details Portia Douglas provided on the day when a large group of students assembled in the auditorium for the first tryouts.

I knew which part I wanted to play. I wished to be cast as Anne Frank.

At this point in my life, if I had ever met a person who was Jewish

I probably hadn't realized it. But this didn't stop me from thinking I could play a Jewish girl.

It may seem like a strange play to have been chosen by a Mormon teacher to be performed before a Mormon audience, with a Mormon student cast. Yet in so many ways it was a perfect choice. Mormons have always felt they understood persecution, as members of the most persecuted religious sect in America in the nineteenth century. Their prophet had been murdered; they'd been driven from place to place, set upon by mobs, seen their property repeatedly destroyed, their family members killed, eventually forcing them to undertake an exodus to the unpopulated regions of the West. And even if this sort of religious persecution didn't in any way rise to the level of what European Jews had suffered, still it touched something and resonated. To be persecuted for what you believe, who you are, as a member of a particular tribe, was something Mormons understood very well.

I bought a copy of the play and read it, becoming even more convinced I wanted to play Anne. I memorized her lines—more than I'd been required to do for the auditions. I practiced saying these lines at home standing in front of a mirror in the bathroom. When the play was finally cast, Mrs. Douglas announced I would play Anne, even though, as she put it, I looked a bit too well fed to be a girl surviving on meager rations. Did I think I could shed a few pounds for the part? Yes, I said, I thought I could. I would do anything to play Anne.

The rehearsals absorbed all my time. I loved inhabiting the feisty, smart Anne, repeating her words, flirting with her teenage attic mate Peter, played by a boy named Rick Bird. I liked arguing with her overbearing mother, who constantly criticized Anne for her behavior and compared her to her more demure older sister, Margot. I loved the way Anne stood up to the cranky Mr. Dussel, the fussy dentist with whom she was forced to share a room, bravely confronting him

in a way I had never been able to with Roland Green, with whom I had been forced to share my house. The play gave me a way of thinking about myself. Playing Anne, I was able to borrow her courage, adopt her words. I redressed old wounds. I sounded as smart and defiant as I wanted to believe I was, or might have been, or perhaps still could be given the right chance.

I began eating less and less in order to feel more and more like Anne, and it soon became natural to me, as if I were learning to do penance. When Anne says, at the beginning of act 2, scene 1, after hiding in the attic for one year, five months, and twenty-five days, *We are all a little thinner,* I could feel her own hunger stalking me. And when she added, *Mother still does not understand me. But then I don't understand her,* I felt as if these words were as true for me as they were for her.

The play ran for three performances in the auditorium of Ogden High School—the cast shown here in a photograph with Mrs. Douglas in the center of the back row, me standing in front. Another photograph, which accompanied the article in the local paper announcing the performances, showed me as Anne, in the same unlikely bouffant, laying my head on the breast of my father, Otto Frank, played by Eric Moon wearing a strange fake mustache. The last paragraph of the article summarized the play this way: *The diary describes the bickerings, the wounded pride, and the tearful adjustment of eight Jews behind locked doors in Germany during Hitler's reign of Terror.* Never mind they had gotten the country wrong and in some strange way made the play sound like a domestic drama, a family of bickering Jews trying to *adjust* to their new lodgings behind locked doors (though in so many respects that's exactly what it is). Although it had been nothing more than a high school play performed by amateurs, people couldn't help being moved to think about its powerful themes—what the Franks represented in their struggle to survive an enormous evil, their deaths in the camps, Anne's youthful confessions that contained such intelligence and self-analysis. It was not the sort of play people in Ogden, Utah, had seen before. What my parents thought of my acting abilities I don't know. Or perhaps I simply don't remember, but it does not seem to me that they took any particular pride in my performance.

And then, after the months of preparation, the performances, the audiences, all the time I had spent preparing, suddenly it was over. And yet I knew I had been changed. For a very brief time, I had inhabited a work of literature, written by a girl my age. And it was the words I had memorized that stayed with me. I had discovered *language*. I had come to own that play.

SEVEN

A year or so before, I had taken up skiing, and when the play ended I focused on this sport. The city ran free buses on weekends, taking school kids to a resort called Snow Basin in the mountains above Ogden. In the beginning I used my brother's skis and poles and found a pair of used boots that fit. I wore layers of clothing, Levi's and long underwear and a woolen jacket. From the moment I discovered skiing I fell in love with the sport and in a short time I became good at it. It was as if again I had discovered a vehicle for speeding across the earth, but unlike Ab Jenkins in his *Mormon Meteor* racing across the white salt I was now flying down mountains on pure white snow.

I loved being in the mountains in the winter, relished the feeling of speed, the fierce sense of skiing down a slope, sometimes very fast, at the edge of control. The world felt dangerously near at such speed. I loved the way a carved turn or linking turns at such speed could feel like riding a rail you were making, solid yet elastic, etching a beautiful line. I often skied off the groomed runs into the stands of tall pines, traversing alone into the thick woods where a particular silence could be found. As the snow fell I would stand quietly in the trees, not moving at all, just listening while the flakes came down around me: it was as if the world became soundproofed and suddenly very still.

I began skiing every weekend, saving up the money I made from a part-time job to pay for a lift ticket and buy better equipment.

❖   ❖   ❖

The part-time job involved being a cashier for Wolthuis Dairy in their drive-up store on Washington Boulevard. The Wolthuis family had operated a local dairy for many years, making house-to-house deliveries, but this was a new idea, a drive-up store where people could just pick up whatever milk products they needed on the run. The store was just a little shack, one room big enough for a couple of refrigerators and a stool and a shelf with a cash register. People drove up to the window where I sat and ordered milk or cheese or butter and I filled the order while they waited in their cars.

The drive-up shack was located on Washington Boulevard, in the black part of town, surrounded by little wooden one-family houses. This was a neighborhood where I'd never spent any time. At first my mother was nervous I'd be working in this area. She thought it might be dangerous, especially as I'd sometimes be working after dark. But I didn't feel bothered by the idea of the neighborhood being dangerous because it didn't feel that way to me, and she soon gave up her objections when I pointed out how much money I'd be making.

A very old black man lived next to the shack and when business was slow I'd go over and sit on his porch and talk with him. He always sat outside when the weather was good. He smoked and watched the people and cars passing by. His eyes were rheumy. I had never seen such yellow whites. He fascinated me. His hands, the way the palms were so pink, the backs so black. The skin drooped from his neck in crenellated folds like a turkey's wattle. There was an attractive calmness about him. He wasn't in a hurry to do anything. He spoke slowly, using slang and certain words that were unfamiliar to me, so I had to listen carefully, straining to understand the stories he told. They were all about when he'd worked for the railroad. All the places he'd gone, the sights he'd seen, being a porter for over forty years. He made working for the railroad sound like a constant adventure. Yes ma'am, he'd say, I seen a lot of things, and then he'd let out a rich, deep laugh. I thought perhaps his politeness and rather formal manners might have come from working in that world. Serving whites. Receiving tips and thanks. Being appreciated for his work. I liked talking to him and he seemed to like my visits. When it was time to go back to work he'd always say, You come over again, darlin'.

At home our lives continued to be absorbed by religious activity and church events but now that my father no longer served in the bishopric he was often home at night and we'd spend the evenings downstairs in the rumpus room watching TV in front of a fire. We'd watch *What's My Line?* and *I've Got a Secret* and try to guess the occupations of the contestants and what their secrets were. My father especially liked programs with music so we always watched Lawrence Welk and Ed Sullivan, Perry Como and Andy Williams, who had started featuring a new musical group from Utah on his show called the Osmond Brothers. They were Mormons, a handsome, clean-cut family that looked like people we knew—and here they were on national TV, the first Mormon celebrities we'd ever seen.

On Sundays we always watched TV in the evening after we came home from the day's church meetings, and we had the same informal supper every week, which wasn't at all like the dinners we had on any other night. We started with popcorn and hot chocolate, then had liverwurst sandwiches with blue cheese followed by banana splits.

On these evenings I'd sit with my parents and siblings and feel that I was only half there in the room with them, the TV screen in the corner flickering and the fire burning in the grate with my father tending constantly to the flames while my mother set out the dishes of food on a card table or the TV trays she put up next to the couch. Part of me would be daydreaming, thinking about skiing the day before, or wondering how Gail was feeling, or maybe I'd be thinking about some boy I'd begun dating who I wished I could be with right then. But I couldn't date on Sunday. This was a house rule. So I'd just sit there staring at the TV.

During these evenings I began thinking about a certain person I had started seeing, though for some time I didn't say anything about him to my parents. He was someone they knew very well and I felt sure they wouldn't approve of my dating him. At the very least they'd have a lot to say. I could imagine the way they'd look at me when I told them his name: John Thorn? they'd say, pulling a face, wondering how he could possibly have turned up again, for the second time, and begun dating another one of their daughters.

The first time I met him I was thirteen or fourteen years old. My sister had just begun seeing him and for some reason they let me go along with them one summer afternoon when they decided to go for a drive north of town in his black Mercury sedan.

We drove up toward the Golden Spike National Historic Site, the place where the transcontinental railroad lines had met in 1869. John and Marcia sat in the front seat and I sat alone in back, staring out at the alfalfa fields and farms we passed, at the horses in the corrals and the lush green pastures where fat cows stood in the dark shade of old cottonwoods.

We turned off the main highway, heading toward the old, mostly empty town of Corinne, then drove even farther north in the direction of the Great Salt Lake on a narrow two-lane road, through dry sagebrush country and past the area marked No Trespassing where the Thiokol Corporation tested missiles. Big DANGER signs hung from the barbed wire fences.

At some point John Thorn asked me if I would like to drive, and I climbed into the front seat and sat on his lap. I do not remember any intimate feeling about doing this: I was more interested in driving the car than in John Thorn. My feet didn't reach the pedals so he worked those, but he placed my hands on the steering wheel and we took off again with me steering the car down the county road.

That was the first time. Driving out in the country in his black Mercury, me sitting on his lap with my sister, Marcia, sitting next to us.

I remember how upset John was later, when he and Marcia broke up. How he had come back from Annapolis that summer—his first year at the Naval Academy—and tried to see her. But it was too late. She'd already become engaged to her returned missionary. It seemed as if my sister had broken his heart.

What happened to him afterward I learned about only later, after we had begun dating. He dropped out of the Naval Academy and enrolled at Brigham Young University, where over the next few years he earned a degree in psychology.

During those years no one in my family saw him, and I don't think anyone thought much about him—a case of out of sight, out of mind. It was a great surprise, then, when I ran into him at a church dance three years later, and an even greater surprise when he asked me to dance.

We started seeing each other regularly. It was as if I had suddenly ascended to the place where my sister had left off with him. I was seventeen, more or less the same age she had been when they had gone steady. I was aware of the years that had passed, how I was four years older now, how different it felt to be near him. When he asked me to dance that night it seemed very natural to say yes, and then to keep saying yes.

He was exceptionally bright, which is why he'd gotten the appointment to the Naval Academy in the first place, and also naturally thoughtful. He had an amiable personality and was quick to make friends. I was attracted to his clean-cut good looks and his maturity. He was six years older than me and had already graduated from college. He seemed sure of himself, as if he already understood what he wanted from this world, and I wanted to feel that way myself. We liked the same things—skiing and horses (his father raised pure-bred Arabians) and camping and the outdoors. We were athletic, both good at sports, and liked being out in nature. In many ways I felt I was a much better match for him than my sister had been.

I must have thought this was smart. Smart in a rather rebellious way. To take up with my sister's former boyfriend. To begin going out with the boy she'd rejected, who really wasn't a boy at all anymore but rather a twenty-three-year-old man.

Eventually when I told my parents I was seeing him they reacted just as I thought they would. They made derisive comments. They were rather incredulous and sarcastic: they could not quite imagine why I'd begun dating him. It wasn't so much that they didn't like him, they just didn't want me to date him. My mother kept saying she didn't understand. What could make me want to do this? My father was even ruder. He made caustic remarks about John, and also about me and my ability to make good choices. They couldn't believe I was going out with him, which only made me want to see him all the more.

I don't remember what my sister thought about my dating him. Again I am reminded of how unaccountable memory is—how those particular episodes from our past that lodge in our minds are often not the most decisive, though they may seem momentous. How we forget all too soon the things we thought we could never forget, as Didion put it. And how in particular I seemed to have lost many memories of my sister, or simply wished to bury them. Now they seem beyond retrieval. I am left with flat blank spaces when it comes to certain portions of the past we shared, including the moment when she realized I was dating John.

When John Thorn proposed to me one winter day while we were out horseback riding, getting down on his knee and presenting me with a small velvet box containing a ring, I didn't think much about it. I just said yes.

While neither my mother nor my father approved of me getting engaged, neither one suggested I should wait to get married. What, after all, would I be waiting for?

I felt defiant about my choice, felt sure I had fallen in love. With

John Thorn, I imagined that I had found a way out. I could see the future, and I thought it looked pretty good. We'd talked about joining the Peace Corps. That's what we wanted to do. Go overseas and help poor, struggling people. I thought the world was just waiting for me to find my place in it, and by that I meant my *real* place, wherever that might be.

We had gotten engaged over the Christmas holidays. When I returned to school and showed my typing teacher, an attractive unmarried woman, the wedding ring I had acquired during Christmas break, she looked at me as if to say, What *are* you doing?

Perhaps she's jealous, I thought when she looked at me that way. Being unmarried and all. Perhaps she wishes she were me.

When I think of that last year of high school, still living with my parents in the house on College Drive in the months before I got married, there is one memory that stands out above all the others.

It's winter. Heavy snow covers the ground outside on the foothills of the mountains. My mother is in the kitchen cooking dinner and my father is in the living room reading the evening paper, waiting to be called to supper. My younger brothers, Jerry and Gregg, are the only children still left at home besides me: the others have moved away, gotten married or gone off on missions for the church. My mother is getting ready to call us for dinner soon. The kitchen is steamed up from cooking, the windows fogged over, including the window that looks out toward the Great Salt Lake. It's so dark there's nothing to see outside that window anyway. Instead it reflects a fuzzy glow, a misted image of the inside of the kitchen, where lights burn and my mother is moving about, putting the finishing touches on our evening meal.

For the last hour or so I have been shut up in my bedroom, attempting to learn how to scream. Screaming is much harder than I'd ever imagined. To scream convincingly at will is a very difficult thing to do. Every effort feels false. There is nothing in that room to elicit a scream, nothing of which I'm afraid. I'm realizing that without fear there's no such thing as a good scream.

But I must try. As Anne Frank, I must scream as part of the opening of act 1, scene 4. Certain acts open to a darkened auditorium with Anne's words, spoken by me, drifting out into the darkness. Portia Douglas has already recorded all my other voice-overs except this one—the scream that erupts in the dark in act 1 when Anne awakens from a nightmare.

And so I am practicing screaming in the room I once shared with my sister, who no longer lives at home. The room she once divided with a string. The room where I once reached up and held the hand of God, and where my father and the elders laid their hands on my head to heal me, where I kissed every picture of Johnny Jones in the yearbook, leaving the thick red waxy outline of my lips on his face, and lay alone at night listening to Nat King Cole. The room where I've spent my teenage years and which I will soon leave to get married.

My throat feels scratchy from all the screaming. I know I haven't gotten it right. I can hear the muffled tinkling of glasses and silverware being laid out on the kitchen table. I can hear my father's voice, talking to my mother from the living room, and the murmur of other voices. My mother is moving pots and pans, lifting them from the stove, setting them down again noisily on the burners. The sink is to her right, below a window looking out toward the Plowgians' house, the yellow Formica counter behind her, dividing the kitchen area from the table where we eat. Heat is coming up through the ventilator from the furnace downstairs, and outside arc lights illuminate the street in front where snow is still falling silently on the road.

I continue to practice my screaming as my family prepares to gather for dinner on this cold winter night, thinking of the lines I memorized earlier, from the scene where Mr. Van Daan says to Anne, *Why aren't you nice and quiet like your sister Margot? A man likes a girl who'll listen once in a while . . . a domestic girl who'll keep a house shining for her husband . . . who loves to cook and sew,* and Anne replies, *I'd cut my throat first! I'd open my veins! I'm going to be remarkable! I'm going to Paris!*

Paris? Mr. Van Daan scoffs.

Yes, Anne cries. *Paris.*

Later she wonders, *Will I ever be able to write well? I want to so much. I am fifteen. Already I know what I want. I have a goal. I have an opinion.*

My mother, who like everyone else in the house has heard me screaming in my room, suddenly calls out loudly from the kitchen. *Judy!* she yells. *We're ready to eat.*

Her voice is sharp and no-nonsense, and she quickly calls out again. *Stop that screaming, or whatever you're doing in there, and come to dinner now!*

She means business. When it's time to eat, you'd better come.

I set aside my heavily marked-up copy of *The Diary of Anne Frank* and leave the room, this room where I have spent my teenage years and which I will soon depart for good to become a married girl, and I join my family at the table, in the warm kitchen where the overhead lights are glowing so brightly against the dense blackness of the cold winter night.

PART FIVE

❖

Art City

ONE

Thinking about those days right after I got married and moved in with John Thorn to our first apartment, I find it is only with the greatest difficulty that I can recall anything of what I had felt during that time or why I had made the decision I did to get married at such a young age. There is a resistance, an old embedded reluctance, to look too closely at this.

It seemed *fated* somehow—that was the word that kept coming back to me. I was fated to end up marrying my sister's ex-boyfriend as part of some deep old familial wound. I was fated to contract an early marriage, as if that *free will* Brother Gallup had spoken of so often in seminary class had somehow been stripped from me. But that's not what happened. I *chose* to marry when I did. Nobody forced me. And still, I could not help feeling there were many factors driving me toward this decision, one of them being the idea of escape.

The wedding took place in June. I graduated from high school one day and was married the next.

We were married in the Salt Lake Temple in order to please our parents, even though we were not worthy to do so. To be married in the temple one had to have never had sex. You weren't supposed to smoke or drink, or consume coffee or tea. You needed to be a true believer. On all counts we were ineligible. And yet when the day came we assembled with our families and entered the temple as a group. My parents were there, and John's father and stepmother, Eleanor, though his mother, Peg, as a non-Mormon was excluded from witnessing the ceremony and had to wait outside. We put on the all-white clothes and moved through the fantastically painted rooms—rooms done up to look like the Garden of Eden, walls covered with scrolls and vines, angels and heavenly clouds floating in blue skies, walls covered in bucolic biblical imagery—and took part in the secret rituals, uttered our vows, passed through the veil, and were pronounced married for time and all eternity.

We began wearing the holy garments under our clothes, which we were told we must always wear next to our skin. These thin, silky one-piece garments, open at the crotch, with their special sacred markings at the navel, breast, and knee. Regular underwear had to be worn over them so that they would always be next to our flesh. In this way the garments would protect us. The only time we could take them off was to bathe or go swimming, though the unspoken rule was it was also okay to remove them during sex, even though some people did not do this.

The reception that evening was held in an older, ivy-covered house in Ogden that could be rented for such occasions. Punch and cookies and an assortment of little cakes were served. No alcohol, of course. Nor were there any toasts or speeches, or dancing or music, except for a woman who was hired to play background music on the piano for a couple of hours.

I stood in a receiving line with my handsome new husband, wearing an ill-fitting white satin dress that had been hastily made by a neighbor, with our parents flanking us as we shook the hands of the well-wishers who passed by. Some of my friends came that night but also a lot of older people from the church, along with relatives and friends of my parents and some of John's friends he'd gone to school with. His mother, Peg, was there, a tiny, vivacious, chain-smoking woman with a raucous laugh. She didn't care that she hadn't been able to attend the wedding ceremony in the temple earlier in the day. She just laughed her gravelly smoker's laugh and shrugged it off. She understood those crazy Mormons and their rules, having lived among us for so long.

We spent the first night of our honeymoon in Wendover, a tiny, wind-blown gambling town on the border of Nevada and Utah. We had traveled across the Salt Flats for several hours in the dark to get there, with the moon shining down on the white salt-covered earth. The town of Wendover had the distinction of straddling two states: on the Utah side strict liquor laws and Mormon influence prevailed; on the other the anything-goes atmosphere of Nevada gambling casinos.

Wendover also had a small Air Force base. It was from here the *Enola Gay*, the plane that dropped the atomic bomb on Hiroshima, departed for its mission and here is where it returned, enshrined in its own hangar. The desert came right up to the edge of town. There were rows of wooden barracks with peeling paint that gave the place a deserted and spent feeling.

As we drove in at midnight a windstorm blew up. Clouds of dust partially obscured the road. We headed over to the Nevada side of town, where there were lots of bright neon lights, stopped at a motel, and for the first time registered as man and wife.

In the middle of the night, as we lay in bed, I felt the pictures on the walls begin to rattle, and then the walls themselves began to shake. At that time, in 1964, atomic tests were still being conducted in the Nevada desert, a couple of hundred miles to the south, and later I felt there must have been a test that first night of my honeymoon.

A few days later I stood in front of an open car trunk in a parking lot near a trailhead in Yosemite National Park having an argument with my new husband as squirrels chattered away in the background and a piney scent filled the air. The argument was my fault. I felt tense and unhappy and I'd picked a fight, though I don't remember now about what. Just that I felt suddenly emotionally volatile. Suffering, perhaps, from those *confused feelings* I'd confessed to Brother Gallup. The honeymoon didn't even pass without a quarrel.

I could not have had any idea of what it meant to be married. I did not know how to cook and I did not like keeping house. In some ways I was a very immature girl, though of course I didn't think so. I wanted to have fun, to feel free, and I thought we could do that together, but there were responsibilities now. I would need to work. I thought it would be easy getting a job, that I might enjoy working, but I didn't.

Because I had done well in a typing and shorthand class in my senior year, I applied for a secretarial position at a savings and loan company in downtown Salt Lake City and was hired, but the job lasted only one week. It turned out not to be a good fit, as my employer put it, and by mutual agreement I quit.

I tried temp work, and hated it. I felt bored doing secretarial work, retyping letters until I produced a perfect copy, filing documents, performing the most menial jobs in offices that felt sterile and inhospitable to me.

I discovered that any work I could qualify for would inevitably be boring. Low-paying office jobs, doing tedious work. Work for girls with only a high school education.

I wasn't much better at domestic chores. I remember buying a package of meat not long after we were married, what I thought were steaks, and taking them to my aunt's house one night for a backyard barbecue and how she laughed at me for buying a cut that was so tough—meat that was meant to be stewed, she said, not barbecued. What did I know?

We moved into an apartment in an area of Salt Lake City called Sugar House, and John went to work for a moving and storage company, giving people estimates for moves. I went to a doctor to get birth control pills. I didn't want to take a chance of getting pregnant since we were going to apply for the Peace Corps when I turned nineteen. The gynecologist, a Mormon with a practice in Salt Lake City, tried to talk me out of using birth control. I was young, he said. Healthy. This was a good time to start a family. I was the perfect age, he added. But I didn't think seventeen was the perfect age. I insisted I wanted the pill, which was then very new, as it seemed like the easiest way to avoid getting pregnant. Reluctantly he filled out a prescription. What I didn't know was he had prescribed the strongest dosage of the pill.

The strongest dosage of the pill turned out to make me very sick. Each day I took it I felt nauseated, and because I couldn't stand this feeling I began taking the pills every other day, then sometimes only when I had sex. Nothing about the pill had been carefully explained to me by the doctor who had provided the prescription.

As a result, by the end of August, a mere two months after the wedding, I found myself pregnant.

I remember crying as I gave my mother the news, standing in the dark, cool basement of the house on College Drive one hot summer afternoon, repeating over and over again in an anguished voice, But I don't want to be pregnant! I can't be pregnant!

Well, she responded gaily—this woman who had always hungered for more babies—there's nothing you can do about it now. She said this as if some part of her was happy for this turn of events, as if she thought perhaps once and for all I would now be tamed, finally collared by my own foolishness.

She was right, of course. There was nothing I could do. Not once, not even in the remotest reaches of my brain, not even in the most rebellious part of my psyche, did the idea of abortion present itself to me.

I was sick. I was terribly sick. For the first three months I was unable to keep food down. I vomited five, six, seven times a day, kneeling before the toilet bowl, clinging to its rim as the spasms hit me. Even a sip of water could set off the nausea. This wasn't simply morning sickness (though that's exactly what it was): it felt more like I had contracted a fatal disease from which I was slowly wasting away.

I had not yet reached my eighteenth birthday. I was carrying a baby, it had begun to take shape inside me and it would continue to do so, willfully, of its own accord, driven by the life force, and it would continue to do this without my consent until that moment when it chose to leave my body. I knew I should want this baby I was carrying but I didn't. But John was happy. He was very happy at the idea of being a father.

I tried all kinds of things to deal with the sickness. Old remedies and new medicines, suppositories and pills, but nothing worked. Finally I became so weak and dehydrated I needed intravenous fluids. I began going to the doctor's office every week, where I would lie down on a gurney while the nurse attached a catheter to a bag of fluids that soon began coursing through my body. Afterward I went home to the apartment and lay on the couch and waited for that day to pass and the next to arrive.

John went off to work every day. He wore a suit and carried a clipboard, driving around and making estimates for Bekins. They gave us a big turkey at Thanksgiving and a ham at Christmas as well as a small bonus. The apartment complex where we lived was new—so new it was still surrounded by mounds of dirt and a gaping hole where the owners had promised to build a swimming pool but no swimming pool was ever built.

We got a poodle, a little black poodle named Jacques to keep me company during the long days I spent at home. I had nothing to do, nowhere to go, nothing to distract me while my husband was away at work. We bought a new car, a silver convertible we went into debt to get, and then we sold the convertible and bought a little used Porsche, which we drove far too fast on the curvy canyon roads above Salt Lake City.

I turned eighteen in October. The morning sickness began to

abate as winter came on, just in time for skiing. Skiing was what John Thorn and I did. We were both good skiers. He had joined the ski patrol at a new resort called Solitude where there was also night skiing. Sometimes we skied all day, and then ate dinner at the lodge and stayed on to ski in the darkness beneath the bright lights that were set up at the edge of runs. The nights were black and cold and brilliantly crisp in the mountains. The stars pressed down, so near to us. Sometimes it snowed in the darkness, and with the snow came a beautiful feeling on earth.

I grew large and still I skied, compensating for the strange shifting mass that was now my body, compensating for the unhappiness I felt at the prospect of being a mother, something I in no way felt ready to be. I skied carefully, very carefully, taking care not to fall, but I also sometimes skied fast as I loved to do, and because I had become a strong skier I was lucky. I didn't fall. The life growing inside me swooshed down the runs with me, bobbing in its amniotic world, unaware of the risk I was taking.

We left the apartment in Sugar House, which we really couldn't afford, and rented a basement apartment on a busy highway that ran between Salt Lake City and Ogden, in a town called Bountiful. It was a dreadfully dark apartment, filled with an odd assortment of furniture. As if to make up for the months of hunger, I began eating. Chili became my favorite dish, and John Thorn made an excellent chili. I ate bowl after bowl of his delicious chili, and then I ate some more. I gained thirty, forty, fifty pounds.

I spent a lot of days alone, sitting in the living room, wondering what to do. Old stacks of *Western Horseman* sat on a table made out of an iron wagon wheel. Looking at those pictures of horses reminded me of what I had lost. Little bugs called silverfish crawled out from beneath the baseboards and flopped onto the floor like tiny landed trout. The days grew short. Night fell fast, like a black cloth suddenly being shook out. The sound of the cars on the highway a constant hissing. Snakes set loose. Sometimes the Relief Society ladies came to visit. I didn't much like that. Their constant cheerfulness. The way they acted like everything was so fine. As soon as they left I ate more chili.

We went to church, not every Sunday but often enough to assure our parents we had not strayed completely from the faith. We often visited them, driving to Ogden to see John's mother, or to have a meal with my parents. We spent time with his father and stepmother, who lived in a town an hour to the south. We wanted their approval. We wore our holy garments next to our skin. Occasionally we visited a temple, more as a kind of social outing with our parents than as anything else. We went through sessions in the Manti Temple with his parents, and the Salt Lake Temple with mine. We did baptisms for the dead. I taught a Sunday school class for five-year-olds, thinking it might be good for me to be around kids. In truth I liked kids very much. I just didn't want to be a mother yet.

I began to feel defeated. Not humbled by the loss of freedom that came with the pregnancy, or the loss of the dreams I'd had when we got married. Just defeated in general, as if I were somehow being taught a lesson I didn't want to learn.

Gail had moved away with her husband and baby. They'd gone to live in the East where he'd gotten a job. I lost contact with other girls I'd known. Most of our social life revolved around skiing and the people we knew at the resort, where we spent a lot of time. We began skiing on Sundays instead of going to church.

After a while, it didn't seem to matter if I went to church or not. I didn't believe or not believe. I was simply habituated to accepting I had been born and raised a Mormon, I lived among them, and none of it seemed to matter much anymore. As Gertrude Stein once said, repetition is insistence. Religion felt insistent, until it didn't anymore.

A dullness began encroaching on my life, blunting my youth, taking the edge off my high spirits. Much of the time I felt sobered, often sad.

Sometimes I thought about the Peace Corps and the plans we'd made. Funny, I thought, how life can be this or that, can go one way or another, and you'd never be able to predict how anything would turn out.

Most days I simply waited for John to return from work. Then everything felt better. Just having him there. I ate more chili. I got larger and larger, lumbering through my pregnancy, finally giving up skiing in the eighth month when I could no longer be sure of my balance.

And then one morning I awoke to labor pains and in the crepuscular light of a not-quite-dawn, John Thorn drove me to the Cottonwood Hospital in Salt Lake City. I was shaved, prepped for delivery, put in a room, and the ordeal began, that ordeal that President McKay said takes a woman to the brink of death. It felt that way to me. The labor was hard. The baby very large. Finally the decision was made to knock me out for the delivery. As I was wheeled on a gurney down a hallway to the delivery room, I called out, I would like to speak to David O. McKay! It was the last thing I remembered saying from my drug-induced state before I lost consciousness. And obviously no prophet appeared at my side.

TWO

I awoke in a large room where three other women were lying in nearby beds.

There was no one there I knew, no relative or family member with me when I came to.

At first I thought I was still in labor, I felt so much pain, and then I realized no, I must have somehow given birth: *the baby was gone from my body.*

A short while later John Thorn came in and said we had a little baby boy. A not-so-little boy, really. The baby weighed nine pounds one ounce.

I asked him where he was and he said he had not seen him yet. He'd been taken away quickly, while he was waiting in another room, and the nurse had told him it would be a while before he could visit him. He said he was tired and going home to rest for a while but he'd come back later.

I slept a little and when I woke up I noticed the three other women in the room were all holding their babies and breast-feeding them. I waited, thinking the nurses would soon bring my baby. But the nurses did not bring my baby. They seemed to be avoiding me, in fact. After a while a nurse came to me and turned me on my side and said she was giving me a shot to help dry up my breast milk because I wouldn't be needing it. Why wouldn't I be needing it? I asked. The doctor will explain that when he arrives later, she said.

All that first afternoon I watched the nurses bring the other mothers their babies and then later take them away. I was still a bit disoriented, confused by the drugs I'd been given, and also in a great deal of pain from the episiotomy that had been performed, and still I thought, Why no baby? Why are they not bringing him to me? When John returned and I asked him if he'd seen our baby yet, he had to admit he hadn't.

After he left that night I lay in bed and thought, Perhaps it's because I'm so young. Perhaps they don't trust me yet. Maybe *I am the problem*. All the other women in the room looked older: maybe they were veterans at having babies. But me? Perhaps I was not yet ready to hold him, still too shaky from the delivery and drugs. Maybe I had to do something, demonstrate some competence before they would risk such a thing.

In the morning, the second day, I confronted the nurse who brought me my breakfast. I screwed up my courage and said, I would like to see my baby. She said she would check on that.

Soon two nurses returned, one holding a little bundle. This was my baby. They stood at the foot of the bed and unwrapped the swaddling and said, Here he is, and held him up quickly so I could see him. I didn't have my contacts in so I asked them to come closer, to bring me the baby so I really could see him and hold him. One of the nurses said, I'm sorry but we have to take him back to the nursery now. But the doctor will be in to see you very soon.

They took the baby away.

Even then I didn't understand that something might be wrong with my son. I still somehow thought the problem must be with me. That I was not yet capable of taking care of my own baby. How naive I was.

My milk must be deficient, I thought, and they can already tell this. He must need them to feed him. That was why the decision had been made to dry it up without even consulting me.

Later on I thought, How could I have been treated that way and not have said something? But at the time I thought I couldn't say anything. I felt confused. I didn't know what to do or say.

When I think of the birth of my son it seems it occurred in another era, if not another world—nineteenth-century Russia, say, or perhaps the Victorian age. There had been no counseling, no choices offered to me. I didn't go to childbirth classes. I wasn't asked how I wished to give birth, or really even told by my gynecologist what to expect except in the most general terms. In that Mormon world, in that era, it was assumed that every girl would know what she needed to know, that her mother and aunts and grandmothers would teach her. Above all it was understood that doctors knew best. They would make the decisions that needed to be made, with or without consulting the mothers. And they would all be male doctors. I wonder now, How could I have even given birth and been completely unconscious of the entire event? How does a body *do* that?

Later that afternoon the doctor came in. He stood at the foot of my bed and asked how I was feeling. I was alone. John wasn't there, nor was any other family member, though my parents had come by earlier in the day and seemed surprised and confused when they, too, were informed they couldn't see their new grandson. I told the doctor I was feeling okay, and then I asked about the baby. I asked why I hadn't been able to hold him yet.

The doctor was a no-nonsense sort of person, not cold exactly, just formal and rigorously precise in a kind of pinched way.

He said unfortunately our baby had some kind of congenital heart defect. The exact nature of that defect had not yet been determined. It could be a minor defect, he said, something called a patent ductus arteriosus, which could be easily dealt with, or it could be something much more serious. A pediatric cardiologist had been called in and certain tests were being conducted to try and determine what was wrong. However, it could be some time before they would be able to make a firm diagnosis, as it was always difficult with a newborn. Because the baby needed constant oxygen he was in intensive care, being kept in an incubator and carefully monitored. I asked him how he knew our baby had a heart defect and he laughed, a sound I found jarring, and said, Believe me it was obvious, he was born very blue, and of course we noticed this right away. We knew he'd suffered a lack of oxygen but there could be many causes for this.

He then looked at me and, seeing I was close to tears, quietly said, Mrs. Thorn, I should tell you that I just delivered a baby that was so badly deformed we couldn't even determine its sex. Fortunately that baby died. Your baby is alive. That's the good news. Then he left the room.

I went home two days later, without my newborn son.

I don't remember now how my parents reacted to the news that our baby had some sort of congenital heart defect, though I am certain they were very sympathetic, especially my mother. She could not have been otherwise. Nor do I remember the conversation John and I must have had when I told him what the doctor had said. Again I am reminded how completely capricious memory can be, eliminating from our consciousness events, exchanges, scenes of seemingly great momentousness, and instead what we are left with is primarily the *feeling* of a particular time, with often just a smattering of seemingly less significant details. Given all that has been deleted, or transformed, or rescripted over the years, I wonder, How can we even trust what remains?

The baby stayed in the hospital as continued attempts were made to diagnose his condition. We did not know when he would be released. They couldn't say. There were still tests to run, and consultations with the pediatric cardiologist who'd been called in. It could be some time before we'd have these answers.

I saw him before I left. He lay in an incubator which the nurse called an "isolette." He wore a little diaper and that is all. Tubes were attached here and there. Oxygen flowed into the little space, and also a faint mist that gave his hair a dewy, moist look. He had dark hair, quite a bit of it. He looked so large and well formed, so *"pretty,"* is the word that came to me. John Thorn and I stared at him a long time.

The incubator had two plastic portals in the side and the nurse allowed us to put our hands inside after we had washed them carefully and we touched him. I held on to his small hand and then cupped my hand around his tiny head. He did not look blue. The oxygen made him appear healthy and pink. It was very hard to believe there was anything wrong with this baby.

It was late April. A cold, wet spring, mud everywhere, the last slubs of dirty snow melting alongside the roadway. We drove home to the basement apartment where the spare room had been set up as a nursery. I did not feel well. Not in body or mind. I felt anguished and guilty. I felt as if I had not wanted the baby enough and this had been an awful thing. I had a terrible sense of failure. I thought of the woman who stood up in fast and testimony meeting who said the Lord had given her a Mongoloid baby because of something she'd done, and even though I didn't believe in such things I wondered, What *had* I done? I felt I might have caused our baby's problems. I must have done something, maybe by being so sick and becoming dehydrated, by taking those anti-nausea drugs, by skiing or eating too much chili, or in some other way not doing the right thing, even though the cardiologist we'd spoken to as we were leaving the hospital said I had not caused our baby's defect. It was an aberration of nature, he said. The heart is one of the first things formed in the embryo, usually before the woman even imagines she's pregnant. He kept assuring me I had done nothing to cause the deformity. Just an aberration of nature, he said.

Dr. George Veasy, the pediatric cardiologist who'd been called in to diagnose our baby's problem, was an easygoing man, affable and handsome, very kind and funny, and even though there was nothing funny about our situation, he spoke to us so gently, with the occasional flicker of humor, and brought a lovely lightness to a very dark time, helping us get through that first difficult period.

Although the exact nature of our baby's congenital heart defect had still not yet been determined, for some reason we were allowed to bring him home the second week after his birth. While I was very excited about this, I also felt afraid. Now the responsibility for the baby would be ours, and he wasn't even a normal baby. Still, didn't the doctors know what they were doing?

One day we simply drove to the hospital and brought him back to the basement apartment. The first day or two seemed to go okay, though every time I looked at him, at his blue lips and fingers and the bluish cast to his milky-white skin, it was impossible not to be reminded something was very wrong. It was also impossible not to feel afraid that at any moment something terrible might happen, something for which John and I couldn't possibly be prepared.

And yet it's not the fear I remember. It's the ordinariness of that time, the feeling I had that this was something for which I had in fact

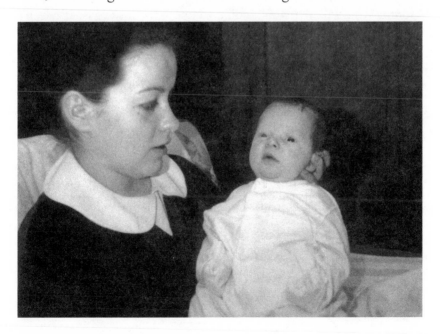

been prepared. To bring a newborn baby home. To hold it and feed it and love it. To know how to care for it, as my mother had cared for us, as I had grown up watching her do.

When was it that the baby began to struggle for breath? The second night he was home? The third? I no longer remember exactly: the events that occurred that night have become rather faint and blurred, as if I long ago attempted to erase them and can now make out only the pale underdrawing. I only know that one night, sitting in the living room in the middle of the night and feeding the baby from a bottle, I began to notice a change in him. He stopped feeding, began struggling for breath, turned even duskier.

We did not call an ambulance. I don't know why. We simply got in the car and rushed to the hospital with John speeding all the way through the empty streets of Salt Lake City in the early-morning darkness. When we reached the hospital we turned the baby over to the nurses, who hurried away with him.

It would be a very long time before our baby would come home again. Months would pass. I would come to know the insides of children's wards very well, become a habitué. Learn to pass my days within their walls, eat the food in the cafeterias, adapt to the smells and the cries of children and the dramas constantly unfolding around me.

This is the other thing I remember about that night. Just one of those insignificant details memory seems to favor. I was wearing a robe I'd made in Relief Society. The Relief Society ladies always had handicraft projects going—things to scrub your tub made out of stiff netting and ribbons, crocheted pot holders, homemade candles with glitter embedded in the wax. Most recently we had been taught how to make a robe out of three bath towels. We had sewn two big bath towels together to make the main part of the robe, and then cut a hole in a smaller towel for the head and folded it lengthwise and sewn it to the other two towels to make the top, basting the cut edges. The result was not only an uncomfortable robe, bulky and binding, but also a boldly unattractive one. Mine was made out of yellow-flowered towels that felt thin and scratchy even after I'd washed them. I had been wearing this robe that night, the night our baby began struggling for breath. It's one of the few things I clearly remember. Rushing into the hospital swaddled in three towels stitched together, crying and holding our baby in my arms.

THREE

Recently I had a dream, a version of the same recurring dream I have had for many years, one that began during the time after the beautiful boy returned to the hospital and the long period of uncertainty began.

The dream is about a child, a little boy. He has no friends. He's so shy and lonely. But I become his friend, as well as his mentor and teacher, and we grow very close, closer than he has ever been to anyone before. He trusts me, this child: he clings to me with such deep affection and this affection is reciprocated. I feel protective of him, this sad, quiet, fragile boy who tells me he has never had a friend. Then his real mother comes into the room and she is critical of the boy and overbearing and he begins to wilt and fade as if her harshness and authority are causing him to slowly disappear. I step in firmly and tell the mother she will have to leave the room. She will have to go away. And she does, she obeys me, and in this way I protect the child.

I've never really tried to understand this dream or spoken about it to anyone. Whatever I don't understand, maybe I don't want to know.

Once, when our son was two and a half and had been admitted to the Variety Club Heart Hospital at the University of Minnesota Medical Center, suffering from serious heart failure, his roommate died one night. This was a little boy about my own son's age. The thing I'd immediately noticed about him was he never had any visitors. Over the course of several weeks, as I sat in the room with my son all day, I never saw anyone come to see him, and I finally asked one of the nurses about him. She said he had no family. He had been abandoned by his parents.

I am no longer even sure what was wrong with this boy, but it seems to me he had some form of leukemia. Day after day he would sit in his crib, his pale, ashen face staring out between the rails at me. His crib was on one side of the room, the bed where my son lay inside an oxygen tent on the other, and I sat between them. I took to bringing him little toys and talking to him every day, including him in the stories I read to my son, even though he was shy and inward and often didn't show any response. And then one morning I arrived and his crib was empty. I thought perhaps he'd been taken away to have some tests. But after a while when he hadn't come back I asked the nurse about him. It was then she told me he had died in the night.

Sometimes I think this is the boy who appears in my dreams. Or perhaps it's my own son. Since I never remember what the boy looks like, I can't be sure. But in some ways it doesn't matter: I know the dream isn't about the boy or my son. It's about me.

When our son was two weeks old his heart condition was finally diagnosed and the cardiologist, Dr. Veasy, called us into his office for a consultation. He said he wished he had better news but he didn't. Unfortunately our baby had a transposition of the great arteries, and this was one of the most serious congenital heart defects because the arteries couldn't simply be switched. It would require a palliative surgery very soon, and then later, when he weighed enough, he'd need a much more complex surgery to reconfigure the inside of his heart.

John and I took this news quietly, trying to understand what it meant. We knew it wasn't good. But how bad was it?

Dr. Veasy took a piece of paper and drew a little picture of the heart for us. He showed us how the defect caused blood from the lungs to flow back to the lungs, and blood from the body to flow back to the body. This was because the aorta and pulmonary artery were connected to the wrong chambers. He pointed out where there was a little hole in the septum between the lower chambers of our baby's heart and how this had allowed a little mixing of oxygenated blood.

This, he said, had allowed our son to survive—also the fact he had weighed over nine pounds, which had been a big advantage. But he would not survive much longer without the palliative surgery to enlarge this hole in the septum to allow more mixing of the oxygenated blood. This was called a Blaylock-Hanlon procedure, after the surgeons who invented it. If successful, this might allow him to survive until he weighed thirty pounds, which is what he would need to weigh before he could be attached to a bypass machine and have the major surgery, called a Mustard procedure. This was a surgery that had only recently been discovered. Until a few years ago, most children born with transpositions of the great arteries had simply died.

After he had finished explaining all this he looked at us, and with the wry smile he often wore—a smile that made you feel his kindness and concern—he said something like, Gosh, you two, you know you guys are so young. You should really think of having another baby.

I didn't resent that he said this. I knew what he was trying to gently say was: I don't think this one is going to make it.

Before our baby was operated on he was given a name and a blessing, though he was not yet a month old, the age at which such blessings are usually bestowed, because who knew if he would live a month?

His father gave him his name and blessing in the hospital, surrounded by his grandfathers, who also placed their hands on his tiny head as he was allowed just for a moment to be lifted from his isolette so the ceremony could be performed.

We named him Todd Freeman Thorn.

And then, a few days later, the time for the surgery came and there was Dr. Mortensen, the pediatric thoracic surgeon, with his large, thick hands covered in black hair, sitting across from us in the Latter-day Saints Hospital in Salt Lake City, saying he believed that even if our baby survived this operation, chances were he would be mentally retarded.

The surgery lasted many hours. It went on until late at night, with Dr. Veasy appearing occasionally to give us an update as we sat in a waiting room. We keep losing him, he'd say, his heart keeps stopping and we have to try and get it going again, but he's a fighter and he keeps coming back.

A three-week-old fighter, I thought. Imagine that.

When he was finally taken from the operating room and wheeled past where we were sitting it was almost midnight. I saw a tiny damaged baby, his chest black and blue from repeated attempts to revive him, a sutured wound running in a half circle from his chest to his back. He had died many times that night. And many times been brought back.

For a long time he stayed in intensive care in the LDS Hospital, but when he was stable enough he was transferred to the Primary Children's Hospital, which was also owned by the church. This hospital was in part supported by the millions of pennies gathered from Mormon children who one day a week attended Primary after school, where we played games and were given religious instruction. I remembered those meetings from my own childhood, how at a certain point the special "penny march" music began and each child walked single file up to the front of the room where there was a receptacle and dropped her pennies into a box. These pennies, we were told, helped sick children get better in a special hospital just for kids. Now my child was in this special hospital I had contributed my pennies to as a child.

It was the beginning of many months spent in children's wards, of seeing the astonishing variety of illnesses and defects that could beset a child, of witnessing the anguish of other parents, the suffering of kids, the tedium of sickness and waiting.

The Primary Children's Hospital sat high above Salt Lake City at the top of a steep hilly area known as the Avenues. Each morning I made the trip from the dark apartment in Bountiful and each evening I made the same trip home. I had nothing to do but go to the hospital each day and sit by the side of the isolette where our beautiful boy was recovering from his surgery, though still very fragile, on constant oxygen. John would come at the end of the day when he'd finished work. We'd sometimes eat dinner in the hospital cafeteria and then go back to be with Todd again. As night came on I looked out the window at the glittering lights of the city far below. Salt Lake a perfect grid of lights, broad main avenues, State and Main Streets, brightly illuminated corridors stretching in a straight line all the way to the Point of the Mountain where the Utah State Prison was located. The next day I would return to the hospital and begin the same routine.

John joined the Toastmasters Club, thinking it would be a good professional move, help him connect with the business community. Automatically I became part of the Lady Toastmasters, the wives' organization. Sometimes I went to an event they held. The Lady Toastmasters sponsored fundraisers for good causes, engaged in good works. Once I went with the group on a trip to the Utah State Prison to visit the women inmates. I remember the drab gray entry room where we waited before finally being admitted and how once inside the women's section, we sat with some of the inmates in a circle on folding chairs. Our leader looked around at the group of sad, unhappy women and said, How all you gals doin'?, then gave them a little pep talk.

Aside from the visits to my parents or John's parents, where we sometimes went for dinner, the outings with the Lady Toastmasters, for a brief time, constituted a sort of social life, even though I had nothing in common with the other women. It gave me something to do: it broke the tedium of the long hospital days.

During this period, John and I in some ways grew closer, drawn together by our fears and hopes for our son's future, by the ever-present need to comfort and help each other. In other ways discord began to set in, the result, I now think, of my growing unhappiness, and the loneliness and anxiety I often felt, both day and night.

And then one day everything changed: we were told Todd could come home from the Primary Children's Hospital. He was five, almost six, months old. Still very frail, but his health no longer as precarious as it had once been. Now the process of learning how to care for him began.

He had spent his first months of life in an isolette, wrapped in a woolly silence, rarely taken out of his little glass box. He'd almost never been held. And he'd only briefly been outdoors, twice carried quickly from the apartment or hospital to the car. I soon realized that even the ordinary sounds of the world were startling to him. Everything took him by surprise. How strange it must have been for him to experience the breeze on his face as we walked out of the hospital that day and headed across the parking lot. To feel the beating of my heart as I held him close to my chest, and smell my breath as I murmured words into his upturned face. How bright the sun must have been in his eyes!

FOUR

A few months after we brought Todd home from the hospital we
left the apartment in Bountiful and moved ninety miles south
to a town called Springville, which was also known as Art City. The
town had gotten this name as a result of a small museum, established
there in the 1920s by a group of Sunday painters and art enthusiasts.
Many businesses in the little town bore the name of Art City: the
Art City Drugstore, the Art City Drive-in, the Art City Cleaners.
But in spite of its name it was really a small agricultural town. The
same town where, a decade later, Nicole Baker would be living with
Gary Gilmore in a neighborhood like ours when he committed the
murders in Provo. It was easy to rent an inexpensive house if, like
Nicole, you were a single mother, nineteen, with two children. But
it was also a stable Mormon town, dominated by churchgoers. The
ranches and farms came right up to the edge of town, and when the
wind blew from a certain direction the strong smell of manure was
carried through the streets. Many of the farms lay in the fertile areas
to the west, near the large body of water known as Utah Lake, which
helped irrigate the region's lush crops.

John Thorn's father and stepmother lived in Springville and also
had some agricultural acreage out by the lake. The Thorns were one
of the oldest families in town, dating back to pioneer times, as were
the Huntingtons, my distant relatives. That was part of the reason we
decided to move there, so we could be near his parents while John
went back to school, at Brigham Young University, located in Provo,

only a few miles away. He wanted to keep going to school, to get his master's degree, become a psychologist with his own practice. I felt he could do this, because he was smart and good at listening to people. He had the sort of mind that liked solving problems.

That he couldn't solve mine wasn't his fault. The kind of unhappiness and anxiety I'd felt since getting married and giving birth didn't seem to me like it had a solution. I often thought, My life is set on a course and I am powerless to alter it. I felt trapped by circumstance. I wondered if there would ever again be a time when I would feel differently, when I wouldn't feel the weight of heavy responsibilities.

It wasn't that I didn't love my son. I had come to feel a fierce love for him. So fierce that the possibility of losing him kept me more or less constantly anxious. So much depended on our ability to care for him until he weighed thirty pounds and could have the next surgery, the major open-heart operation he needed. Thirty pounds, I would think, thirty pounds. There were months, years to go before he weighed that much, and during that time so much could change.

In Art City we rented a small white wooden house not far from John's parents on a street where a little canal ran down the center of the road. Nice trees, big old elms, lined the street. The house was only a few blocks from the shops on Main Street. I could put Todd in a stroller and walk down there if I got bored.

John began attending his classes that fall. At no point do I remember the possibility of my going to college being discussed. The idea was never even raised. Why? I ask myself this question now and the answer that comes to me is: You were a woman. And you were in Utah. It was my job to stay home and care for Todd, help him stay well. Just as it was John Thorn's job to support us and begin working toward his advanced degree.

Provo was full of fervent believers, young people who had just returned from their missions and were eager to get married and start families, couples who liked living close to the university, devoutly religious professors who taught there. We didn't socialize with these people. We made no friends among them. For the most part we kept to ourselves, went skiing on weekends when we could find a babysitter, had dinner with John's parents now and then, settled into small-town life.

We no longer went to church. Instead we skied on Sundays. We wouldn't have gone to church even if we hadn't gone skiing. Slowly, bit by bit, we'd simply fallen away. We'd stopped wearing our garments. One day I'd decided I couldn't do that anymore. I took them off and never put them on again. Later John would follow suit—but much later. I was the first to defect.

I didn't feel guilty about this. I felt relief. Life had been hard over the last couple of years. I didn't feel religion made it any easier. It made it harder, in fact. The rules and restrictions. The pressure to conform. The boringness of it. For many years I felt I'd been leading something of a double life. We liked having a beer after skiing. I still smoked when I felt like it. We didn't want to feel guilty about this, or hide what we did. But my aversion ran even deeper than these superficial things. I resented the way men ruled over everything in the church. The way some of the brethren had behaved toward me in the past. I did not have that thing everyone in the church talked about, and that was a *testimony*. I wondered if I ever had. Instead I had questions, objections, and disbelief. There was no pleasure left in attending meetings. I didn't like going to church and didn't feel I had to anymore. If I was old enough to care for a sick baby, wasn't I old enough to make my own decisions?

I felt an oppressiveness lift from me as I grew farther and farther away from the church. I found myself caring less and less what my parents thought. They still occasionally made remarks to others about my marrying John, though they treated us well enough to our faces. But why try to please them anymore? And why attend a church I no longer believed in, if I ever had?

My parents seemed to accept that I had drifted away. I had, in some way, always been incorrigible in their eyes. Why try to reform me now? Especially when I was no longer their responsibility? When my actions didn't necessarily reflect badly on them, since I lived seventy miles away and not in the same town? It would be wrong to imply that they didn't show John and me many kindnesses during this period, or that they didn't surround Todd with love: they did. I often felt their empathy. I knew they understood how difficult things had been for me, how at a young age I'd been forced to shoulder so much responsibility, as they often put it. Perhaps this is why they didn't interfere, why it didn't seem to matter much to them when I stopped going to church.

It seemed to me Art City was full of young women like myself, bored girls who had married too young, then gotten pregnant and had a kid or two and now felt the insistent heel of responsibility pressing down on their necks. Teenage mothers who spent their days pushing strollers around town, struggling in the heat in the summer and hauling their children around in bulky snowsuits in the winter. Soon I joined their ranks.

The house we'd moved into was cold in the winter, with frigid air leaking in around the old windows and doors. We stapled plastic sheeting over the outside of the windows to keep out the wind, and the world became a gauzy-gray place, nothing outside distinct anymore.

We had no money and many bills and it soon became clear I needed to go to work to help us get by. John had found a part-time job selling water softeners but it wasn't enough. We sometimes argued about money now. We both felt stressed.

I got a job at the bank on Main Street working as a teller. Todd went to day care in a private home with four or five other kids, all of whom freely passed their germs around, causing colds that in him occasionally turned into pneumonia. For months he would be doing pretty much okay, and then an illness would strike and he'd be back

in the children's ward, in a hospital in Provo or Salt Lake City, and I'd feel guilty, and yet we couldn't afford for me to stop working. The truth was, I liked getting out of the house. I didn't mind the work, getting dressed up and going into the bank every day.

He slowly learned to walk on his stick-thin legs, waving his tiny blue hands in the air for balance. His stomach was abnormally distended, his lips blue, his tiny teeth dark from a lack of oxygen, but for the most part he had begun to look more like a normal little boy, though one who was seriously underweight. Still, it was becoming clear to John and me, as it was to anyone else who spent any time with him, that he was in no way retarded. Dr. Mortensen had been wrong. The beautiful boy, as it turned out, had a beautiful mind.

The drive-in window of the bank where I worked was its own tiny room, a partially glassed-in box where I sat alone on a stool, closed off from the rest of the bank, and waited for a customer to drive up. Sometimes when it was slow I wrote a poem. I didn't really know how to make a poem because I hadn't really ever read poetry, but I wrote what I thought a poem might be.

There was a carpeted room in the basement of the bank where we sometimes took our breaks, and I remember being down there one day and asking the vice president of the bank, whose name was Cal Thorn, if he'd like to hear some poetry I'd written. He looked at me with something like alarm on his face. When I'd finished reading two or three poems he said, Well . . . , indicating he needed to get back to work, and got up and left.

I wrote the poems as I sat on the stool in the drive-up window, thinking about things, waiting for a customer to arrive, looking out across the black parking lot toward the Art City Bowling Alley. I think I wrote them out of boredom and sorrow. The poems I wrote this way, though I have long since lost them, were no doubt just as predictable and shallow and sentimental as one would imagine, capable of flummoxing Cal Thorn, who probably didn't like it that I was writing poetry on bank time anyway.

I don't remember reading any books during the years we spent in Art City. Did I, and I just don't remember? What books would they have been? The truth is, I hadn't yet become a reader. Literature was an unexplored universe, though I know I must have occasionally looked at one of John Thorn's books from the classes he was taking because I still have some of those books on my shelves.

I do know during those years I felt a hunger that manifested itself in a kind of yearning. I was always reaching for something, I just didn't know what. John had an open, questioning mind and I know he must have discussed the ideas he was picking up in his classes with me but I can't recall these conversations. I just know that we were always capable of talking to each other about many different things, and his intelligence stimulated me during this time, his excitement about what he was learning.

Still, I went through periods of terrible blackness. I remember
one night when Todd had been sick for days and we'd gone through
many sleepless nights and I stood over his crib in the middle of the
night and held him by his shoulders and shook him as he screamed,
pleading with him to stop, until I frightened myself and collapsed in
tears.

Later John would say to me—much, much later—I now know
that you were very depressed during those years, but I didn't realize
it then. I just couldn't see it.

Sometimes when we were short on money, as we often were, I stole
a twenty from the bank and when my shift ended made it look like
an inexplicable mistake that my cash drawer didn't properly balance.
I justified this wrongness in various ways. To steal from a bank that
had so much money, this wasn't like taking something from a person,
but of course this was shady thinking. In later years I would come to
understand that stealing anything, at any time, anywhere, from anyone, is what keeps you feeling poor. It's what traps you morally, as
well as psychologically, in a warp of bereftness.

Some days when I wasn't working at the bank I'd ask my father-in-law
if I might come over and take a ride on one of the Arabian horses he
kept stabled in his backyard. He'd saddle a beautiful little bay mare
named Scheherazade and have her ready and I would head out toward
the countryside and into the foothills, the way I had done as a girl in
Ogden, and for a while I felt an old happiness return. In this way I
dispelled some of the anxiety I felt, the fear about a lack of money,
the anxiety about leaving Todd in day care, the unresolved question
of his future.

At work each afternoon I'd take a break with some of the other
girls who worked at the bank and we'd go to the Art City Drugstore
next door and sit at the counter and drink cherry Cokes and I'd listen
to them talk about the missionaries they were waiting for and what

they were going to do when they got home. Mostly what they were going to do was get married right away and quit their jobs and have children.

Some afternoons I'd walk over to the little art museum and wander around looking at pictures. The beautiful old building was filled with many early landscape paintings by Utah artists. Many of the paintings were made in the early part of the twentieth century when the church had paid for a group of Mormon artists to travel to Europe and study the latest styles in painting with the idea that when they returned they could make art that would be a credit to the religion.

It was my first experience of an art museum, this little museum in Art City. I liked wandering around and looking at the paintings. Many depicted a rural world, farms and ranches, horses and sheep, pastoral bucolic scenes familiar to me. Others celebrated the majestic red-rock country of Utah. There was one painting I especially liked, by a painter named Roy Butcher. When I thought of his name and what he'd painted, it seemed funny, though the painting wasn't humorous at all. Roy Butcher had depicted the slaughter of a hog. Why did this painting draw me so? The people didn't even have facial features, just round fleshy ovals. Loosely rendered figures bent over a table set outside under some trees, where a slaughtered pig had been laid out and was being sluiced with water. The workers were washing away the pig's blood. Light fell through trees onto the slaughtered pig and illuminated the red blood and the bright clothes of the farm workers. I could feel the action in the scene, smell the odors.

John's father, Bernell, and his uncles Roe and Kent were all pipe fitters and shared a close bond. Bernell and Roe and their wives lived next door to each other and the two brothers both worked at the local Geneva Steel plant, but Kent had taken a job overseas in Libya. He and his wife would spend months there and come back and tell stories about the life they led among the American oil workers and the local Libyan people, regaling us over the Sunday dinners we shared. Libya seemed as far away and unreal as the countries I had once imagined traveling to for the Peace Corps.

Every so often we'd drive the two hours to Ogden to visit my parents and have a meal with them. My youngest brother, Gregg, was the only child still living at home. But my sister, Marcia, and her husband, Denny, lived nearby on a farm once owned by Denny's father. The same farm where as a girl I had kept my horse.

Marcia had very much wanted kids but she'd been unable to conceive. It seemed ironic that I, who had not wanted to get pregnant, did so easily, while Marcia, who had so longed for children, was unable to conceive. Marcia and Denny had adopted a baby around the time Todd was born, a girl named Kelli, and a year later they adopted a boy, Mike. Now, when I visited her, our children could play together, though looking at her pink, healthy kids always reminded me of just how sick Todd still was. She was very kind to us, however, and often very helpful, as were my parents. But now, instead of feeling a kind of low-level censure from them for having married John and later left the church, I felt their pity for having had a baby with so many problems. Neither sentiment left me feeling very good.

Once we visited my parents when my grandmother Freeman from Snowflake was staying with them and she met Todd for the first time. This was when he was about a year old and his fragility and blueness, his dark lips and nails, could easily shock someone. Later my grandmother mentioned our visit in her diary: *Judy came to dinner,* she wrote, *with her afflicted babe.*

Her afflicted babe. I knew this was how other people saw him, but when I looked at my son, what I saw was the beautiful boy.

It was during one of these visits to my parents that they announced they were moving to Spain. My father had arranged to be transferred from Hill Air Force Base to an American Air Force base just outside Madrid called Torrejón. He would keep the same job, do the same work over there, and their move would be entirely paid for by the government. They were going to rent out their house in Ogden. Ship their car and furniture to Madrid. Take my youngest brother, Gregg, thirteen years old, their last child at home, and go to Spain to live.

I think my father saw this move as maybe his last chance at adventure. It fit with the image he had of himself as somebody who could do something daring, like take a raft down the wild rapids of the Green River. And he did have this side to him—the daring, adventurous side. Still, it surprised me when he said they were moving to Spain for a few years, at least until he was eligible for retirement. I thought it was a very exciting idea, but they were almost sixty. Never mind that they had never traveled much beyond the American West and didn't speak Spanish. They wouldn't need to, my father said. He'd be working on an American base where everyone spoke English. And besides, as my mother pointed out, they could go anywhere in the world and they'd find people like them. All they'd have to do, she said, is go to church and they'd have *instant friends*.

There came a point during the following spring when Todd was sick more often than he was well. He turned two and still was nowhere close to weighing thirty pounds. He began to manifest the symptoms of heart failure. He began sliding backward.

He grew listless and cried easily. It was clear he often felt distressed. At his next appointment with the cardiologist, Dr. Veasy sat us down and talked to us frankly. He said nothing more could be done for Todd by the doctors in Utah. He was unlikely to grow any stronger or gain much more weight. He felt his condition was worsening and it was better to consider an operation now than to wait any longer. We needed to take him either to Texas or to Minnesota, where such operations were being performed. Both places had excellent surgeons—the best in the country for the procedure that Todd needed. We should consider taking him to one of these medical centers very soon. As risky as the surgery would be, it would be better not to wait any longer.

We chose Minnesota. Arrangements were made with the Variety Club Heart Hospital at the University of Minnesota Medical Center to check him in as soon as we could arrive.

We had decided to move to Saint Paul. Some months before, John had applied and been accepted into the doctoral program in psychology at the University of Minnesota. Todd could have his surgery there. John would begin school in the fall. And me? I imagined I'd do what I had always done. I'd take care of the beautiful boy.

We were leaving Utah. We were going someplace where Todd might have a chance of surviving the surgery he badly needed. This was all that mattered.

And so on a hot July morning in 1967 we drove away from Art City, heading east for Saint Paul.

PART SIX

❖

Reconfiguring the Heart

ONE

I had never been east of the Rockies until that summer when we drove to Saint Paul with our belongings loaded in a VW Bug and our dog, Jacques, nestled atop a stack of blankets piled on the backseat.

The farther we drove into the Midwest, the more overcome I felt by the humidity and heat. After so many years of living in the West where the air was dry it was a startling change. The journey was long, hot, and very worrisome, with Todd growing sicker each day. There was no air conditioning in the car. I held him on my lap for much of the trip, with the hot wind blowing in through the open window. He was two and a half years old but still small for his age, and he was growing worse by the hour. He became more and more listless as the trip wore on. We stopped at fast-food restaurants and ate in the car so we could just keep driving. We ended up driving late into the night, sleeping a few hours, and then pushing on.

When we arrived in Saint Paul we drove directly to the Variety Club Heart Hospital at the University of Minnesota Medical Center, where the doctors were expecting us. Todd was immediately checked in. He was running a fever. His liver was depressed due to the enlargement of his heart. One of the first things they did was submerse him in a bath of ice water to bring down his temperature, with him screaming as I stood by his side feeling helpless.

And then he was checked into a room, and when he'd gone to sleep that night we walked away and left him there, in yet another hospital, in a strange city.

Before we left Utah John had been in touch with a professor at the University of Minnesota who had helped him get into the doctoral program. This was Dr. Clyde Parker, a Mormon originally from Utah. He and his wife, Eileen, were planning on spending the summer in Utah with their three children, and they had offered us a housesitting job while they were away. We went to the Parkers' that night after leaving the hospital. They had not left for Utah yet: they wanted to be there when we arrived so they could show us how everything worked.

I liked Dr. Parker and his wife immediately. They felt to me like the sort of people I had known all my life, except they were better educated, had a worldliness and sophistication. They were a handsome couple, had traveled and spent time in India on a Fulbright. Their children were beautiful and smart. They lived in a large house in a wealthy suburb of Saint Paul, just a few blocks from a small lake where they kept a canoe and often picnicked.

During the few days we spent with them before they left for Utah, I felt enfolded by a happy family, safely ensconced in a beautiful house. It seemed to me things might be okay here, that they might work out in this place we had moved to, if only Todd could be made well.

But he could not be made well, or at least not right away. The pediatric cardiologists who assessed his situation felt that he would need to stay in the hospital for at least a few weeks to build up his strength and bring him up to the best possible condition for the surgery. There was no guarantee he could even be operated on. This would be up to the surgeon, whom we would meet later.

The time we spent alone in the Parkers' house after they had left for Utah, during this period when Todd was awaiting the surgery, felt rather like a vacation to me. I was in a new and interesting place. I still spent hours every day at the hospital, and I was never without worry, but when I came back to the Parkers' I sometimes walked down to the lake and lay on the sand in the late-afternoon sun and felt a peacefulness enfold me. I watched the clouds, or took a swim, or simply rested until the sun set. One night John and I took the canoe out to the middle of the lake and sat quietly in the darkness. You could hear the wind, creatures stirring on the bank.

Our relationship seemed to improve for a while. Fewer arguments. Less tension between us, less worry about money. It was as if the new environment, the nice house and neighborhood, so pleasant, so full of comforts, so much nicer than anything we'd known, lifted us up and made us both feel better. John was excited by the prospect of starting his classes in the doctoral program in the fall. I was simply happy to be in such a safe, pleasant place, where I felt I could relax, take walks, sit by the water when I felt like it, explore my new surroundings.

One day a neighbor of the Parkers' invited me to a picnic at the lake with her children. It had been a long time since anyone had asked me to do something like that. We sat on blankets at the edge of the water and watched her children play. We talked about Todd. She knew I was a Mormon, like the Parkers, but she didn't make a big deal out of this. In fact she didn't even mention it. She had brought oxtail soup in a thermos for the picnic. It seemed like strange picnic food to me, but I found it delicious. Later she offered to give me the recipe. It seemed terribly complicated. I couldn't imagine myself making such a thing. Oxtails! She was a handsome, sophisticated woman who treated me as an equal, even though I was much younger, and I went away from the picnic feeling happy.

I felt as if something were finally happening to me. Something *different*. I was twenty years old. Hadn't I longed to be out in the world? And wasn't I out in it now?

Through Dr. Parker, John got a job that started in the fall. It was at this moment that everything changed.

He was hired to be a counselor and dorm director at Macalester College, a small liberal-arts college in Saint Paul. The modern, five-story dormitory on campus, Dupre Hall, had for the first time gone coeducational that year, with the men and women students separated by floor. We were going to be the dorm parents in Dupre Hall during the first year of this new experiment, and John would also act as the in-residence student counselor.

In the fall we moved into the ground-floor apartment of Dupre Hall, which, with its Danish modern furnishings, two large bedrooms, and contemporary decor, felt like the nicest place we'd ever lived. At the age of twenty, never having gone to college myself, I became a dorm mother in a dorm where half the students were older than me.

I found out that as the wife of a faculty member I could take classes at Macalester for free when the fall semester began. Any class I wanted, as long as there was room. It was as if, with no particular effort on my part, I had just won the grand prize in a contest I'd never even known how to enter.

TWO

I can picture distinctly the moment when we first met the heart surgeon.

One day, a few weeks after we had arrived in Saint Paul, John and I were summoned to a hallway outside our son's room in the Variety Club Heart Hospital to speak with a slim, elegant man who introduced himself and told us he would be operating on our son the next day.

He wore a crisp white coat with a stethoscope hanging around his neck. The coat was open and I could see that his initials had been monogrammed on the pocket of his shirt. He wore thin tortoiseshell glasses, had a lean, handsome face with high cheekbones, and his light brown hair was swept back from his forehead. His hands were beautiful, with long, delicate fingers. He held his chin in one hand as he first looked at us, and that is why I noticed his hands.

When he spoke I heard an accent, though his English was perfect. His name had previously been mentioned to us as the man who would perform the surgery Todd needed, and this name had sounded Spanish to me. I felt surprised to see how light-skinned he was. He seemed to be one of those men who might only rarely have to shave.

He spoke in a very professional manner, but somehow from the beginning I sensed he was very curious about us. Right away he made an effort to get us to talk about ourselves. I liked that he had done this. It helped me relax for the conversation to come, and no doubt he knew this.

He said he understood we were from Utah, which he had heard

was a very beautiful place. He asked us how long we had been in Minnesota. This sort of chitchat went on for a few minutes, with him studying us intently all the while, and then he turned to the subject he'd come to talk to us about.

He said he had examined our son and looked at his medical records and as we must know, the situation was not ideal. In fact, he said, pursing his lips slightly as if pondering how to put it, the situation is rather lousy.

"Lousy," I would later realize, was a word he favored and used a lot. In time I'd come to see how much he loved American slang and got a kick out of flattening his vowels and adding a little nasal twang to certain words, as if emulating a hickish American. He would do this just for his own amusement and to entertain me. I would come to understand how much he loved the elasticity of American English, how it could engender in him a certain kind of intellectual play.

Yes, he said, the situation was rather lousy. This couldn't be denied. It wasn't ideal, he added, not at all what he would wish. Our son wasn't in the best condition for surgery, as we no doubt knew, but to wait any longer was to take a chance he'd deteriorate further. So he had decided to operate the next day. The surgery would begin early. Todd was the first patient he'd scheduled in the morning.

We talked a bit more about the operation. He added a few details, and then he said that to be honest he thought there was a fifty-fifty chance our son could make it, given his condition and the difficulty of the surgery. But—and he uttered this word crisply, giving it full weight and then pausing as if to take the sting out of the percentage he'd just given us—but, he said soberly, looking at us, we will do everything we can. We'll do our best.

He looked at us directly and held our eyes for a moment, and in that look I felt his heart going into everything he had said.

The odds, for some reason, didn't frighten me. I thought they were fairly good. What John thought I didn't know. At least, I reasoned, there's a fifty percent chance he'll make it.

I was aware of the way the heart surgeon continued to study us. I could feel him thinking, A young couple from Utah—*very* young. But now I was the one who was curious. Who *was* he?

He offered to draw a little picture for us, showing what he'd be doing during the operation. With a blue pencil, he began sketching a heart and some vessels on a pad of paper, and then added a complicated pattern of arrows.

After he drew the picture he asked if we had any questions.

I asked how long the surgery would last, just to say something.

He didn't know, it would all depend, but perhaps a few hours.

John asked if anyone would be able to come out of the operating room to tell us how it was going during that time. He said possibly someone could come out if needed.

As he prepared to leave I asked him if I could have the little picture of the heart he had drawn. He smiled and looked down at me. Of course, he said, and handed it over.

Then he touched my shoulder and shook John's hand and turned to leave, saying he hoped all would go well tomorrow.

I watched him stride away down the hallway, not hurrying, but walking slightly bent forward, his head down and his long white coat flapping, making no noise whatsoever in his crepe-soled shoes.

This walk, too, I would come to know. The light but purposeful stride. He moved like a very fit man. Every move he made was dictated by his light frame, his natural elegance, like an athlete to whom a lifelong love of sports had lent agility. He had the walk of a younger man even though I put his age at around thirty-five or forty, which at that time seemed rather old to me.

Todd made it through the surgery, the long and complicated operation. Apparently, he was still a fighter. Still capable of beating the odds.

When the surgeon came out he still wore his scrubs and a green elasticized bonnet over his head.

He said Todd was far from being out of the woods but for now the news was good. It had been very touch-and-go during the operation. The next few days were critical. He was now in intensive care, where he would remain for a time. The surgeon said we could see him for just a brief few minutes.

What I saw shocked me. He was lying on his back, connected to machines by various tubes. He had a massive incision running down his small torso, from his neck to his small swollen belly. It intersected the old scar running under his arm. Tubes were stitched into his sides for drainage. Naked and heavily sedated, his eyes were slightly open, a look so dull showing in that small space it made it hard to believe he was even there. We stood over him for a few moments, touching his small curled fingers, and then were led from the room.

A day or two later, the heart surgeon asked to talk to us. He did not look happy. He looked very grim.

Our son, he said, had somehow developed a staph infection in his wound.

That's what he called the incision: a *wound*.

The incision would have to be reopened so the staph could heal from the inside out. This was the way it worked, he said. Staph must be dealt with by opening an incision and then leaving it open.

For how long? I asked.

Until the wound heals and the staph is expelled from the body.

But how long does this take? I asked again.

Several months, he said. Perhaps a bit longer in this case. His sternum, which had been split for the surgery, had already been unwired and the wound reopened. He had been moved to an isolation room where everything was kept sterile. In order to visit him now we would have to wear a gown and mask and paper slippers over our shoes and we would not be able to touch him. He was very sorry, the surgeon said. Very, very sorry. It was a complication that hadn't been foreseen, and a very serious one.

❖   ❖   ❖

We went home that afternoon to the apartment in the dorm we had recently moved into. Two days earlier, my parents had arrived. They wanted to be there when Todd was operated on, and they had made it just in time, arriving the night before his surgery, but now they were leaving. They seemed exhausted. I could feel how deeply worried they were about Todd. My father, especially, was very frail. They both were anxious to get home.

They had come to us directly from Spain. Spain hadn't worked out for them. Todd's operation had given them a good excuse to return to the States, but they had already by then decided to move back to Ogden.

My father hadn't been happy in Madrid. Things hadn't turned out the way he'd hoped they would. I think he found it hard to live among foreigners in a strange city. And he didn't much like his job. Less than a month after he arrived he began to feel homesick, and one day in the commissary during lunchtime he'd suffered a grand mal seizure that was so severe his spine had been wrenched and his arms severely injured as people attempted to hold him down. He had crushed vertebrae and dislocated both shoulders and spent a month recuperating in the hospital on base, and during that time all he could think about was returning home, by way of Minnesota, to be with us in time for Todd's operation.

They both looked different to me after their ordeal in Spain. My father had lost weight, my mother had gained pounds. Neither one looked terribly well. I was glad they had come. I knew it hadn't been easy for them to get there in time. But I could also see how anxious they were now to leave.

The day they left I went to visit Todd, who had been moved to a special isolation room. I had to put on the gown and booties and cover my hair and put on special gloves and a mask in order to enter.

He was still heavily sedated, though more conscious than the last time I'd seen him. Still, he showed no signs of recognizing me. There was a nurse in the room with him and she offered me a chair by the bed. When a young doctor arrived—a doctor I had not seen before—the nurse asked him if she might leave for a minute and said she'd be back shortly.

When she didn't come back right away, the doctor asked me if I'd be willing to help him. He needed to irrigate the wound, he said, and it would help to have my assistance. Of course I agreed.

What I was not prepared for was what happened next. The young doctor—I wondered: Was he an intern? A resident?—raised the head of my son's bed so his torso was elevated. He filled a sterile syringe with a sterile saline solution, and unwrapped a small curved metal pan that had been sterilized, and then he began removing the bandages from Todd's chest, revealing something I could never have imagined.

He was open from his neck to his stomach. An opening several inches wide. I looked at the inside of my son's chest. I could see the two sides of his sternum where it had been split, the end bones visible. Between them were organs, vessels, cartilage, an unidentifiable pink interior, glistening and bright. Slippery, slick stuff, shifting as he breathed.

It was all I could do to hold steady. The young doctor seemed unaware of my discomfort. He handed me the little curved pan and told me to hold it against Todd's belly at the bottom edge of the wound to catch the water as he squirted it into his chest, flushing out blood and bits of stuff.

When he finished he thanked me, then gently patted the wound dry with sterile squares of gauze and rebandaged his chest. Throughout all this Todd made no noise. He seemed barely conscious, unaware of what was happening.

The nurse returned and the doctor left. And then I took off the protective coverings and also left the room.

I went directly to the ladies' room at the end of the corridor, where I sat in a stall and sobbed.

❖   ❖   ❖

Later that night I had a miscarriage. I hadn't been certain I was preg-nant because I hadn't yet seen a doctor but I had missed a period and I'd begun to feel the old familiar sickness that had plagued my first pregnancy. I don't think I had even told John yet that I felt sure I was pregnant again.

I had returned to the hospital that night and that's where I was when the severe cramps began. I went back to the same ladies' room I'd visited earlier in the day and sat in the same stall, bent over in pain, until I finally expelled something I knew was not a blood clot.

What did I feel at that moment?

All these years later I struggle to remember and I find it hard to sort out this difficult moment from the others that engulfed me that day. The shock I'd experienced looking down at my son earlier in the day and seeing not just the outside of him but the inside as well. The feeling of that life slipping out of me. Both moments retain an imprint of interior life suddenly being exposed to an exterior sphere, and these two abnormalities had somehow melded, so that what was happening to my son's body and what was happening to mine became somehow connected in memory, embedding themselves in my mind as one thing that happened that day, and not two.

I couldn't have managed another pregnancy, not sensing what was going to be required of me in the months to come. Yet I would never have ended that pregnancy on my own. I was shaken when I stood up and left the bathroom stall that night. But I know I also felt relieved. Of course this was only one of the things I felt, perhaps the most unacknowledged, the least pressing, the most deeply buried, as I made my way out of the hospital and headed home.

THREE

Each day he grew a little stronger and more alert in spite of the large opening in his chest. Often now when the bandage was changed I stayed in the room and watched in order to learn what I would need to know when he was finally well enough to come home, and although he remained critical I did believe that one day this would happen. He would be well enough to leave the hospital.

Once again I found myself living between worlds. My days were spent at the hospital, and in the evenings I returned to the apartment in Dupre Hall, which still did not feel like home to me—these rooms on the ground floor of a five-story dormitory filled with students I didn't yet know.

The campus of Macalester College was to me a new and exciting place to be. So much activity all the time, all of it occurring right around me in the dormitory and the common areas just outside our apartment. The moment I left "home" I stepped outside into the world of students and professors, with the wide lawns and old brick buildings creating a feeling of a contained and slightly separate realm, bordered by two busy streets, Snelling and Summit Avenues. To have just come from Springville and the drive-up window of a bank, to have lived such a quiet life in that little white house in that small farming town, and now to find myself in this different world in Saint Paul. It might have been uncomfortable or intimidating but it didn't feel that way. Instead it felt as if I had finally come to the place where I wanted to be.

I began meeting the students in Dupre Hall. There was a girl from Mississippi named Judy B. who had long dark hair and an intense presence. Her Southern accent and manners seemed very exotic to me. I had never met anyone who wanted to be a writer, who had already decided this is what she would be. She was so smart—so knowledgeable about books and music. She introduced me to Leonard Cohen. The *Concierto de Aranjuez*. William Faulkner. She came from Greenville, Mississippi, and she talked about that place as if it were a different country.

I met a tall, lively girl from a wealthy suburb of Chicago named Connie and her boyfriend, David. Also a beautiful blond girl from Dubuque, also named Judy, and her Italian boyfriend, Franco, an exchange student at Macalester.

There was a girl from the East named Mary with a blooming red birthmark on her face who refused to hide it with makeup and who would later return from an internship in Europe where she had witnessed the Prague Spring. She was a theology major and struck me as the most intellectual woman I had ever met.

There were students studying art, others studying dance, some who wished to be writers. Dupre Hall was filled with interesting young people with active, vibrant minds who were eager to get to know us, this young couple from the West who had moved into the director's apartment.

Mrs. Stryker, a portly, affable middle-aged woman, sat at the front desk, just inside the entrance to the dorm, greeting students as they came and went and announcing visitors. The students liked to hang out with her; she had an easy way about her that made her very popular.

All of these people took an intense interest in our lives. In the fact we'd come from Utah, had both grown up as Mormons. But here everyone had a background of some sort, and it could often appear unusual. Everyone came from somewhere different. It was all part of the greater curiosity of being a college student.

They knew we had a young son in the university hospital recovering from open-heart surgery and in some way this made us even more interesting. When would he come home so they could meet him? they'd ask.

When would he come home? Not for some time. We knew that. Meanwhile John Thorn had a job to do, and in certain ways so did I.

On Parents' Weekend, when I was introduced to the fathers and mothers of the students as the dorm mother in Dupre Hall, I knew these parents looked at me as if some mistake had been made. How could I, this girl who looked younger than their daughters and sons— who *was* younger than many of them—possibly be the dorm mother?

This was the fall of 1967. Every week demonstrations against the Vietnam War were held on campus. Students stood at the corner of Snelling and Summit Avenues, just beyond the windows of our apartment, holding signs and chanting antiwar slogans. In Utah the Vietnam War was something I had hardly paid any attention to but here it was front and center. The students constantly discussed the war and their objections to it, and the faculty often joined in. For the first time I saw how the country was being divided. I felt the immorality of the war. It did not take me long, in the presence of students who were always discussing Vietnam, to decide how I felt. I began to form opinions about things I hadn't paid much attention to before.

This was the height of the civil rights movement, which also deeply engaged the students. Macalester was a liberal place with a racial mixture to the student body. It wasn't at all like Brigham Young University, the only other campus I was even slightly familiar with. At BYU the students were almost all white. Their behavior and appearance were tightly controlled. If there was any question, the girl students had to kneel down to prove their skirts touched the ground and weren't too short, and the boys' hair couldn't reach below their collars. Classes often started with prayer. Everyone believed in the same religion, leveling the intellectual field. And everyone was required to obey the authorities, both the church leaders in Salt Lake City and those on campus. This was one of the first principles of the gospel, this obedience to authority. It was what made us *good* Mormons.

Here at Macalester the students and faculty hadn't gotten that message. Here the questioning of authority was encouraged as part of developing a critical and independent way of thinking.

In the beginning I didn't talk much about my past: I wanted to minimize the great difference I felt. But I could see how the students were emboldened by their questioning, even the questioning of their own lives, and their parents', the ways in which they'd been raised. I could see it was part of their strength, what made them *students*. Their mistrust of the establishment tapped into feelings I could share. And gradually I began to reveal more about myself and the place I had come from—the patriarchal culture that had formed me, the religious culture in which I'd been raised. I had something to contrast it with, a different way of trying to make sense of it.

The students in the dorm were taken up by discussions of the free-love movement, the hippies and beats, the speeches of Dr. Martin Luther King, and books and films from different cultures, and they began to pass these enthusiasms on to me at the discussions that were often held in our apartment at night, and at various events held on campus, from the screening of foreign movies to debates in the student union.

I felt my mind being challenged and stimulated. I had come to the place where this could happen. I began to understand that Macalester wasn't just *any* college—it was a very, very good one, really top-notch, a kind of elite private institution costing a lot of money to attend. I knew luck had favored me beyond anything I could have imagined. Only a few months earlier it would have been impossible for me to envision myself in a place like this.

I took note of everything. I noticed how the students wore interesting clothes. Tie-dyed shirts. Bright colors. They dressed very creatively, wore their hair long, even the boys, and the girls often didn't wear makeup the way the Mormon girls did, affecting that Marie

Osmond look. They didn't appear to be interested in superficial glamour. They felt it was better to be natural.

The students—both the men and the women—talked openly about sex. They felt no embarrassment or shame. They used birth control, took responsibility, seemed mature about these matters. This is what surprised me the most: the girls were just as sexually active as the guys and they didn't pay a price for it. I couldn't sense the same double standard here that I'd always known at home.

This was the moment, during these first few months at Macalester, when I began to feel relief in various senses.

There was the relief of relaxing with the students who were becoming my friends—I who had not really had many friends since high school.

There was the relief from the tension and tedium, of feeling my life was fated to forever be set on a course I couldn't alter.

There was the relief from financial worry. We had a free roof over our heads, as well as a paycheck and even free meals at the cafeteria on campus, which meant I didn't have to cook if I didn't feel like it, and the cafeteria was right next to the dorm.

I felt relief as each day passed and Todd grew a little stronger, regained his mental alertness and physical strength, and the doctors began expressing a cautious optimism about his future. I felt relieved to see that each day he was in less pain.

And I felt a sense of relief in another, quite profound sense: it was now that my Mormon background began to stand out in a way it never had before. In Utah I remained a kind of undifferentiated part of the norm, but here a Mormon was anything but the norm. Here my own strangeness was brought home to me, and not in a bad way but as a kind of ineluctable feature of my biography. I began to realize this Mormon background would retain an inescapable prominence in my life, whether I wished it to or not, that it would always color the perception of who I was, both in my own mind and in the minds of others who met me.

❖ ❖ ❖

I knew I was different from the students who surrounded me, but they didn't make me feel as if my difference was a liability. They didn't seem to care that I hadn't been to college, that I didn't know the books or music they were always talking about, that I married young and already had a little boy. What they seemed to accept was my curiosity and my interest in learning, my eagerness to discuss everything with them that they were talking about. They treated me as if I were just as smart as they were. Almost everyone had come from the East or the Midwest and just as they seemed rather exotic to me, I understood I appeared exotic to them. I was a Westerner. I wore cowboy boots and jeans on campus when almost no one else was wearing cowboy boots. I must have talked a lot about my love of the West, because one day Judy B., who had become my closest friend in the dorm, made me a little book of drawings and words titled "Out West Where I Come From."

I think this must have been something I said a lot in those days: Out west where I come from . . .

I saw that my Westernness was a great part of what had shaped me and made me who I was. Everything about where I was born and the people I came from began to appear more distinctive to me, and, in a way, more *peculiar*.

Connie, one of my friends in the dorm, turned out to share my love of horses, and together we began driving out to a stable in a suburb of Saint Paul to take riding lessons from a strict German instructor named Herr von Blucher. I learned how to ride English, how to take his well-schooled horses over jumps, and I found this new way of riding exhilarating. We rode even in winter when we had to dress in thick layers of clothing to withstand the cold in the unheated indoor arena.

It must have also been Connie who took me to the nearby Unitarian church one Sunday to attend a service for the first time. What

struck me was how liberal and open-minded both the congregation
and the pastor were—how engaged with social issues. The sermon
that day revolved around the antiwar movement. I understood for
the first time what great differences there were in what religions
allowed—what got discussed from the pulpit, what might constitute
a subject worthy of spiritual or moral consideration. I went back
the next Sunday, intrigued by the sermon I'd heard. I saw how the
Unitarians, as opposed to the Mormons, were unafraid to promote
questioning and free thinking. They encouraged individuals to follow
their moral conscience. It wasn't about obeying religious authority.
Nor was it about saving the world through proselytizing.

Ecumenism was then a very popular idea on campus and the students often talked about this notion of unity and parity among all
the world's religions. I found this way of thinking very liberating and
attractive. There was no *one true church* as I'd been taught. There was
no Church of the Devil but rather a universal, all-embracing idea of
religion that took its name from the Greek word *oikoumene,* meaning
"the inhabited earth."

Even before I enrolled in my first classes that fall I had begun to
receive an education simply by being with such bright students and
joining in the discussions held in our living room. The students liked
John; they trusted him and came to him with their problems. They
liked to hang out with us in our apartment. The talk sessions held
there often felt like some combination of group therapy and an informal party where books and music, as well as politics and social issues,
got discussed for hours, late into the night. Religion. War. Justice. As
well as Fellini, Antonioni, Faulkner.

Todd was still in the hospital when the semester began. I enrolled in
a literature class taught by a man named Roger Blakely and also an
art class, drawing from the nude. These were my first two college
courses, art and literature.

The syllabus for the literature class included books by Thomas

Hardy, Virginia Woolf, D. H. Lawrence, John Galsworthy, and Henry James. I wasn't sure I'd ever even heard of these authors. But now all that would change. The important thing, I understood, was that I simply begin somewhere, and that somewhere was here.

The first book we read was Hardy's *Tess of the d'Urbervilles*. There were a dozen students in the class and many were already familiar with Hardy's writing; I could tell this from the comments they made in class. These students seemed almost as smart as the instructor, Mr. Blakely, a small, wizened man with thick glasses and a slightly pocked complexion who sat behind his desk at the front of the room with a cigarette in hand, perpetually squinting at us through the rising smoke. He cultivated a sort of impish persona and delighted in provoking spirited debates.

When he found out I came from Utah he smiled slyly and said, Ah, those Mormons! As if he understood something I didn't.

Tess claimed my full attention and interest. I felt taken up by Hardy's tale of a young rural girl from a poor family who is seduced by a roué, left pregnant and shamed, whose baby is born frail and sickly and dies at four months and who later is courted by the son of a minister, who refuses to hear about her past. I felt I knew this girl. This child of nature who preferred being outside. A girl with six siblings and a weak mother and a domineering dreamer of a father. I recognized the way her father put on airs when he discovered his aristocratic lineage, though he remained dirt poor. I recognized the landscape Hardy was writing about. Wessex wasn't the American West but it could have been. The fecund sense of the earth pervading Tess's world—the *oozing fatness and warm ferments* of spring coming on, the connection to nature and birds and the rhythms of the seasons. This is what I had felt in my youth.

Tess's unsophisticated open-air existence and her ripe beauty, which, as Hardy wrote, *required no varnish of conventionality to make it palatable to the opposite sex,* also struck a note. I remembered the easy attractions, the elder standing on his porch waiting for me to ride by, the looks I was wont to receive as I grew older, the male gaze with its burden of guilt—which Hardy described as *the wretched sentiment that had often come to her before, that in inhabiting the fleshy tabernacle with which nature had endowed her she was somehow doing wrong.*

Tess's life was tremulous—*there be very few women's lives that are not,* Hardy wrote—and I had felt that tremulousness. Tess, in the face of her accusers and those who judged her, had a passivity I understood all too well. And Tess was a pagan, a nonbeliever: she had come to dislike the *scheme of religion* and instead believed in having an ethical system without the dogma—a religion, as she put it, of loving kindness.

Still, for all the connection I felt to the story and all the enthusiasm I tried to bring to the discussion of the novel in class, at the end of that discussion I found myself unable to answer the question that Mr. Blakely put to me. Who, he asked, do you think was the greater evil to Tess—the wealthy roué Alec d'Urberville, who deceived and impregnated her, consigning her to a shamed existence but who later comes to her rescue, or Angel Clare, the would-be gentleman farmer and son of a minister who fell in love with the milkmaid Tess, never allowing her to reveal her sordid past, and then upon discovering it on their wedding night abandoned her, leaving her to toil in poverty and misery?

Who *was* the greater evil? How could I judge this?

I couldn't answer the question. I didn't begin to know what to say, and I told Mr. Blakely so. Instead, I spent years thinking about it, wondering if in fact there even was an answer to such a question. Weren't both men injurious to her? How to determine the greater blame?

FOUR

Todd slowly grew stronger over the course of that fall. He could not yet leave the hospital but he was eventually moved from isolation into an ordinary room in the children's ward. He had a roommate now—the boy who had no visitors. He could walk about during the day for short periods on his delicate little legs, with the thick bandage beneath his shirt puffing out like a bird's breast. Poking along down the hallway like a little robin. Great care had to be taken that he didn't fall or bump his chest, but he could now spend time in the common room playing with other children.

One day several of the children began throwing wooden blocks at each other. Stop it! I cried, jumping to my feet. Stop it now! And they obeyed.

The heart surgeon continued to follow Todd's progress, stopping by to check on him almost every day. Often he did this early in the morning when I hadn't yet arrived at the hospital but occasionally our paths would cross. When this happened I noticed he always took time to talk with me and I often felt him studying me, as if trying to figure something out, though I had no idea what this thing might be. I only knew he was very kind to me, and I found his attention reassuring and helpful. I thought he went out of his way to humor me, to make me feel optimistic about Todd's future. He had a lovely, intelligent lightness about him. It was as if this lightness meant he couldn't stay in a room too long, but during the time he was there he captivated you so easily you weren't even aware how this was hap-

pening until he'd gone. His foreignness lent him a certain exoticism,
though I knew nothing about his background. Just the accent. The
completely different manners, and the very cultured way of speaking.
Compared to the other doctors, he seemed aristocratic to me.

One day I sat alone on a bench outside the double doors leading to
a wing of the hospital where a test was being performed on Todd to
evaluate his progress. His reconfigured heart seemed to be working
well but still tests had to be run. John was attending classes that day
on the campus of the University of Minnesota, a short distance away.
We'd agreed to meet later. I had been sitting alone for some time,
just outside the double doors, waiting for the procedure to end, for
Todd to come out so I could accompany him back to his room. I
had been daydreaming, letting my mind wander, half-bored by the
waiting.

It was midday, the beginning of winter. A kind of calm whiteness
surrounded me, the whiteness of the hospital corridor and the white
doors I stared at and the white light of a bright sunny winter day,
with white snow covering the ground just outside the nearby window. I found myself staring out of this window from time to time.
The sun glinted off the windshields of the cars in a parking lot, creating pinpoints of bursting, dazzling light. In all this whiteness and light
I found a kind of calm. I felt as if everything had been arrested, as if
time had stopped moving forward and instead was rising upward in a
steady column with me suspended at the center.

Suddenly the heart surgeon came out through the double doors
and for a moment I felt startled by the disruption his appearance
caused. I must have frowned or looked startled. He strolled up and
said hello and stood looking down at me.

Are you all right? he said. You look very sad today.

I told him I felt fine. I wouldn't have bothered telling him anything
else.

He indicated the spot on the bench next to me and asked if I would mind if he sat down for a moment. I said no, and he sat down next to me.

He said he had been thinking about my being from Utah. He had heard the skiing out there was very good. Was that true?

Yes, very good, I said, and added, We get the lightest snow, the deepest powder.

He said he was thinking of planning a ski trip out west. But he didn't know where to go. Colorado? Or maybe Utah? He'd never skied in the West before. He could use some advice.

Are you a skier? he asked me.

Yes, I said smiling, warming to the subject.

You must be very good, not a lousy amateur like me.

From the way he said this, I knew he was not an amateur at all.

I told him I had taught skiing before I left Utah. This was true. I had become certified to teach the winter before and taught on weekends at Solitude, the same resort where John Thorn had worked on the ski patrol. But as soon as I said this I felt embarrassed. It sounded like I was bragging when what I really had meant to say was a simple truth, that I loved to ski.

Aha, he said. An expert. I knew it.

Not really, I said. But there is great skiing in Utah. If you're interested I could tell you where to go.

You know, he said, hesitating for a moment, there's a little ski area a couple of hours north of here called Afton Alps. It's nothin' to write home about, he added in his slangy voice, but I've been there a few times. Perhaps we could go skiing there sometime. I have a day off next week.

He looked at me, his expression at once open and serious, as if this were an informal, rather natural suggestion for him to make.

The ease with which he presented this idea made it seem as if it were something he'd been thinking about for some time. But it caught me off guard. And yet immediately I said, Sure, I'd like to go. I could do that next week. I had heard about this place to ski in Minnesota and knew that it wasn't far away and I'd hoped to ski there one day.

Okay, he said, and then stood up as if he had somewhere to be. That lightness propelling him, the sense he had places to go. I felt he did not want to linger over his invitation. He named a day and a time in the following week when he would pick me up early in the morning, and we agreed to meet at the intersection of Snelling and Summit Avenues, on the corner of Macalester's campus near Dupre Hall. We'd ski for the day, he said, and be home by evening. And then he prepared to leave. He would see me next week, he said. He looked forward to it.

When he walked away, I knew that something had happened. Something beyond an invitation to go skiing. What had largely escaped me up until that moment now became very clear.

He was attracted to me.

Something had now been initiated.

And I knew in that instant it was something I wanted.

FIVE

When exactly did Todd come home from the hospital? Was it just a few weeks after that first day when the heart surgeon and I went skiing together?

His chest was still open when he was released. He had been in the hospital over two months and the doctors believed he would now do better at home, as long as John and I felt we could properly care for the wound. Each day we would have to irrigate it with sterile saline solution after removing the bandages, and then afterward carefully bandage his chest again. The day he was released, we were sent away with supplies of sterile syringes and bottles of saline solution and boxes of square gauze bandages and the special tape we would need to use to attach the bandages to his flesh. By this time we were familiar with the procedure, having watched it often. This was something we felt we could do. We took him back to the apartment in Dupre Hall and he began meeting the students, who immediately rallied around him. They were delighted to have a child in their midst, even one so frail. It was, in part, his vulnerability that made them so eager to help. They began appearing at our door, asking if they could watch him for the evening while we went out, or take him to the student union for an ice cream cone. They wanted to know if they might gently kick a ball around with him for a while on the grass. Everyone understood the need to be very watchful and careful with him. It would be disastrous if he should receive a blow to his chest. They understood this and they were mindful and I trusted them completely—Judy B. and Connie and David and Franco and Ken and Mary and all the others who wanted to help us. For so long I had felt protective of him, and now I wanted to let him go. I wanted our beautiful boy to begin having a beautiful life.

He began to lose his hospital pallor. He acquired color to his cheeks and his blond hair became lighter the more time he spent outside. It grew long and was now often wind-tousled when he came in after playing with the students. He gained weight, grew happier and more confident every day. And slowly I began to feel a new independence and freedom as well.

When the heart surgeon arrived to pick me up for skiing that first day, he pulled up in a little green sports car. We managed to somehow fit my skis inside next to his. He looked very different in his ski clothes. He seemed younger, more casual, not just in dress but in attitude. He wore blue stretch pants and an expensive-looking sweater and appeared rather debonair in his little sports car.

When we arrived at Afton Alps, I had to laugh: it looked like more of a hole in the ground than a ski hill. Nothing could have been more different from the big ski resorts I'd known in the Wasatch Mountains, but still, there were several chairlifts and the runs were covered with snow. At the bottom of the hill a little lodge was nestled in a stand of pines near the parking lot. I felt happy to think I was here. That I would soon be skiing again.

What soon became clear is what an excellent skier he was, though he made jokes about his advanced age and decrepit state as we rode up the lift together. He used the Arlberg method, a rather elegant style of skiing perfected by Austrians involving an erect stance on the skis and a countermovement of the shoulders during a turn, which made sense once he explained he had spent a part of his youth in Germany. This is where he'd learned to ski, he said, in the German and Austrian Alps.

That day, as we rode the lift and talked, he told me more about himself. He had been born in Italy, though his parents were both from Central America and this is where many members of his family continued to live. He often went back there to visit them. His youth, however, had been spent in Europe, where his grandfather had been an ambassador. He had lived in both France and Switzerland. His grandmother had been living in Germany during the war and while visiting her he and his mother had become trapped there by circumstances and had been forced to settle in to wait out the war. This was when he was a teenager. He had acquired his love of sports during this time, becoming not only an enthusiastic skier but a Ping-Pong champion and an avid tennis player as well.

We skied all that day, taking only short breaks for hot chocolate in the lodge. In his stylish ski clothes, with his strong good looks, he made an appealing sight. He carved his turns perfectly coming down the packed runs. He skied so smoothly he looked rather balletic: all was synchronous and lovely, rather elegant. It became clear to me that day he loved skiing just as much as I did.

I skied much faster, but I found myself slowing down for him because he began teasing me, saying I was going to kill him if I insisted on skiing so fast. And yet I could tell he, too, wanted to go fast. I found him often surging ahead of me on the runs.

It was clear, very clear, that first day that we were both having a good time. It was evident we would do this again. This would be just the beginning. That was the unspoken agreement we forged that day. I think we both understood that what we were doing would lead to an affair and knew that this was not only inevitable, it was also what we each wanted.

I don't remember now what John Thorn's reaction was to the idea of me spending a day skiing with the heart surgeon. Many years now separate that moment from the present, and much in my memory has become fused into what Irving Howe once called "fables of factuality"—those safe havens we create for ourselves in our stories about the past. But it seems to me it didn't lead to any sort of immediate trouble or terrible arguments between us, though I feel he must have been jealous.

In time we would be forced to admit that what we had gone through during the first hard years of our marriage had not caused us to grow closer but had pulled us apart. And it was now that we began to feel the unraveling.

SIX

When I discovered, at the age of twenty, the books of Thomas Hardy, Virginia Woolf, Henry James, and D. H. Lawrence, those writers Mr. Blakely had introduced me to, I felt I also discovered what I wanted to do with my life. As improbable as it sounds to me now, this was the moment I decided I would become a writer.

I remember thinking even at the time, What makes you think you can do this? What stories do you have to tell, a young untutored woman from Utah?

To the first question I had no answer.

As for the second, I could convince myself I did have stories to tell. I didn't know yet what those stories might be, but I did believe I had stories in me and I would find them as I learned how to write.

The next semester I enrolled in a creative-writing class Mr. Blakely was teaching. He had introduced me to great books. Could he now guide me into the world of writing?

Macalester had established an International Center of its World Press Institute on campus that attracted journalists from many different countries. The man who directed this program and his wife, a pretty blond Southerner, became friends of ours, and John and I often went to parties at their house. There were always interesting people there, and great music and food. It was here that I first heard Otis Redding singing "(Sittin' on) The Dock of the Bay"—a thrilling experience akin to the first time I'd heard jazz. I discovered B. B. King and Screa-min' Jay Hawkins.

At these parties I came into contact with a group of foreigners for the first time, journalists from various countries who were visiting Macalester on scholarships. One of the men who ran this program would sometimes corner me at a party and tell me he thought I was lovely and he wanted to go to bed with me. I needn't worry about his wife, he said, because she wouldn't mind. They had an open marriage and she was sleeping with the handsome South American journal-ist. I never went to bed with him, but his attention wasn't entirely unwelcome.

The art teacher, too, showed an interest. One day while critiquing a drawing I'd done, he touched my face and told me I had very sad but beautiful eyes and would I come to his studio and pose for him? I declined, yet I felt flattered all the same. It seemed that men could see something in me I could not yet see myself.

A woman came on to me for the first time. For a while I didn't realize this was what was happening. My experience of such things wasn't just limited. It was nonexistent. To my surprise I found myself attracted to her.

All around me I felt sexual energy stirring. The so-called Summer of Love lingered on through that fall and winter. The sixties, for all I had known, might not have been happening in Utah, but they were definitely happening here. Here husbands and wives had agreements: they could sleep with whomever they wished and still stay married. Students coupled and uncoupled with an ease and nonchalance I never before could have imagined, and they did so without guilt or guile. Love, after all, was everything.

Perhaps this is part of what made it possible for me to do the pre-viously unthinkable and engage in an affair, to explore my own sexu-ality without the sort of shame and guilt I'd been made to feel in my youth at the idea of such a thing. I'd always known this sexuality was a deep part of my nature. Now I felt it rising to the surface.

❖   ❖   ❖

Among the clusters of memories—those fables of factuality I retain from the first months when the heart surgeon and I were falling in love—is the memory of an evening we spent dancing at a supper club on the outskirts of Saint Paul.

He loved to dance and was very good at it: during his university days he had won dance contests. I remember him saying to me that night, *It's all in the hips,* and then he showed me what he meant. Everything was about moving the hips very fluidly while the upper body remained quiet. This, I understood, was a Latin way of dancing.

I wore a sleeveless gray linen sheath that night and felt happy and confident in this dress. I had begun noticing the women at the parties at the director of the International Center's house, the women from Argentina and France and Italy, what they wore, how they moved. Their simple sense of style appealed to me. I could see how it was so different from the kinds of frilly, colorful dresses women at home often wore. I had begun to feel I understood this difference for the first time, and something had happened recently that caused me to think this was true. The first night I made love with the heart surgeon he had said to me, as we sat on the bed in the motel room getting dressed, You have a very nice sense of style, do you know that? You dress very well.

In truth I felt as if I were learning something new every day—how to eat properly with a knife and fork, how to talk and hold conversations, how to dress, how to parry sexual advances, how to read, what books to choose, what music to listen to, what clothes to wear. That night at the supper club I learned to dance in a slightly different way. I, who had spent my youth going to church dances, let myself be guided by his expertise, and we were soon dancing together as if our bodies understood the same language, the language he was teaching me. Dancing would become something we liked to do almost as much as skiing. It carried with it a romantic aura. Both activities came to feel intimate, this physicality of our bodies in motion, together and apart.

I felt myself falling more and more deeply in love with him. I understood what it meant to be madly in love. To desire someone so very deeply, and in every way. I waited only for the next time we could be together. I thought of him all the time now. We talked to each other every day, and soon we were meeting almost every evening, even just for a short time. I felt passionately happy when I was with him, and for him it was the same. There was an ecstasy to our feelings. We found ways to be with each other very often. We grew less cautious.

Of course I thought about the fact that he was married, but in the beginning, in those first months together, it didn't seem to matter. All that seemed to matter was the overwhelming desire I felt for him, and the way that desire was reciprocated.

Sometimes we went to dinner and spent a whole evening together, choosing some out-of-the-way restaurant. One night at a German restaurant in one of the suburbs, a small scene ensued when the waitress refused to serve me wine because she said I was too young. The heart surgeon became indignant. He couldn't believe I couldn't have wine and he politely confronted the waitress, expressing his incredulity. In Europe, he explained, even children were given a little wine at dinner! Finally the waitress relented and served me.

America astonished him with its prudery. America was crass. It was brash and a bit barbaric, its citizens provincial for the most part. And yet I could tell he also admired this country. He admired its energy and the possibilities present in the culture that had adopted him and given him such excellent opportunities.

He was, in essence, a sort of grandee. I came to understand that, what this word meant, how literally it suited him. He had grown up with great privilege and wealth and he still lived in that world. His wife was from an even wealthier family. He had the exquisite manners of his class, perfected during his years in Europe, and this too was a revelation to me. I had never been around men who behaved this way. Who held a chair for you, and rose from their own chair if you excused yourself to use the restroom, and then stood again when you returned.

He was fascinated by my Mormon background. He had come across Mormon missionaries in various parts of the world and found them curious—their oversimplified views, the way they handed out toothbrushes to potential converts, their clean-cut Anglo appearance such a contrast to the poor indigenous people they often lived among. He wanted to know about my past. He treated me as if he were attracted to my mind as well as my appearance. He praised and listened to me. We had long conversations, covering many subjects. He gave me books to read. He was interested in politics. I remember one book in particular he gave me during this time, by the Russian writer Andrei Sakharov, with the title *Progress, Coexistence, and Intellectual Freedom.* This was a book he greatly admired. Another time he recommended Albert Speer's memoir, which he'd also found fascinating. He was always thinking about such things. He had a global view of humankind. He taught the young residents who trained with him that they should not restrict their interests to medicine but should also pursue a broad education in the humanities.

He'd grown up looking at paintings in the great museums of Europe and this too he talked to me about. He believed an education in the arts, history, and philosophy was essential. In many ways he became my tutor during this time. He gave me confidence in myself, and he encouraged me when at last I told him about my plan to become a writer.

You should try to do this, he said. I think you could.

There came a crisis: his wife found a receipt from a motel in the pocket of one of his jackets and confronted him. He'd been forced to tell her the truth. Yes, he was having an affair. She was a very sophisticated and worldly woman, more European in her sensibilities, and I don't think the idea of an affair would have so deeply rattled her if it hadn't so clearly been such a serious one.

The night she learned of our affair she took a midnight train to Chicago. Why Chicago? I don't know. And why leave so late at night? He told me they had stood on the curb in front of their house, waiting in the dark for the taxi to take her to the train station while he pleaded with her not to go. But when she asked him if he would end the affair if she stayed, he said he could not do that.

What else did they say to each other that night? Did she try to tell him it was wrong to get involved with the mother of one of his patients? That there might be ethical issues involved? Had he revealed this to her? Did she find this even more distressing? Did it upset her to learn that I was nearly half her age? Had they discussed any of this?

I didn't know. These were not things I ever asked him about.

It had never troubled me that he was the doctor who had operated on my son. I had not considered that because of this I might have been especially vulnerable to his advances. Or that his actions might have appeared somewhat predatory. That he might have played upon my sense of gratitude. I don't remember thinking about any of these things at the time. Had I fooled myself into thinking these considerations had nothing to do with my feelings for him? Did I imagine I could separate these things out?

Yes. I did separate them. I didn't see any connection. I was oblivious to such concerns.

Once it happened, however, that was it. I had fallen deeply in love with him. Nothing else mattered. Nothing else was even considered. And he had also fallen very deeply in love with me. If he had imagined he was entering some casual affair, he must have been caught by surprise.

No, he told his wife that night. He did not think he could stop seeing me.

And so she got into the taxi and left for Chicago and didn't come back for a few days.

After she returned, they went on much as before, and so did John and I. I don't remember at what point, or how, he found out I was having an affair. From this point on, however, things would become more complicated, more dramatic and intense, though outwardly, for all practical purposes, it might appear to others that nothing much at all had changed. The heart surgeon and I continued to meet. We even grew bolder about where and when, as if it no longer mattered who might see us together.

Our lives went on in Dupre Hall, much as before. For the most part, John and I were civil, often even kind, in spite of the distance that had set in. We did this for Todd's sake, and also for our own. We retreated from our unhappiness into separate emotional worlds where a different kind of happiness could be found.

I watched Todd grow stronger by the day. I knew he would make it now. The doctors had warned us that he might never be able to be very physically active: perhaps, they said, he might one day be able to do a little ballroom dancing, a comment I found rather odd. But his newly reconfigured heart was already allowing him to be more active. He could run now when he played with students on the lawn, and ride his tricycle around the living room. The open wound didn't seem to trouble him, as if it had just become another fact of life, though of course we all remained cautious. In the spring we enrolled him in the preschool on campus, and he started meeting other children. He began to experience a new freedom, and so did we.

John had become very popular with the students. They trusted him and often confided in him. He spent a lot of time talking with them about their problems, just as we now spent time talking about ours. Sometimes he conducted group therapy sessions in our living room

and I sat in. Many of these sessions included a trust exercise: someone would stand in the middle of the room with several other people
standing behind him and this person was then told to fall straight
backward without making any attempt to catch himself before he
hit the floor. The others were meant to catch him before he did. If
you tried to break your fall by reaching out, you had to repeat the
exercise until you could keep your arms locked at your sides and fall
straight back.

I never understood the purpose of this exercise. It seemed so
counterintuitive, so opposed to the need to learn to protect oneself
from harm rather than rely on others. But psychology was very big at
this time and all sorts of new approaches and ideas were being tried.
Group therapy had become popular. Everybody, it seemed, wanted
to share, except me. The most important things happening in my life
were not things I felt I could speak about with others.

A nurse was sent from the county social services department to
ascertain that Todd was being properly taken care of at home. That

his wound was receiving the right care. Because of the massive medical bills and our low income we qualified for public assistance. The welfare nurse sat in the living room of the director's apartment in Dupre Hall and watched me boil the glass syringe in a pot of water to sterilize it. She observed me as I carefully washed my hands and filled the cooled syringe with sterile saline solution, then removed the soiled bandage and irrigated the wound, cleaning away the dead tissue from the edges with Q-tips, and then opened packets of fresh bandages and redressed it. Todd very calmly helped me, as he always did, by holding the little curved pan against his own belly, and then pressing his small fingers to the ends of the tape while I stretched it in place. The nurse said I had done a fine job and left.

I wrote a story over the summer in Mr. Blakely's class, about a little girl who becomes obsessed with another little girl in kindergarten and waits for her in the coat closet in order to wrestle her to the ground and smother her with kisses among the galoshes. She is eventually caught doing this and told it's wrong and later takes her revenge. I wrote another story called "County Road D," which had no plot because I didn't yet understand plot and instead simply evoked a rural landscape in spring, that sense of oozing fatness and warm ferment Hardy had observed in his Wessex as the winters waned and spring came on.

I met a woman in the class who had a passion for the poet Wallace Stevens and we became friends. Every week at the beginning of class she would slip me poems by Stevens written out in colorful markers on bright pieces of construction paper. In one note she wrote to me she said, *One thing I don't really understand is the correlation between creativity and intelligence. Maybe you got to have a whole lot of both to be immortal. In you I see both—I mean, the skull-power comments you make in class—Zounds! I just could never. So I know you got an IQ, and you also have the creativity—example: those summer stories of yours.*

I, who had thought of myself as struggling to keep up with such bright students, felt deeply encouraged by her comments. Sometimes she gave me her own wildly exuberant writings. She was the first to show me how you could blast the language open and create wild and improbable patterns of sense and senselessness that nevertheless could cohere and convey the kind of deep subterranean content of visions and dreams. Still, I thought the best stories were written in simple language, with a strong presence of voice. Those were the stories I wanted to write.

At the end of the summer a contest was held in class to pick the best story written during the semester and everyone got one vote. My story "County Road D" won. The prize was a paperback collection of literary novellas, on the inside flyleaf of which Mr. Blakely had written in his spidery scrawl *First Prize*.

I carried the book back to the apartment that day, feeling an outsized sense of happiness. It helped me to believe I might actually learn to write well one day if I just kept reading, if I just kept trying. In my hand I held the collection of novellas by Joseph Conrad and Henry James and other writers whose work I had only begun to discover. I must read them all, I thought. This is how I would learn to do it. I would teach myself how to write by reading the great writers.

My ambition, I knew, was sprinting ahead of any idea of what I could possibly accomplish, but I thought if it didn't run ahead, as James Wood once said, there might be no race at all.

Over that summer the heart surgeon and I continued to see each other as often as we could. We met in motel rooms, in restaurants and cafés, on the tennis courts near the university. We began playing tennis once or twice a week now that we could no longer meet for a day of skiing. Sometimes we played mixed doubles with one of his colleagues from the hospital and his wife. Surely they knew we were having an affair. By this time it must have been obvious to everyone who saw us together, but we no longer cared who knew.

His wife and children left for Europe for the summer. She told him he should think about what he wanted to do. Make some decisions about the future, determine whether or not he wanted to remain together. Her absence made it easier for us to see each other.

He lived in a large house on Summit Avenue, not far from the Macalester campus. Summit was lined with graceful and lovely old houses, some so large that it looked as if you'd need servants to run them. I had walked down the avenue many times to the point where it ended on the banks of the Mississippi River, taking my time, strolling along and admiring the houses and gardens, turning around at the river and walking back. I liked to do this at night when I could look into the lighted windows of the houses and admire the little domestic scenes being played out in the beautiful rooms.

The first time he took me to his house that summer when his wife was away in Europe I felt uneasy. I knew I didn't belong there, in this place where he carried out his family life, even though that family was now far away. The house was very beautiful inside, filled with paintings and nice furniture and objects. We walked around looking at the paintings on the walls. This is a Siqueiros, he would say, stopping in front of a small painting in the living room, or This is by Diego Rivera, pointing to another. He showed me a number of paintings but he kept coming back to the smaller painting by Siqueiros. He was the best, he said. The most talented and original of all the Mexican painters.

We went upstairs to his bedroom, the same bedroom he shared with his wife, and we made love in their bed. The room had shutters over the windows that cast a slatted light upon the walls. I had been reading Robbe-Grillet's novel *Jealousy* that summer and I looked at the slatted bands of light on the wall and thought of a scene from that book where a similar light from a jalousie infused the room.

Jalousie. Jealousy. There was danger here.

His children were much on his mind that summer. He missed them. He loved them very much, and was especially close to the youngest, a little boy only five years old. In their absence he began thinking what it would be like to live without them. We often talked now about divorcing our spouses and starting a new life together. The greatest obstacle for him was the idea of his children. He struggled with the thought of leaving them, disrupting their lives, of how much he would miss them.

I thought of them too, just as I thought constantly about my own son and wondered what a divorce might mean for him. Even though I felt my own marriage would break up no matter what happened, I didn't want to be responsible for his decision about his children. I was resigned to this. I worried. Besides, I did not see how I could fit into his world even if he should decide to leave his wife. How would this be possible? For some reason this thought frightened me very much. I felt inferior to him in ways I could not deny. What if I failed and could not measure up? What would I *do* in his world?

It wasn't only my age, though at twenty-one I was younger by sixteen years, and this seemed a considerable gap. The real problem, however, was the difference in our backgrounds. I could see this would be a problem even if he couldn't admit it, and very often he couldn't. Perhaps he could imagine me as his wife because he saw how malleable I was. Maybe he thought he would shape me, prepare me for a life with him. But I had no experience of the kind of world he effortlessly inhabited. I spoke no language but English, I hadn't traveled, I had no education, was nakedly naive about many things. How would I make up for this difference in our experiences? And what if our love should wear thin? What would I be left with then? Guilt as well as remorse?

In the fall John and I made the decision to separate and file for divorce: it was made mutually. He would stay at Macalester and continue working as a counselor until he finished his doctoral degree.

And me? What would I do?

I could see only one path and I took it. Because in the end, after everything was said and done, it felt like the right thing to do.

SEVEN

He sent a letter that arrived as I was packing to leave. The letter had been written from a hotel in San Francisco where he was attending a medical conference. I read the letter sitting in the living room among the boxes I had filled with books and clothes and Todd's belongings, all the things I was taking back to Utah with me. I was returning to Ogden with my son, moving back in with my parents until I could figure out what to do.

The first line of his letter read, *I am trying to unravel what made us fall in love.*

He admitted the surrounding circumstances were very complex. He was alluding, I knew, to his role as Todd's surgeon as well as the fact we were both married when we met. He said he was absolutely honest and true in his feelings—that it had never crossed his mind to exploit me, but that yes, he had been selfish. From a personal point of view he said he had no problem deciding what he'd really like to do. But there were others to consider. He meant his children.

He said he was writing this letter with tears in his eyes and a feeling of compression in his throat. He was going to try and see if he could preserve his family, though he understood there were limitations to this plan. He said he respected me more than ever for my sharp analysis of our situation and the desire I had expressed to unravel my (and our) problems on my own by returning to Utah.

He had an overwhelming desire to spend the rest of his life with me, but he also felt his children had the right to a full-time father, and thus he was caught in a dichotomy. He had me constantly on his mind. He loved me, he needed me, and he desired me, and he begged me not to treat him as an outcast now, because he was trying his best to be fair. I know, he wrote, that there is unfairness toward you and as a matter of fact toward myself. But on a scale it's a two against six.

I looked at this letter for a long time. At the sentence where he'd calculated the unfairness to each of us in our present situation: two to six, I thought. In that equation I found a certain elegant accuracy.

I left Minnesota as I had arrived, with great uncertainty about the future. I could see no way of staying on. One day I had been playing tennis with my lover on a court in Saint Paul and dissecting *Tess of the d'Urbervilles* in class, winning a little prize for my story, living each day among the brightest students in a richly interesting world, and the next I was back in my parents' house, living again in the town where I'd grown up, working in a department store over the Christmas holidays. There was one life, and then there was another. It was as if I had turned a page in a book and suddenly discovered myself in a different story.

For a long time after I had returned from Saint Paul to my parents' house I continued to see the heart surgeon. We met in various locales. New York and Aspen, Park City and Chicago, Los Angeles and Sun Valley. We stayed in nice hotels, visited museums, looked at art together, spent afternoons wandering through parks. We skied in resorts I'd never been to. I never got over the feeling I had been right to go away from him in the way I did and return that fall to Utah. I did not believe in breaking up his family. I did not ever really believe I could. I didn't see myself living in his world, adapting myself to it. But that didn't mean we couldn't go on being lovers. Which is what we did for a very long while. So long it is difficult to say when it all ended.

PART SEVEN

❖

Home

ONE

Long after this time, toward the end of the summer of 2014, I
made a trip to Driggs, Idaho, on the other side of the state, where
John Thorn lives in a little nearby town called Victor. I wanted to sit
down with Todd's father and talk with him. There were questions I
needed to ask that I thought he could help me with and John said
he'd be happy to see me. My husband, Tony, agreed to make the drive
with me and we took along our dog, Ava, only a year old. This would
be her first driving trip. We planned to spend the night in Driggs.
It would take about four hours to get there from our place on the
Camas Prairie in the southern part of the state, where for many years
we have lived, for at least a part of the year, on a small farm.

It was raining hard the afternoon we arrived in Driggs and checked
in to the log-cabin motel I had booked earlier. The motel was just out
of town, on the main road that leads to the ski area. Had the rain not
been so heavy we might have been able to see the backside of the
Teton Peaks from the porch of our little cabin, set back from the road
in a grove of aspen trees dripping with rain.

The next morning I left Tony still sleeping and drove the ten miles
south to the smaller town of Victor, where I'd agreed to meet John
for breakfast in a café on Main Street. It was still stormy outside. We
sat and talked for two hours as the rain beat down steadily and a sea-
soned waitress named Ramona kept our coffee cups refilled. He still
works as a psychologist, treating clients out of an office in Jackson
Hole just over the hill. I would have recognized the bearded, burly

man who sat down opposite me anywhere, even though it had now been fifty years this summer since we took our marriage vows in the Salt Lake Temple.

There were facts I wanted to check. When we learned that Todd was in heart failure and needed surgery right away and we had to leave Utah quickly, had we really driven straight through to Saint Paul in the middle of that hot, humid Midwestern summer? Yes, we had, he said. Don't you remember how we stopped one night alongside the road at a pullout and rolled out our sleeping bags because we were so tired and we slept for a few hours beside the road with Todd between us?

I did not remember this, and there were other things I'd remembered incorrectly. When I mentioned the basement apartment in Bountiful, John frowned and said, But it wasn't a basement apartment, it just seemed that way because it was so dark. There were no windows in the bedroom and that's where you spent most of your time because you were so sick during the first months of your pregnancy. It must have seemed like a dark basement to you.

In talking with him I found that our memories of most of the major events in our life together were very similar. I also knew there was a question I wanted to ask that seemed so sensitive I wasn't sure it would be appropriate, but I realized that I could trust him to understand, that there still existed between us a kind and good feeling, and so tentatively, toward the end of our conversation, I brought up the subject that had really driven me to seek him out.

I said that one of the things I had been thinking about a lot lately was why I had chosen to get married so young, putting myself on a trajectory that would affect the rest of my life, and why I had chosen to marry my sister's ex-boyfriend—him, in other words. I told him I had avoided thinking about these things for most of my life but that I could no longer do so. I was trying to figure out whether, or how much, his earlier relationship with my sister, Marcia, had influenced his attraction to me, or for that matter my attraction to him.

These were really two questions, and he addressed the former first.

He told me that when we had gotten engaged during my senior year in high school our plan had been to wait for a year and a half before getting married. Then I would be nineteen years old and we could join the Peace Corps as we dreamed of doing. But when we told my parents we were engaged, my father insisted we get married right away. He said he wouldn't allow us to wait.

This news hit me with the force of a powerful revelation. I had not remembered my father had done this and I told him so.

Oh yes, he said. That's why we got married when you were seventeen. Your father insisted on it, even though my parents wanted us to wait.

And we wanted to wait?

Yes, we wanted to wait, too. That was the plan.

I knew he was right. I knew he wasn't making this up, that my father had done this, had served me up on the marriage altar prematurely, and at that moment I also clearly understood it was because he wouldn't have minded simply being rid of me. My waiting to get married would have complicated his life. I might have hung around, another mouth to feed, another kid to deal with. But still I could hardly believe what I was hearing.

Did you know that your father threatened to shoot me, not once but twice? John said quietly to me.

This, too, was news to me.

The first time was when I was dating your sister, John said. He never liked me. He said I was a divorced child. Because I came from divorced parents he said I would never amount to anything and he didn't want me to date his daughter and he'd shoot me if I kept coming around. But Marcia and I kept dating anyway until I went away to the Naval Academy and she met Denny. The second time he threatened to shoot me was when you and I got together a few years later.

He stopped speaking for a moment to let me absorb this news. He could tell I was stunned by what he was saying. And then he went on, in that same quiet, calm voice I imagined he used in therapy sessions.

He had such a terrible temper, your father. He couldn't control his anger. And when he got angry he hurt people. I've often thought your whole family suffered trauma because of how he behaved, both physically and emotionally abusive.

I listened. And again I thought, He's right, even though I thought it might be a strong diagnosis for a whole family, because in truth not every child was treated the same. Marcia, for instance, had a very different experience with my father than I did.

John continued, Don't you remember how your father would punish you kids for making too much noise in the car during family vacations and how he'd just grab any two kids—it didn't matter if they were the guilty ones—and drag you out of the car and bang your heads together? It didn't matter who he punished, he just needed to hurt someone.

And of course I did remember this. There we would be, driving through Zion or Bryce National Park or along the Kaibab Plateau or passing the Grand Canyon, surrounded by such sublime scenery— six or seven kids packed into the backseat of the car and getting bored and beginning to fool around—and suddenly he would pull over and stop the car and yell, I'm going to bang some heads together! And he'd get out and open the back door and haul out two kids, any two kids, and drag them to the roadside, and holding our heads in his big hands he'd smash the tops together, and then maybe he'd grab us by an ear and twist it and drag us back toward the car, kicking us in the butt from behind, and shove us inside and say, I hear any more out of you kids and you'll get it again even worse the next time, and then he would get back behind the wheel and ease the car back out onto the road, and with our ears burning and the bones on the tops of our heads still thrumming with pain and with shame seething inside we would sit mutely as we again sailed down the road through the immensely beautiful world.

Yes, I said to John. I do remember him banging our heads together. And it's true, it really didn't matter who was at fault.

Maybe, I thought, I'm wrong about him not treating everyone alike. Maybe we all suffered in the same way. But part of me could not believe this. I knew that Bob had received harsher treatment, and when he was young Jerry as well, and I knew that I had also. Perhaps others.

He just couldn't control his temper, John said quietly, could he?

John now addressed the question of my sister.

It's true, he said, he had loved Marcia very much and been upset when she'd rejected him. It's also true that Marcia and I looked very much alike, he said, and it happened to be a look that matched his standard of beauty—small, dark-haired women with large brown eyes. He said he didn't really know how much a part Marcia had played in our later getting involved. Yet he did not believe he'd fallen in love with me because I was Marcia's sister. He'd been attracted to *me,* to who I was then.

But I was just a girl! I said. And you were six years older! You already had a college degree. You'd been out in the world.

He looked at me for some time, as if expecting me to say something else besides simply stating well-known facts. I realized it sounded like I was accusing him of something, and in a way I was. But really, what had he done wrong? Except propose to me, even though I was so young, because, as he put it, he didn't want to lose me.

My father was the bully, not John. My father was the one who'd threatened to shoot him. Who had humiliated him as the *divorced child.* My father was the one who had forced us to get married before we had planned to. And all of this—*all of this*—I had buried for years.

Why had I buried it? And why had I written my father all those letters over the years, letters filled with such loving concern and affection—letters written over decades, from 1970 through 1990? I think you are my best correspondent, he once said. And why had I denied his cruelty, preferring to whitewash his behavior until finally he had alienated me by attacking my first novel and turning so cruel?

Because, I thought, I had been taught to revere one's parents as a principle of the gospel. Because this had been pounded into my head as a child: *Honor thy father and thy mother, that thy days may be long upon the land.* And most of all because I had so longed for his love and approval, and I had so feared him all of my life, that I could grovel, year after year, in letter after letter, and visit after visit, hoping for whatever crumb of acceptance or affection he might throw my way. And often he had tossed me something, and not just a crumb: he offered brief but lavish meals of love and behaved in ways that could make me feel exactly how much he really cared, how sorry he really was, how he wished things could have been different. After all, he was a very smart man.

I knew that in some way I had made John uncomfortable by asking the questions I had. But he was enough of a professional and a gentleman not to try and turn the tables and put me on the couch, as he might have. He might have pointed out that it was my own complex relationship with my sister, not his, that was really the problem, though we had all somehow gotten caught up in the sort of tangled psychological family drama I knew I could spend years trying to unravel.

The thing is, John Thorn said, for all the difficulties we went through, we had a son, Todd, and he survived against incredible odds. When I think of that everything else falls away and becomes rather inconsequential.

Later he would tell me something else that I had forgotten. When Todd was so critically ill in the days following the surgery in Minnesota, John had performed a laying on of hands with the help of one of his Mormon classmates, administering to Todd and giving him a blessing. The next day John was contacted by a Mormon intern who worked with the heart surgeon who called to say that the night after the blessing, when they did the rounds, the heart surgeon had told his assistant to "pull all the support stuff off," that they had done all they could and that everything they were doing was making things worse. He said it was up to God and Todd at that point. The next day, John told me, the tubes were taken out, and Todd began to improve, slowly starting down what proved to be the road to recovery.

I must have been present at this blessing performed by John, but I had no recollection of it. And again I thought, How is it possible we forget the things we thought we never could?

We said goodbye, not knowing when we'd see each other again. The rain was still coming down hard as I walked to my car, which I'd left parked in the mud behind the café. I picked up Tony and Ava at the motel and we checked out and drove north under lowering skies, heading toward Tetonia, a small town just north of Driggs where my great-grandfather had homesteaded in the late 1800s. My mother's father had been born here in this valley, and a beautiful valley it was, stretching westward from the magnificent Teton Range, peaks so domineering in their purity and simplicity and grandeur that all other elements in the landscape had to adjust to their majesty. It began raining harder and the sky turned ominously black. *We live in a world ruled by fictions of every kind,* J. G. Ballard wrote. *We live inside an enormous novel . . . The fiction is already there. The writer's task is to invent the reality.*

What sort of reality, I wondered, had I been creating? What sort of fiction did I live inside?

We pass through Tetonia, with its tall grain elevators and even taller black steeple on the Mormon church. In every one of these little towns in eastern Idaho there is a Mormon church with a steeple tall enough that it's the first thing you see as you approach. It had been Brigham Young's plan to establish a religious fiefdom in the Western territories, a theocracy over which he would rule, and this fiefdom would include not only the territory of Utah but adjoining territories as well. He set about expanding the kingdom into Idaho and Arizona and Nevada, even all the way to San Bernardino, California, where some of my Flake relatives ended up. This is why the Flakes and the Freemans were all sent to colonize Arizona, and the Pauls, my mother's relatives, came north to Idaho and settled in the country we were passing through. And as the Mormons settled in these places they selected the choicest land—the land closest to rivers and streams, claiming water rights that stand to this day. Throughout the West it is the Mormons who often hold the oldest and first rights to the water.

For a while the clouds lift here and there and ragged bits of pale blue sky show through. The lush, wet piney valley we're passing through is so unlike the wide, treeless prairie where we live for much of the year. White cattle graze in green fields and the green looks so lurid, like fake turf on miniature golf courses. So much rain has fallen in one small town the main street is flooded and we plow through a small lake with the water splashing around us. A brown horse paws the earth in a field at the edge of town and I feel the attraction I always feel when I see a horse. I look to see how straight the horse's back is, if it's young or if it's swaybacked and old, and I look to see what sort of shape its coat is in, if it's shiny or dull, and I look to see if it has a fine head or a common one.

The heavy black clouds return and it begins to rain again. Looking out through the mist at the farms and the broad agricultural landscape I think of Tess and Hardy's Wessex. Tess working on the dreadfully bleak Flintcomb-Ash farm where she ends up after Angel abandons her. Digging up the winter turnips from the cold plowed earth with her raw red hands, working without cease in the bitter cold from dawn to dusk. *There be very few women's lives that are not tremulous.*

How could I be expected to know? Tess cries out to her mother when she returns home pregnant with Alec's baby. *I was a child when I left this house four months ago. Why didn't you tell me there was danger in menfolk? Why didn't you warn me?*

North of Tetonia we stop at a little cemetery and during a break in the rain walk about on the wet grass looking at tombstones to see if there might be one with my ancestor's name on it. Although the cemetery does have some older markers, none date back to their time. What I do see is what I always see when I stop at old cemeteries in the West, and that is all the graves of the children who died young. *My darling is at rest,* one tombstone reads, a child who died at two. Another says simply, *We Loved Her.*

We pass potato cellars covered in earth and haystacks in various shapes and the rain hits the windshield and runs upward in little spermlike drops and then it begins to hail and the hail beats down on the car so hard it seems it could dent the metal. Ava cowers in the backseat, terrified by the sound of the hail hitting the car, and I reach around to calm her and I feel how she is shaking.

I think about my cousin Diane, who has been transcribing my grandmother's handwritten diaries. She recently sent an installment from the year 1964, the year I got married. My grandmother came to see us that summer, just a month after my wedding, and recorded her visit: *Arrived at Roy's evening of July 15th. Alice fixed a lovely birthday dinner. Met Judy's husband. He seems nice. But she's having a hard time.*

Married a month and having a hard time. Even my grandmother, to whom I wasn't even that close, could see that something was wrong. I had wondered how she knew that. Now I understood.

We head home across the broad Arco plain. There are no farms or ranches here, only thousands of acres of government-owned land, a flat lava plain covered in scrub desert plants growing out of the dry volcanic soil, home of the Idaho National Engineering Laboratory. The road stretches for miles in a straight line through the open, flat, empty land.

At one point we stop at a pullout for a historical marker in order to change drivers and let Ava out. We stand in a strong wind, gazing out over the land, the sky dark with lowery clouds. The historical sign is labeled ELEPHANT HUNTERS and this grabs my interest. I stroll over to read the text:

> Early day big game hunters who occupied lava caves around here more than 12,000 years ago had a diet that included elephants, camels, and giant bison. When a gradual change to a warmer, drier climate made local grasslands into more desert, the elephant herds left for cooler plains farther north. But 8,000 years ago bison were still available here. Indians continued to hunt buffalo on these plains until about 1840.

Elephants, I think.
Woolly mammoths.

Farther on down the road we stop at another historical marker, this one labeled NUCLEAR REACTORS, and this time we stay in the car as it has begun to rain hard, and read the text through the windshield:

> Since 1949, more nuclear reactors—over 50 of them—have been built on this plain than anywhere in the world. This 900 square-mile Idaho National Laboratory site is the birthplace of the nuclear Navy. Commercial power reactor prototypes, including reactors that breed more fuel than they consume, were also developed here.

A Wagnerian dark has enveloped the mountains to the north and as we set off again lightning bolts flash against the blackness—crisp white-hot bolts that hit the earth with frightening power. Soon it begins snowing to the north in the tall mountains of the Lost River Range: snow and lightning together in August.

❖ ❖ ❖

We're almost home now. The sun has finally come out and you can see where the storm passed over the mountains in a narrow swath, leaving a skiff of snow like a coating of powdered sugar. We pass through the little town of Arco, where many of the older buildings on Main Street are built out of black lava rock, including the town hall with its sign above the entrance announcing FIRST CITY TO BE LIT BY ATOMIC ENERGY. Most of the businesses on Main Street are closed, the stores empty now, restaurants shuttered. Only the Pickle is left, a burger-and-sandwich place on the highway leading out of town.

We pass Craters of the Moon, winding along a curvy two-lane road through miles of nothing but the jagged black lava rock from an ancient volcanic flow, until we come to Carey, another small farming town, this one founded by Mormons and still dominated by them. It's Sunday and the parking lot of the Mormon church on Main Street is full. I imagine the congregation inside. The solid women sitting in the pews, the hardworking men beside them, the farmers and ranchers and their wives, portly men with sunburned necks, their shapes proof of the abundance in their lives. I think of the water they control. Their two-year supplies of food. The strong sense of community and inestimable wealth of the church, and the patriotism that has helped stock the CIA with the sons and daughters of good Mormons like those inside this small-town church, and provided workers for the NSA megadata collection center in Utah. I think of John Gardner's last novel, *Mickelsson's Ghosts*, his description of the *earnest young Mormons pressing through the world . . . They would prevail, no question about it. They . . . were the Future. The terrible survivors.*

Lying back in the passenger seat I look up at the sky, at layer after layer of dense white clouds, one layer behind the other, clouds stacked and staggered into infinity and lending the sky an astonishing feeling of depth. Satellites and God up there, I think. And not just God but Mrs. God.

Whether or not they exist, we're slaves to the gods.

We pass the blinking light at Highway 75. Only seventeen miles to go now. We'll make it home before the pitchy blackness of the prairie night settles in. The cats will be waiting for us, milling about the yard in the evening light. The chickens already roosted in the barn. I begin thinking about dinner. The eggs I'll need to collect. The corn that has only this week begun to ripen in the garden, from which I plan to make a fresh corn polenta. I'll use the heavy cast-iron pot I always use to make this dish, the red enamel one, now blackened from years of use.

EPILOGUE

The beautiful boy grew up to be a beautiful man, a teacher in an alternative high school in a small town in Idaho, working with teenagers who have a hard time fitting in and who struggle with learning. It's a military town, site of an Air Force base, and the kids he teaches have grown up knowing only war—a perpetual war in the Middle East in which many of their parents have fought, often serving more than one tour of duty. A good number of the girls in his school become pregnant in their teens. He does his best to help them. He helps the boys too, arranging for them to be excused from class so they can accompany the girls they've gotten pregnant to their doctor's appointments. He is among the few adults born with a transposition of the great arteries who received that early surgery to survive to middle age without further medical intervention.

If the heart could think, wrote Fernando Pessoa, *it would stop beating.*

But it cannot think. So it goes on, beating every second of every day, even one that's damaged or been reconfigured, and now pumps backward.

I often think of the heart surgeon, of something or other he said to me during those times we spent together. How the way to tell if a restaurant is really good is by looking at the dessert menu. How a fountain pen is such a personal instrument, its nib so shaped and conditioned by the owner's writing, that to ask to borrow one was like asking to borrow a toothbrush. How shoes were very important: it's where outfits often fell apart, he said.

Nineteen years would pass from the time I left Saint Paul, having decided I would become a writer, and the publication of my first book, a collection of short stories that appeared when I was forty. When the book came out I sent my parents a copy and my father called to congratulate me.

Who knew, doll? he said.

Meaning: Who knew you could write?

He'd been able to recognize himself in some of the stories I'd written, and not always portrayed in the most flattering light, but overall he thought I'd done a good job and he said he was proud of me.

When my first novel, the story of a young woman who'd grown up in a big Mormon family in Utah, was published a year later, I got another sort of call from him. He was angry I'd written the book I had, though I was surprised that what upset him didn't seem to be the family stories I'd told but the way he felt I'd portrayed Mormons. He thought it made the Mormons look bad. Like racists, he said. He thought I had revealed things in my novel I shouldn't have. Discussed the holy garments, the temple rituals. He said I must have imagined I'd sell lots of books this way. I must not have realized I'd be held accountable for what I'd done. But he was going to hold me accountable. He'd even looked up the meaning of the word for me in case I didn't know, and he was going to read it to me. When he finished reading the definition of "accountable," he told me the whole family was against me; everyone had been upset by my book. Not just him, but my mother and sister and older brothers. I had no way of knowing if this was true, but his words hit me very hard, as if I had suddenly, and without warning, been ejected from the fold and hurled beyond the pale. And then, just before I hung up, he turned cruel, delivering his coup de grace:

This book you've written, he said. It isn't even very good. There's nothing there. It's boring.

❖   ❖   ❖

What upset your father about your novel, my mother said to me not long before she died, was the way you had made us look poor. The bunk beds with kids stacked up like chickens in a coop. The hand-me-down clothes. You hurt his pride. He believed he'd always been a good provider for his family.

When a writer is born into a family, Czesław Miłosz once famously said, *the family is finished.* You could forget about having any more secrets. You could forget about hiding what you didn't want others to know. You were going to be exposed, hung out to air, and by a traitor from within.

But later I wondered, Is it the family that's really finished or simply the writer's place within it? Could a family still be a family with parts missing?

My father died in 1990 from heart disease, just six months after that phone call. My mother died a year later. And Jerry, the brother who could have been my twin in our youth, died in 1994 from complications of AIDS. With these deaths everything changed. My sense of family was forever altered. I became the outlier I always knew I was, and I found my place, which was really no place at all—more like a transient camp of memory, a mutable, sheltering landscape, where often nothing seems missing, and the coherence of the past lives on in the bounty of the present.

ACKNOWLEDGMENTS

It is with affection and gratitude that I wish to acknowledge the friends, family, and colleagues who have supported and nourished me over the years.

My first thanks must go to Laurie Winer, writer and editor at the *Los Angeles Review of Books,* who helped shape the essay that led to this memoir, and to *LARB* for publishing it. I'm grateful not only for her humor, patience, and advice but also for the deep friendship we've forged.

For their unfailing affection and encouragement, I thank Rae Lewis, Dylan Landis, Louise Steinman, Colleen Daly, Elissa Kline, David Francis, Jane Weinstock, and Teresa Jordan. Through the conversations we shared, they contributed such helpful and illuminating thoughts and provided endless comfort and good cheer. I am also indebted to my first readers, Sonja Bolle and Barbara Feldon, women whose beauty is matched by their intelligence.

To Tina Barney, I owe a special thanks for being such a constant and loving friend throughout the many years we've known each other. The late Digby Wolfe, brilliant writer, mentor, friend, and companion, is no longer here to thank, but I remember him with love and gratitude—he who would tell me to just go into that room and write and he would take care of everything else.

Will Bagley read an early version of my manuscript and offered very helpful suggestions, saving me from factual errors. His knowledge of Mormon and Western history is unmatched. Diane Ellerton transcribed our grandmother's handwritten diaries, and her painstaking labors were of great help to me: my thanks to her.

I'm grateful to John Thorn for his generosity and kindness, and to Daniel Gundlach for being such a supportive and kindred spirit. Marcia Garner kindly provided me with family photographs and I offer her a grateful bow. Michael Wilder prepared the photographs for the book, taking such meticulous care, assisting me in unusually creative ways, including singling out the detail used for the jacket of this book.

My thanks also to Kay Samples, Judy Betterton, and Connie and David Cole—old friends with whom I share so many good memories. To Gerald Howard, my first editor, thank you for believing in me. Patrick Dillon, Kevin Bourke, and Oliver Munday each made important contributions to this book, and I thank them for their fine efforts.

To Joy Harris I owe more than a thank you—as my first reader, my first advisor, and the very finest friend I could have. I am indebted to this resourceful woman who is as brilliant at knitting me a cashmere scarf as she is at analyzing my first drafts and serving as midwife to my books.

Dan Frank and Betsy Sallee gave themselves over to the life of this memoir with such devotion and care. I am grateful for the insight they brought to my story, and for their creativity and encouragement. I'm also indebted to Betsy for suggesting the title, just one of her many contributions to this book.

To Marnie Mosley, Todd Thorn, and Hailey Thorn, my deepest love and gratitude.

Finally I thank Anthony, whose perseverance as an artist has long shown me the way. His steadiness and love holds the world together. It was my great good fortune to have met him, on that night very long ago, as he stood in a crowd outside a museum. Each day I am grateful for his presence in my life, for which I thank my lucky stars.

Judith Freeman is the author of four novels—*Red Water, The Chinchilla Farm, Set for Life,* and *A Desert of Pure Feeling*—and of *Family Attractions,* a collection of stories, and *The Long Embrace,* a biography of Raymond Chandler. She lives in California and Idaho.

A NOTE ON THE TYPE

The text of this book was set in a typeface named Perpetua, designed by the British artist Eric Gill (1882–1940) and cut by the Monotype Corporation of London in 1928–30. Perpetua is a contemporary letter of original design, without any direct historical antecedents. The shapes of the roman letters basically derive from stonecutting, a form of lettering in which Gill was eminent. The italic is essentially an inclined roman.

COMPOSED BY NORTH MARKET STREET GRAPHICS,
LANCASTER, PENNSYLVANIA

PRINTED AND BOUND BY BERRYVILLE GRAPHICS,
BERRYVILLE, VIRGINIA

DESIGNED BY IRIS WEINSTEIN